write
your
novel
in a
month

write your novel in a month

how to complete
a first draft
in 30 days and
what to do next

01 02 03 04 05 06 07 08 09 10 11 12 13 14 15 16 17 18 19 20 21 22 23 24 25 26 27 28 29 30

WD

WRITER'S DIGEST BOOKS

WritersDigest.com
Cincinnati, Ohio

jeff gerke

For more resources for writers, visit www.writersdigest.com/books.

17 16 15 14 13 5 4 3 2 1

Distributed in Canada by Fraser Direct
100 Armstrong Avenue
Georgetown, Ontario, Canada L7G 5S4
Tel: (905) 877-4411

Distributed in the U.K. and Europe by F&W Media International
Brunel House, Newton Abbot, Devon, TQ12 4PU, England
Tel: (+44) 1626-323200, Fax: (+44) 1626-323319
E-mail: postmaster@davidandcharles.co.uk

Distributed in Australia by Capricorn Link
P.O. Box 704, Windsor, NSW 2756 Australia
Tel: (02) 4577-3555

Edited by James Duncan
Interior designed by Bethany Rainbolt
Cover designed by Claudean Wheeler
Production coordinated by Debbie Thomas

dedication

To Gregory Manchess, Stephan Martiniere, and Eric Velhagen—artists who send me flying to other worlds, who inspire my own artistic endeavors, and whom I have had the pleasure of meeting. And to Cézanne, Van Gogh, Goya, Caravaggio, Vermeer, Friedrich, and John Conrad Berkey—artists who inspire me but whom I never did get to meet.

acknowledgments

Thank you to Writer's Digest for the opportunity to help novelists better do what it is they are trying to do. To James Duncan, for the editing and excellent feedback. And to my wife and children, for being in my life.

about the author

JEFF GERKE trains novelists how to better do what it is they are trying to do. He trains through his books for Writer's Digest, which include *Plot Versus Character* and *The First 50 Pages*. He trains through his online video training program Fiction Academy, a part of Bestseller Society. He trains through the many writers' conferences he teaches at all over the country every year. And he trains through the freelance editing he does for clients. Jeff is the founder of Marcher Lord Press, the premier publisher of Christian speculative fiction. He lives in Colorado Springs with his wife and three children.

table of contents

01
02
03
04
05
06
07
08
09
10
11
12
13
14
15
16
17
18
19
20
21
22
23
24
25
26
27
28
29
30

introduction

One of these days, I'm going to sit down and write that novel...

It's on the bucket list of millions of people. To write a novel—ah, it is one of the great achievements a person can realize. It's right up there with running a marathon or traveling to Paris or the Holy Land or climbing a massive mountain peak.

But it's the very difficulty of those things that can make them seem unattainable. Hopefully no one would set out to climb Mount Everest without first having gone to incredible lengths and expense to prepare for the attempt. Anyone who takes off on a marathon having not trained for it will rue the decision. Preparation, training, expense ... these things stand like the Grand Canyon between people and their biggest dreams.

So it is with writing a novel. Lots of people begin writing their heartbreaking work of staggering genius, plunging ahead with great fervor, only to run out of gas after a few pages or chapters. Just like trying to run a long-distance race or climb a mountain without training for it.

Is there no hope, then? Must it take you ten years to write all the way to the end of a full-length novel manuscript? Do you have to quit your job, leave your family, and move to a Tibetan monastery to have the time and focus to write this thing?

good news

I'm happy to tell you that the trip to Tibet is not necessary. (Unless, of course, that's on your bucket list, too!)

It is possible to write that novel in under a decade. Under a year. In fact, it's my intention to help you write it in one *month*.

Wouldn't that be incredible? To look at the calendar one month from today and know that your book was done? In the bag? Checked off the list?

There are a variety of reasons for wanting to write a novel this quickly. It may be that you've not yet written a novel and need help getting that first one done. Perhaps you've written one or more already, but now you're faced with a blinding dead-line—previously, you've had ten months to write your novels, but now it has to be done in four weeks. Ack. Or you don't nor-mally struggle with writing, but you're about to have one month between contracts, and you'd love to crank out this "pet" book you've been wanting to write.

Maybe, like so many other people, you've either lost your job or are looking for another opportunity. People have always told you you're a good writer. Before finances get too tight, you'd like to pump out that novel manuscript and let it make the rounds with publishers while you're out doing job interviews. Maybe that's how money will come in? It certainly won't have even a chance of happening until you've written the novel.

Perhaps you've accepted the NaNoWriMo (National Novel Writing Month) challenge to write a novel in thirty days.

Whatever the reason you've come to *Write Your Novel in a Month—How to Complete a First Draft in 30 Days and What to Do Next*, I'm very pleased you've come. We're going to have fun together, you and I.

the trick

The trick to writing a novel quickly is to knock out most of it in a very short period of time.

Sounds obvious, I know: "If you want to write quick, write quick."

But here's what I mean: Once you get a goodly portion of a manuscript behind you, it will build inertia on its own. After you pass that milestone, finishing the journey won't even be an issue. I'm not one to go all mystical and say that after you reach that point the book will write itself. But I will say that once you pass the highest elevation on the trail, everything after it becomes easier. It's like you're walking downhill. My job is to get you to—and over—the high point. If that works, you won't need me much anymore. I'll miss you, but I'll cheer for you as you sprint the rest of the way home.

this guy and this book

I've been writing my own novels—and helping other authors write theirs—since the mid-1990s. I once had to research and write a 100,000-word novel in six weeks. While that doesn't seem to be a novel in thirty days, it really was. Within those six weeks, I had to do enough research to convincingly write about life in the Sudan *and* plan the novel *and* create the characters *and* write it in six weeks. The actual writing time was four weeks.

It was backbreaking work to get 100K words written in that time, but it was worth it.

My goal in this book is not as aggressive as that. Because the NaNoWriMo challenge is to write 50K words in a month, that's where I'm going to set the bar for us. We'll do your planning work first, and then you'll just have to get to the 50K-word mark in those thirty days. Absolutely doable.

The techniques for writing quickly that I present in this book are drawn from my own experience and from the experiences of authors I've known and/or helped over the years. So if my own techniques don't work for you, some of the others might.

A bit about me. I entered the publishing industry in 1994 when I received contracts to write a trilogy of near-future techno-thrillers (under the pen name Jefferson Scott). A few years later, I wrote a trilogy of military thrillers. Parallel to my fiction-writing career, my career as an editor was taking off. I worked on staff as an editor for three publishing houses before going freelance in 2006. Then in 2008, I launched my own indie publishing house, Marcher Lord Press. Between that, my freelance editing, and the fun I have teaching novelists how to better do what it is they're trying to do, I'm *busy*.

In this publishing career I've become friends with over two hundred multipublished novelists. As I mentioned, the tips and techniques you'll find in this book come from my own experience as novelist and editor as well as from these friends, all of whom I polled as I was researching this book. You're getting the expertise of multiple successful authors—not just one—on how to write a novel very, very fast.

Even if you're not writing a novel quickly, though, I hope you will find this to be a useful resource for you. It is the compilation of all my best teaching on how to plan, write, and revise a novel that will engage and satisfy your reader and please agents and editors.

This book is arranged in three sections:

1. Planning Your Novel
2. Writing Your Novel (Fast)
3. Publishing Your Novel

First, we'll do all the preliminaries you need to have in your pocket before writing the first word. This includes your character creation, inner journey work, three-act structure, genre, villain, setting, and more. If you're a seat-of-the-pants writer who wants to plunge ahead trusting your muse, you can do so. But for the rest of us, this early work will save you headaches later. We'll also talk about a few fundamental craft issues as well, though the main craft discussion will come in Part 3. On these main things, it's easier to do it right the first time than have to redo it all later.

In Part 2 we'll talk about how to write this novel in a hurry. All my own tips and the tips from the colleagues I interviewed will be presented there.

In Part 3, we'll talk about revising your novel (that's where the rest of the craft discussion will happen) and what to do with this work of fiction awesomeness you will have created.

the only easy day

When I was writing my military thrillers, I learned the motto of the Navy SEALs: "The only easy day was yesterday." I think it fits as a motto for what we're doing here as well.

It's not a small thing to write a novel. If it were, everyone would do it. It's going to take your best work—a lot of it, all in a row—to get this done. As much as I'd like this book to magically write your novel for you, it's not going to happen.

The main thing that separates the people who could be writers from the people who are writers is a completed, novel-length manuscript. There's nothing glamorous about writing a novel. You might think there is, but there really isn't. On the other hand, there can be lots of glamour in having written a novel, especially one that gets fabulously published. But actually writing it...? Not so much.

It's a long road of concentrated days sitting alone with your keyboard, looking like you're doing basically nothing. It requires the kind of mental discipline that regularly brings very smart and capable people to their knees. It's not for the faint of heart. For the most part, no one cares if you write it or not. You're creating something from nothing, and until it's created, no one will wonder why it had never been created. It's only when they read it that they can see the value you've brought into being. But in that period when you're writing it, it's a lonely time, and some people won't understand what you're doing or why it matters.

But if you have the mental toughness of a Navy SEAL and the stick-to-itiveness of an Olympic athlete—and you are willing to devote the time to writing a novel in a month—you can absolutely do it. It will mean saying no to a lot of great opportunities during that month. It may mean not seeing family and friends very often until you're done. It may require extra expense, like if you need to go live in a hotel or rent an office for thirty days. Your Facebook time will definitely be nipped in the bud.

Face it: If you're going to do this in one month, you're going to have to become a book hermit for a while.

Many things worth doing require such sacrifice. After the 2012 Summer Olympics in London, swimmer Michael Phelps said he was ready to have a life again. He'd given over half his life to swimming, pressing his incredible physical abilities to their utmost, and he'd become the greatest Olympian in history. But it had cost him. He'd essentially missed out on being a kid and a typical teenager. I wouldn't have been surprised if he'd never hit the pool again and instead spent the next ten years locked in his room playing video games. He's earned it.

One life truth we've all learned is that any great endeavor requires great commitment. Rome, as the saying goes, wasn't built in a day. Nor were Olympic champions.

Nor are novelists.

No, for us, it takes *thirty* days!

Yesterday was an easy day compared to what we're about to do now. So clench your willpower muscles, and let's attempt something amazing.

the horrific but true phases of writing a novel

There is one thing that keeps more novelists from finishing their book, one factor that defeats more authors than any other.

Fear.

Perhaps you're that exception who doesn't have any doubts about her own abilities. But the probabilities are that you do, as I do, struggle with fear when it comes to writing fiction. Even if you're not Stephen King, most of your novels will be horror. Maybe not in genre, but certainly in the writer's experience!

What if I stink? What if I can't convey what I am trying to convey? What if my story idea is just stupid? What if I embarrass myself? What if I start but can't finish? What if I do my best but it's just not good enough? What if I use up all this time and money and it ends up being a total waste?

Here's a fear you might not have anticipated: What if what I write ends up revealing all kinds of things about myself I don't even know I'm revealing?

Years ago I went to see a counselor for a while to help me work through some psychological issues. At the end of one of my sessions, I handed him my fourth novel, which was the first in my military trilogy. The next time we met, he handed it back to me and said, "Well, that certainly explains a lot."

Gah! *What* did it explain? What was I revealing through the book that I didn't realize I was revealing? This revelation of your inner thinking can be frightening, and it can lead to a lot of stalling and procrastinating. But if you're going to write your novel in thirty days, you have to kick this fear out on its keester. You don't have the luxury of waiting around forever to finally do it. And, frankly, I suspect the reason you picked up this book is that you're tired of waiting for "one day" to come. You're ready to write this puppy *now*. Good for you.

But if there's still a temptation to delay that fateful moment for as long as possible, try this: Just don't promise to let anyone read it. Maybe you can dodge that one for a while. Go stealth. On the other hand, your significant others, who might be allowing you to hole up in a writer's cave for a month, might demand they get to read it as payment for letting you go do it. In that case, hand them someone else's manuscript.

Kidding! Hand them your manuscript. Seriously, you can't let fear rule you as you write this novel. Take it from me: Lots of people less capable than you have written novels. I know you can do this.

And here's another thing: If you're expecting everyone to love your novel, you're in for an unpleasant surprise. Some people will love it—even some people not related to you. But some people will not like it. Some will be *meh* about it. Others will actively dislike it and will go out of their way to blog their dislike to the world. (Most of those folks are jealous of you, but that's a discussion for another day.)

You can take solace in the fact that even the grand masters of literature suffered the same fate. A reviewer of *Anna Karenina* by Leo Tolstoy called it "sentimental rubbish" and challenged anyone to "show me one page that contains an idea." Ouch. Even the Bard himself had critics: "Shakespeare's name, you may depend on it, stands absurdly too high and will go down." Ah ... no.

Nor will all of your fellow novelists hold you in deepest respect simply because you have joined their elite club. Apparently Mark Twain didn't like Jane Austen at all: "Every time I read *Pride and Prejudice*, I want to dig her up and hit her over the skull with her own shinbone."

Wow.

Who knew that being a novelist could be so brutal?

so what?

Okay, so there are things that might cause you to feel trepidation when it comes to writing a novel. That's why I mention them at the outset. It's good to arm yourself now.

The fact that there are dangers in the writing trade only serves to reinforce that you're undertaking something many people would never even try. Are there dangers in attempting an ascent of Mount Everest? Are there dangers in attempting to circumnavigate the globe on a sailboat? Of course.

With fiction, the dangers threaten your sense of self-respect rather than your life and limb (though Stephen King's *Misery* shows us that the latter can occasionally happen).

So what? So somebody doesn't like your book? Big deal. You probably don't like everything everyone else has written, right?

Write a novel for the right reasons. Even if you were to climb Mount Everest, run a marathon, win an Olympic gold medal, *and* write a novel, it would not prove that you're a good person. You have to answer that question through means other than accomplishments. If you're writing a novel to prove that you're an important person, it's likely to be empty. Don't even start. If you're writing a novel to get everyone to like you, you will fail. You'll never make that happen.

You have to write this novel because you want to, because it's burning a hole in your heart, and because no one else is writing exactly the kind of novel that ought to be out there. You have to write it for you.

A word about the examples I use in this book. I'm a movie guy—a film school grad, an Akira Kurosawa fan, and a screenwriter—so my examples are often from movies. I do that without apology, even though this is a book about writing novels.

Film is the highest, most powerful form of storytelling in our culture today, in my opinion, and the principles that make for strong cinema also make for strong fiction. It's much more likely that you have seen *Star Wars* than that you've read some novel I might name—and even if you haven't, it would take you only two hours to become familiar with the whole movie.

Besides, if you write your novel according to the principles of good film storytelling, it may come in handy when it's time to turn your book into a screenplay!

But at the moment, you're going to write this novel—and I'm going to show you how. And you're going to do it in thirty days. Afterwards, I'm going to teach you how to seek publication for this work of fiction. Take a minute to picture yourself having written it all. Stay in that moment for a while. Savor it.

Because when you do finally write that novel, when "one day" is *today*, you will have overcome fears, detractors, and difficulty, and you will stand on that mountaintop knowing that you have achieved something very, very few others ever will.

part one

planning
your
novel

the ultimate story

Writing a novel is all about victories. Certainly completing a full novel is a great victory. But there are smaller victories along the way. Consider them supporting triumphs that unite in an irresistible rush toward your eventual coup.

In those moments when you're not feeling especially triumphant, remembering the victories you have already achieved will hopefully inspire you to press onward. You'll see that you're heaping up victories here. If you're on Victory 8, that means you must've achieved at least seven victories before then, and that's got to encourage any writer. You're winning this contest of will and endurance. You're going to emerge the victor.

your first victory

If you could write any story at all, what would it be? The ultimate novel. The story no one else has written—or written *right*—that you would love to see brought to reality. If you were given the keys to the vault of creative wonders and told to go inside and pick out ten items that ought to be in the most amazing novel ever written, what would you bring out?

Unleash your imagination here. Give yourself freedom to dream way, way big. Throw off those voices that say you're not ready to write *that* story yet or the fear that says you could never accomplish something so beautiful. You're in a realm of perfect liberty. Your creativity is unfettered now, freed of the burdens of "reality" that would keep you looking at the two feet of concrete ahead of you instead of to the stars. Lift your eyes.

Don't censor yourself. If you've always longed to see how *Gone With the Wind* would've gone if Scarlett had chosen differently, write that idea down on a sheet of paper or a blank page in a word processing program.

Don't listen to the voice that says, "Well, you're not Margaret Mitchell," or, "You'd never be able to get the copyright clearance to do that story." You're brainstorming right now, so don't shoot down any idea. You're after a creative spark that will power you through a long and difficult journey. Besides, you could write a story that was like that other one but different enough to avoid legal problems. Just reach for the exciting idea right now.

Have you always wanted to write an epic fantasy about intelligent hermit crabs who rise up to defeat their blowfish overlords? Write it down! Have you always wanted to explore the lengths a mother would go to protect her child from a predator? Write that idea down. Have you wished you could learn what it would've been like to live in another time or in another culture or in another family or in another career or as a celebrity or in an alternate history?

What you're looking for here is the idea that makes your brain go, "Whoa! Could I really write *that* story? Could I truly have permission to write something as abso-stinkin'-credible as that?"

When you've found the idea that lights up the pleasure centers of your brain like a Christmas tree with twenty strands of lights, you've found the story you should write in thirty days.

And when you've found that, you've won your first victory.

Because, as I mentioned in the Introduction, writing a novel is hard work. Even if you're doing it all in thirty days, as opposed to a year or more, it's still a very long project. How many garden or yard projects have you worked on for thirty days in a row, all day, every day?

Anything you work on that long and that intensely is going to make you want to stop the insanity! So you'd better have a great reason for doing it, a compelling engine that will drive you to keep doing it.

An incredible idea that fires your creative juices like nobody's business is the best engine for your project. What would that idea be ... for you ... today? Write it down.

You see what I'm doing, don't you? I'm getting you to come up with the idea for the novel you're going to write in thirty days. Sneaky me.

You may have already thought you knew what book you were going to write. You may have had a specific purpose and story in mind. You may even have an assignment to write a certain novel in a very short time. All of that may cause you to write some other novel besides the ultimate novel you've been thinking of as you've read this chapter, and that's okay.

But if the story you were going to write doesn't stoke your imagination like the story idea that came to your mind just now, maybe you're headed toward the wrong story. If you have the freedom to choose any story (and I realize you may not), why not choose to write the most exciting story you can possibly imagine?

In the end, that story kernel may be the most important part of this novel.

the greatest commandment

If you've spent much time learning about the craft of fiction, your writing teachers have doubtlessly imparted the rules and laws of fiction. Perhaps you've been told to avoid "to be" verbs or "-ly" adverbs, or maybe you were told to use—or avoid—certain points of view (POV). You also may have heard that you should show and not tell, even if you're not sure what that means.

And if you've *really* been studying fiction craftsmanship, I suspect you've encountered something else: Fiction experts disagree!

Most aspiring writers don't see that one coming. They assume fiction writing, like most activities, has a fixed set of rights and wrongs—or at least best practices to follow. And they expect the acknowledged masters will teach them the large but not infinite set of commandments of writing great fiction. Then these admirable novelists expect to take those rules to heart and head down the path to writing great fiction.

The problem is that there is no universally acknowledged set of rules when it comes to fiction. For every *law* engraved in granite, there's a glaring exception. For every expert saying, "Do X," there are five others saying, "Whatever you do, don't do X."

"Prologues are bad and should always be eliminated!" some fiction experts say. While others, including me, say that prologues are awesome and should be in every novelist's toolkit. Now, I understand that prologues are often done poorly and contain nothing but backstory, and I agree that those prologues should be cut. But it's the poor execution and the presence of backstory, not the fact that it is a prologue, that is the problem.

The point remains: Fiction teachers disagree. And not just on small rules that might be forced to live side by side, but on irreconcilable matters. I mean, you can't simultaneously have and not have a prologue, right? You can't both use and not use description or omniscient POV or "–ly" adverbs.

The poor novelist, seeking with all earnestness to apply every teaching from every fiction authority, is rendered paralyzed. What's a body to do?

Allow me to simplify.

There is only one commandment for fiction. Only one law that, if broken, will kill your novel. All other rules are optional, unfixed, and up for debate. Isn't that great?

I'm not saying there aren't gatekeepers in your life who will approve or disapprove of your novel even if you get this commandment right. I've seen an editor reject a novel simply because it had a prologue. I've seen novels declined because they had too much (or too little) description, bad dialogue, telling instead of showing, poorly drawn characters, and a hundred other violations of the "rules" of fiction.

But if you were somehow able to collect and analyze one thousand rejection decisions all made on this one date in history, you would find that the reasons for the rejections did not form a cohesive, codified system of thinking. You'd find radical inconsistencies across the lot of them.

The sad truth is that there is no consensus. Nor will everyone agree with my one commandment. It's not something that fiction editors and agents will rise up and herald. It's not even directed to industry professionals. The one commandment of fiction is about readers and why they come to fiction at all.

It is this: *You must engage your reader from beginning to end.* That's it. Keep your reader hooked. An engaged reader reads your book. A disengaged reader stops reading it.

How to gain and retain reader engagement is the topic of upcoming Victories, but for now just keep in mind that this is the only thing you must do to keep your novel from failing.

I have to confess something to you about this commandment: I don't like it. It goes against every writing-teacher instinct in my being. I want to be able to tell you that high fiction craftsmanship is what will make or break your novel. Otherwise, why in the world am I working so hard to help writers elevate their fiction craftsmanship?

But if you look at what makes a novel a blockbuster, be it *Jurassic Park* or *Fifty Shades of Grey* or the Harry Potter series or The Hunger Games trilogy or the Twilight Saga or whatever else, it's probably not the refined skillfulness of the author that made it work. The author may indeed have what industry insiders would consider high craftsmanship (or not…), but that isn't what made the book a phenomenon. The thing that made each of those books become huge was that each one engaged readers from beginning to end. They obeyed the Great Commandment of Fiction.

For the typical person, reading a whole novel is hard. Most folks don't have massive blocks of undivided time in which to do something optional like reading a book. They have to read it in fits and starts, which will inevitably cause them to pick the novel back up again at random spots in the story—like halfway through a paragraph. There's a hurdle to overcome every time the reader tries to start again. The only thing that keeps them hurdling (outside of being directly related to the author) is being *engaged* in the book.

John Q. Reader wouldn't know a paragraph of backstory if it bit him on the nose. He wouldn't know or care that the author is hopping around into everyone's point of view. He wouldn't stop reading the book if he encountered one too many sentences in passive voice.

What John Q. Reader knows is whether or not the book is boring him.

This fact should encourage you. Write a story that enough people consider truly interesting—with a great premise, engaging action, compelling characters, and so forth—and your novel will succeed, despite a few broken "rules" here and there. Or despite a lot of broken rules.

Now, I hope you'll pay heed to what I think makes for strong fiction craftsmanship, and I hope you won't point to broken fiction rules in popular novels and say, "See, you don't have to work so hard for your book to be a bestseller!" The sad truth is that it's reader engagement, not a mastery of craft, that plays a larger part in a book's likeliness to succeed.

You may have to deal with the literary elite to get your book published, and some of those folks may reject your book because it fails on whichever craftsmanship issue they most treasure. But if you can get past those obstacles (and I hate to put myself in the category of *obstacle!*) and place your book into the hands of John Q. Public readers, then it will be down to whether or not your book engages them through to the end.

And that's what it should be about. A thoroughly engaging novel covereth a multitude of fiction sins. It is, in the final analysis, the only thing that matters about your novel.

the premise

Think about your favorite novels. What delighted you about them? Why are they your favorites? Probably the story was intriguing to you. Possibly the characters were especially fun or memorable. Maybe it was an excellent example of what makes your favorite genre so great. Maybe it gave you a new insight or took you to a place that lit the fires of your imagination. Perhaps the book made you laugh or cry or feel motivated to make a change.

As you contemplate new novels to read, what informs your decisions? Many readers tend to return to authors and series they have enjoyed in the past. They also tend to have favorite genres, so they'll browse in those areas when looking for a new book. Perhaps they'll read a novel because of good reviews or because it's famous or influential.

Readers may not even know what they're looking for. Maybe they're waiting to be grabbed by something that looks and sounds interesting.

In other words, sometimes readers read a novel because of the premise. Someone tells them about a book they're reading, and it sounds intriguing. Or they read the back cover copy or see a book trailer or read someone's Facebook comment, and think, "Wow, that sounds awesome. What's the name of that book? I have to read it."

Premise, in my opinion, is the single largest component in what makes people want to read a novel. This is especially true if the reader has had no prior connection with the author, the series, or the genre. They're going to weigh the idea of reading your novel against the idea of reading some other novel, and the thing that will tip the balance is which book they think sounds most interesting.

What's the difference between premise and core idea? Earlier in this victory I had you contemplating the ultimate story idea, the central spark that lights the fire in you, the engine that can power you through thirty days of writing. How is that different from premise?

Well, they're similar. In the end, it doesn't really matter. They're sort of interchangeable. But if I had to define them, I'd say that the core idea is, as I mentioned earlier, the "incredible idea that fires your creative juices like nobody's business." It's what makes you want to sit down and write it. Premise, on the other hand, is what makes a reader want to read it.

The core idea for my first published novel was two combatants locked in the mortal struggle of a virtual reality battle across the Internet, the combat careening through various Web pages such as a NASA telepresence operation of a lunar rover, a big corporation's annual report meeting, and a tourist site giving 3-D tours of ancient Egypt. It was a moment, or really, a feeling, an amalgamation of events that could lead to creating that moment. That's why I wrote that novel—to get to that moment.

But that wouldn't have translated very effectively into back cover copy for the potential reader. So I wrote up something that would work better to convince readers to pick up the book. I came up with a premise: "Someone is killing people across the Internet. Don't log in. You might be next." Or something along those lines.

The premise of *Raiders of the Lost Ark* might be something like, "An archaeologist struggles to rescue the lost ark before the Nazis can use its power." That might not be why Spielberg decided to do the movie, but it's why a lot of people went to see it.

What will the premise of your novel be? You've already given some thought to what might be the ultimate story ever, and that should be the book you write. Now consider how to articulate that idea so that it appeals to the largest audience possible. Make it a big idea. Or, in Hollywood terminology, make it "high concept."

Make it an intriguing idea.

recipe for success

Here's my recipe for a novel that has the best chance of becoming a blockbuster (outside of your already being famous or having an unlimited marketing budget):

- Up to 4 points for premise
- Up to 2 points for genre
- Up to 2 points for an enjoyable first page
- Up to 1 point for cover art
- Up to 1 point for author reputation or the reader's past experience with the author
- A fraction of a point for intangible mystery (fiction craftsmanship, strong edit, good copyedit, artistic typeset, etc.)

Some of these ingredients are about what makes a person buy the book, and some of them are about what could make the book become huge. Those are different things, but they obviously overlap.

The thing that could make it go huge isn't even on the list. What causes readers to love a novel is that the author adhered to the Great Commandment of Fiction. If she is engaged from beginning to end, she won't care that it has a terrible cover or lots of typos or low fiction craftsmanship. But she probably won't find out that it engages her from beginning to end unless the ingredients above are met. So you have to do both.

I think the typical fiction shopper looks at that list and does some mental calculus when deciding whether or not to read a given novel. She's looking for a book that scores at least a 4 on that bulleted list. So if the premise grabs her, she's at a 4 already and will buy the book. Hence the importance of a great premise. If the premise is merely okay, she'll look for other things to get that book to a 4. She'll browse her favorite genre (2 points) and look for an author she likes (1 point), cover art she likes (1 point), or at least a partially interesting premise (0–4 points). She might even read the first page to see if it appeals to her. If all of those elements add up to a 4 or more, she'll buy it.

See where great fiction craftsmanship ranks in her mathematics? Dead last. She probably couldn't even gauge that when she's just shopping, anyway. But if she does read it, she may find that it has "a pinch of intangible mystery" that enhances her enjoyment. That's how it seems to the general reader, anyway. Professionals know the mystery includes craftsmanship, structure, character work, excellent editing, a good copyedit, an attractive typeset, and more. The general reader may not be able to articulate why the book seems solid, professional, and well done, but you and I know what creates that aura.

Still … dead last. Really? Probably, yeah. Typical reader here, remember.

Earlier in this chapter, I had you think of an idea for your story, and now I want you to think about your novel's premise—the question or theory that drives the idea to the end. In other words, the "sound bite" that will make a reader want to check it out.

Don't worry if you can't think of anything that feels high concept right away. The main thing is finding that core idea that will energize your thirty days of writing. You can articulate your premise later.

your story core

You may have a strong premise in mind, but let's dig deeper and further develop your story's *core idea*.

isolating the core idea

Look over your list of brainstormed ideas. Rank them in order of how much joy you get from just thinking about them.

Now look at the top one on the list. Is that the novel you most want to write? It's great, but would it be absolutely perfect if it had elements of the other top ideas on your list?

Why not combine them all? Now is the time to cherry-pick the most exciting elements of all of your top ideas and drop them into one basket. You'll figure out later how they can all work together. Details, right? For now, you just want to assemble the most audaciously mind-blowing multiheaded warhead of awesomeness you can think of.

Write a sentence—even an egregiously long one—stating the top elements that send your excitement level through the roof. Go ahead, write it out.

This will become your focus statement. Your lodestar. Your premise. Your *core idea*. It will guide you as you write, and it will return you quickly to the right path if you veer off it.

celebrating the core idea

Now take a moment to wax poetic about what you love about this core idea and what makes it so wonderful. Go ahead and gush. Write a whole page or more. Mention every last thought that occurs to you concerning what you hope to accomplish and why this idea thrills you so much.

You're going to need this later—trust me. Here's why: As soon as you start writing this book, you will lose all objectivity about it. Guaranteed. It happens every time, no matter how many novels you write or how accomplished you become. And when you reach that point of lost objectivity, the doubts emerge from the shadows and pounce on you. You will be assailed by voices telling you the idea is stupid and not worth working on. And you won't be able to resist those voices, because you won't "feel it" anymore. You won't remember why it's such a good idea.

That's why you need the page you're writing right now. When those doubts come, just pull out this page and reread it. It will remind you that it really was—*is*—a good idea. If you can just press on and accomplish all the things you knew would make this story wonderful, then you will emerge on the other side of it and will eventually begin to believe again. You can say, "Well, I can't see it anymore myself, but I successfully wrote the story I thought would be cool, so I just have to trust that it really is cool."

developing the idea

Now elaborate on your übercool core idea. What else do you already know, just by having that idea, and what do you need to find out?

For instance, if the idea that lights your creative fires is to bring to life the story of Chen Guanming, the Chinese farmer who rode his rickshaw 90,000 miles from Jiangsu province to London to watch the Summer Olympics (an amazing true story, by the way), then you already know some things about your story.

You know you'll need to do some deep character work to understand Mr. Chen. You know you'll need to research his story and his path. You know it's a contemporary story, not a historical or a science fiction. You know it's an intimate character study, not an epic, so there probably won't be many story lines outside of Chen's. You even know the rough outline of your novel: Chen before the trip, Chen's decision to make the trip, the trip itself (the main portion of your book), and his arrival and reward.

If your idea is about a man who in 2015 gets abducted by extraterrestrials and taken to their galactic empire far away, then you know that you'll need to create the aliens and their civilization and technology, for starters. Maybe the man is terrified at first, but later he doesn't want to go home. Why is that? Now you need to know the backstory for the man, his problems at home, or maybe the things that make him realize he needs to stay. Maybe he's in love, or wants to help a revolution, or is just a curious scientist. You will know some things right away, but you will need to know more. (Note that I said *you* need to know his backstory; that doesn't mean the reader necessarily needs to know it—more on show and tell in a future Victory.)

So take a look at your lodestar sentence and ask yourself: If this is the story I'm going to write, what do I already know about the task ahead?

Start writing your lists. List the things you automatically know, things to research or invent, characters who will probably populate the story, main movements of the story, the era and setting and genre (if you know them), and anything else you can derive just by thinking about your core story idea.

Keep these lists handy, as you'll probably think of things to add to them later.

goals

Here at the outset, I want to make explicit the goals that will help you accomplish the novel that you're going to write in thirty days.

word count

First, we're shooting for at least fifty thousand words. Fifty thousand is the bar set by the NaNoWriMo people, so that's a good one for us. Does that mean your novel can't go beyond 50K—or fall short of it? Absolutely not. But if you get approximately fifty thousand words in your pocket, the hardest work will be over.

So don't worry if you finish your book and it's either below or over the fifty-thousand-word mark—or if you reach the end of your thirty days, have "only" 50K written, but still have 50K more to go. The point is to get over the main hump in a hurry, and that's what I'll help you do in thirty days.

a usable rough draft

At the end of thirty days, I don't expect you to have a polished draft ready to be sent to publishers. I hope you're not expecting that either.

What I do hope you'll have in your hands is a workable rough draft. You'll have something there that wasn't there before. You'll have a lump of clay that looks more or less like the vase you were trying to make. It doesn't matter if it's not finished yet—that wasn't the goal. Now you can go back and revise and rewrite and polish. But that's a whole lot better than looking at a blank page and a blinking curser that chants, "Loo-zer, loo-zer, loo-zer," at you.

something proved

The main thing I want to do for you, especially if you've never written a novel before, is to prove that you can do it. That you really can be a novelist.

My own first novel—which shall live in infamy and shall never be published—was only around 45,000 words. But that didn't matter. What mattered was that the exercise proved to me that I could actually write a long story. The longest fiction I'd ever written before that was probably ten thousand words, so I honestly didn't know if I could do it.

Just getting through that first draft was a confidence booster. What's more, I'd found my groove. I realized that, if I needed to, I could've kept going and going. I'd broken through a psychological barrier, and on the other side was freedom and the knowledge that I really could do this writing thing.

I suddenly realized beyond a doubt that I had it in me to be a novelist.

That's what you're going to see about yourself, too.

genre

After putting your finger on your novel's core idea, your next Victory will be to decide on its genre.

Genre refers to what type or category of story this is going to be: science fiction or romance or Western or horror or chick lit. Your novel doesn't have to fit into any genre if you don't want it to. And there's nothing preventing you from blending genres or even inventing your own, but most books tend to fall into one category or another. Where will yours fit?

Let me pose the question another way: If your novel were already written and published and a bookstore received five of them to put on display, in what section would the books be shelved?

genre alternatives

Depending on how your übercool story idea came to you, you may be pretty well locked into the genre you want to write. I mean, if your idea is to write the most romantic Regency Romance ever penned by a human, you're probably going to write it as a Regency Romance, right?

But it's also possible that yours is a story idea in search of a genre. If your core idea is more thematic, like an exploration of man's inhumanity to man or the Problem of Evil, that may not automatically suggest a genre. In that case, you have some fun ahead of you. The field is wide open.

Always wanted to try your hand at a historical novel set in World War II Stalingrad? Why not explore your story idea against that backdrop? Is your idea about a boy's ascent to manhood? A story like that could be told in any genre, but fantasy is a natural choice, as it lends itself so well to the mythic and symbolic and tends to feature coming-of-age stories.

Even if you think you know what genre you want to write your novel in, I challenge you to consider alternatives.

Yes, your idea to write the plight of a young pioneer woman going West to settle in the Oregon Territory would work very well as a historical novel. But what if you wrote it as a science fiction about a young female astrophysicist heading out to deep space to colonize the first habitable Earthlike planet? See how you can explore the same situations in both genres? But one might give you the opportunity to look at the idea from a different perspective.

Or better, the alternative genre might allow you to do some things—or *say* some things—that the original choice wouldn't let you. For example, what if you wanted to talk about how one of the Native American leaders wasn't a very nice guy? Well, the Political Correctness Police would be all over you for that if you wrote that in a historical novel. But if it was a science fiction and the Poombah of Rigel-9 wasn't a very nice guy, you'd be in the clear.

I used to write puppet scripts for kid shows. The things puppets could get away with saying was amazing. If adults got up and said the same things, there would be an uproar, but puppets could say them all day long. That's the benefit of using a storytelling technique that is once removed, such as an unexpected genre for your story. The reader can really see the issues rather than having the knee-jerk reaction that comes with a more traditional setting.

So what about your story idea? Did you have a genre in mind when the core idea came to you? If so, write that down.

Then, just for fun, write down seven alternative genres for your book. Now give at least thirty seconds of thought to each one. Would your story idea become very interesting if told in that way? You're watching for the proverbial lightbulbs to go off as you cast your mind across these ideas. Don't worry if none of the alternatives gives you a better jolt than the original genre idea you had. In that case, you'll be that much more confident that you chose wisely.

If you had no genre in mind when you came up with your story idea, you should write down at least ten genre alternatives. Go to Amazon.com and browse through the genres of fiction. Write down any that strike your fancy, even if you don't know what they are or how to write them.

The following examples caught my eye when I glanced at the Genre Fiction page in Books at Amazon.com:

- Action & Adventure
- Coming of Age
- Metaphysical
- Sea Adventures
- War

There are also major categories for "Science Fiction & Fantasy," "Historical Fiction," "Mystery, Thriller & Suspense," and more. Clicking on these categories reveals multiple subcategories. Like Books > Science Fiction & Fantasy > Fantasy > Epic—a sub-subcategory that includes over thirteen thousand titles!

As you browse through all the choices, keep your core idea in mind. It might be a good idea to have that sentence in front of you so you can keep all the main components of your idea in mind as you look. When any genre choice sets off a fun little glow in your brain, write that genre down (along with a note of what you thought was cool about that genre choice for your story).

After half an hour of this, you'll probably have a nice little list going. What's more, you'll probably be feeling a buzz about your story idea all over again. Rarin' to write, even.

Keep in mind that you can combine genres if you want to. Like the idea of a road/journey novel but also want to have a murder mystery going on? Why not do both? Unless you're writing for Harlequin or some other publisher that has a fixed framework that you must write to, there's nothing preventing you from getting all wacky when it comes to your genre choices.

Just remember: All things, even your choice of genre, need to serve your core idea. Not the other way around.

genre implications

Your choice of genre has ramifications for the story. Fun ramifications. Ramifications that will help you accomplish what it is you're hoping to do with this novel.

For instance, if you choose to write your book as a vampire romance, the genre automatically hands you some elements for your story. You know you're going to have at least one vampire main character and probably at least one human main character. You know you're going to have a romance, which itself suggests some story elements: how the main characters meet, how their romance begins, and so on. There will probably be do-gooders out there trying to go all Van Helsing on your poor misunderstood creature of the night. You'll have the trappings of vampires as well, including those famous hungers, a preference for nocturnal activities, and a four-poster bed made of fine cedar.

If you wrote it as a police procedural, you'd be handed entirely different—but equally useful—elements. The Victory here is to choose a genre that will amplify what your story is about.

Once you have chosen a genre, use every item in that genre's kit. Exploit the genre's potential to push your idea to its limit.

If your story idea could fit in any number of genres, look for one with characteristics that will allow you to explore several sides of that idea.

For instance, if your core idea is to explore the limits of a man's faith in the face of persecution, you could certainly tell it as a contemporary novel. But what if you picked a genre that took conflicts like this to an extraordinary level? Perhaps a legal thriller à la *Inherit the Wind* or a historical novel set in the midst of a pogrom, or a fantasy in which the hero stands alone against a godless villain who would enslave the world? It's all about the impact of your core story idea. What genre would give your idea the maximum support in your effort to accomplish the things you love about it? If you've found yourself drawn to a genre you know almost nothing about, you're in for more fun. Do a Google search on the genre to see what people are saying about it. Search for it on Amazon and read some sample chapters. Better yet, read a whole novel. If movies have been made in this genre, watch a couple of them. The idea is not to copy these other stories, but to begin to get a feel for what constitutes the genre. Talk about your pleasurable research projects!

setting, era, and backdrop

Another way to draw out aspects of your story is to carefully choose your setting, era, and backdrop. Whatever your genre, these selections can further amplify your idea.

For instance, if you wanted to explore a woman's struggle to rise to her potential despite the forces arrayed against her, you could do it as a modern-day tale set in the corporate jungle. Or you could consider another setting, era, and/or backdrop that would add color and commentary to her struggle. You could set it in 1893 in New Zealand during the time when women fought for suffrage (New Zealand was the first nation to extend the right to vote to all women). Or you could set it against the backdrop of the Women's Liberation Movement of the 1960s or against the social repression of Victorian England.

By *backdrop* I mean the larger social issues going on at the time; e.g., things like the Vietnam War and the Antiwar Movement, the Salem Witch Trials, Prohibition, the Great Depression, the Crusades, the Black Death, and the Dot-Com Bubble.

Take a moment to let your mind roam across cultures and nations and all of history to see if you might not find a backdrop or an era or even a setting (like a sailing ship vs. a maximum security penitentiary vs. a soldier's trench) that gives you an *Aha!* about your story. If it gives you an angle or a handle or a flash of inspiration, maybe that's the way you should go with your novel.

In all of Part 1 of this book, what we're looking to do is find the optimum jewelry setting for the diamond that is your core story idea. What will best make it sparkle and showcase its brilliance? What combination of factors will best ensure that you achieve all the levels of coolness you wrote down when you had the idea at the outset? A thoughtful selection of genre, setting, era, and backdrop will help you get there.

your hero

Good fiction is about someone. Some-*one*.

Yes, it might be about lots of people, or you might have dual protagonists or ten viewpoint characters, and on some level your novel might even be about everyone. But in the end, as far as the reader is concerned, it's about one person.

I think this is because we all view the world as being about one person: me. We go through this life in first-person perspective—one person's story—experienced through one person's eyes and ears and mind. We are certainly aware of other people and can enjoy their presence in our lives, but we generally perceive the world as the story of one person at a time.

So when we come to fiction, we're looking for our surrogate, our keyhole character, the one person either most like us or with whom we can most identify.

Because, in the final analysis, what we're really looking for is a way to vicariously live the events of this story. We want to walk in the shoes of someone else, not necessarily to escape our own situation but perhaps to see how someone else might respond to these events—and to compare that to how we would respond. We wonder what it would be like if we were faced with that choice or living in that future or forced to go through that tragedy.

It's not voyeurism so much as a desire to expand our own experiences and learn from other people's lives how to better live out our own.

Your novel, too, is about some-*one*.

It's great if you want to have an ensemble cast, or co-protagonists, as in a romance, but despite your efforts or preferences the reader is going to pick one person to be his or her *person* in this story.

Think about your own experience. If you loved the movie *Steel Magnolias*, did you love all the characters equally, or was one your favorite? You might've pulled for everyone in *Band of Brothers*, but probably there was one main guy who most claimed your allegiance. In a romance with co-protagonists, I'm guessing you probably identified with one or the other of the main two.

Male readers, research has shown, connect best with male protagonists, while women have a much greater ability to connect with a hero of either gender. So keep your target readership in mind when you choose your protagonist.

Speaking of whom ...

who is your hero?

Go back to the elongated sentence you wrote that encapsulated all the coolest features of this core story idea. Read it again, along with the surrounding notes. Once again get into the wonderful mood that idea put you in.

As you think about that idea, who do you see right in the middle of it all?

Who is the person most affected by those events? Who is the intrepid mover making things happen? Who is the person at the helm of—or at the mercy of—what's going on in this story?

Depending on what kind of novelist you are, as you will see below, you may or may not have anyone in mind to be your protagonist. No worries.

plot first vs. character first

In my Writer's Digest book *Plot Versus Character*, I outline in detail my theory that every novelist is one of two sorts. According to that theory, you are either what I call a plot-first novelist or a character-first novelist.

The plot-first novelist comes up with story ideas with ease. This person says, "Ooh, wouldn't it be cool if..." and completes the sentence with some plot idea, be it alien invasion, action scenario, or epic quest.

If that's you, your core story idea sentence is probably plot related.

The character-first novelist, by contrast, comes up with ideas for *characters* all day long. This writer says, "Ooh, I can imagine this person who…" and completes the sentence with an idea for a person in some situation or beset by some challenge—maybe a single mother living in the Great Depression or a Wild West gunfighter with nothing left to live for after the death of his beloved wife and family.

If this is you, your core story idea sentence is probably about a person in an interesting predicament.

Neither is better than the other. You work the way you work depending on how you're wired. Also, you might be a character-first novelist normally, but in this case your story kernel was plot related, or vice versa. That's okay. I'm speaking in generalities here to make a point. Your story idea might not even be especially plot or character related; perhaps you want only to explore a theme. That's great, too.

In other words, if you're a character-first novelist, you probably already have some idea of a main character for this story. If you're a plot-first novelist, or if your story idea is philosophical in nature, you may have no idea who your novel's main character might be.

It's all good.

Whether you already know who your hero is or not, let's take a minute to think about this person (or *being*, if you're writing speculative fiction).

who your hero needs to be

As I said at the outset of this Victory, fiction is about some-*one*. Your reader is expecting this novel to be about one main person, the reader's surrogate, even if there are many other characters in the book.

Who will that someone be for your novel?

It must be someone who is on the front lines of all the action. It needs to be someone who will take an active role in what's going on. It needs to be someone who will be present for all the main events. It needs to be the person who, at the climactic moment of the story, is doing the key thing to try to win the day. And, as we'll see in a future Victory, that person needs to be transformed during the course of the story.

Who—or, rather, what kind of person—does the hero of your story need to be?

Go back to your core story idea sentence and ask that question. Look at your genre and era, too. If you're going to be writing a novel about Occupy Wall Street, who might your protagonist be? An activist living in the tent city and striving for social justice? One of the policemen trying to keep order? One of the women raped by the protesters?

If your novel is going to be a romantic comedy about love among the staff at a ritzy hotel, will your main character be a young woman newly hired on the housekeeping staff? A happy-go-lucky greensman on the landscaping crew? The ambitious assistant manager climbing the corporate ladder?

If you're writing a novel about the revolution in 2013 Syria, will your hero be a soldier fighting to preserve the regime? A rebel trying to overthrow it and establish Sharia law? The parent of a child hung by the neck by one side or the other? A foreign "observer" from some country far away? A journalist? A Red Cross worker?

Just wade around a while in your story idea and genre/era choices. Begin thinking through how you would actually accomplish the story you want to tell. What kind of person would be ideally positioned for every major event that will happen?

Some people like to ask it this way: Who hurts most in this story? I think that's a useful question, because the reader is going to closely connect with whoever suffers the most in your book.

Might as well use that connection to your advantage and make this person your hero.

So think about your novel idea. As you've read over this section, has a picture of a hero begun to emerge? Write those thoughts down in your chapbook or journal or whatever notes you're keeping about this story.

connect your reader with your hero

In the next Victory, you will begin to create your hero's character and personality. But even before you know what those will be, it's appropriate to talk about connecting your reader to your protagonist.

The reader wants to form a fond connection with your hero. She comes to the book like someone with a crush on you. You have only to give her some positive attention, and she'll commit. She's yours to lose. But lose her, you can. A reader who can't connect with the hero in a novel is a reader about to put that novel down and never pick it up again.

This doesn't mean you can't have a hero who starts low and then has a transformation for the better. Indeed, that's what I recommend you *do* have in your novel. But he can't begin so low that we hate him. If he offends the reader on some bottom line issue, you've lost her. No one wants to spend four hundred pages with a jerk. And if he *is* a jerk at the outset, that's okay so long as—and this is vital—you show the reader a glimpse of the wonderful person concealed within and struggling to get out. Even the Godfather, a brutal killer of men, was a doting grandfather.

Have all of this in mind when you're thinking about your protagonist. He or she can be an antihero or even some sort of scumbag, but the reader needs to see that heart of gold—very early on—or else.

There are at least five strategies for making your hero a likable person with whom the reader wants to connect. You don't have to decide now which one (or ones) you're going to use for your hero, but it's good to drop them into the pot on the front end of this project.

the selfless hero

Selflessness is one of the principal virtues in our culture. Putting someone else's good ahead of our own is considered truly heroic.

Thus the single mother who works two jobs but still somehow manages to do homework with the kids and go out for ice cream once in a while fits the bill, as does the soldier who volunteers to stay behind to cover his buddies' retreat and the silent partner who lets someone else get the glory for work that was actually shared.

Because this is a major quality that endears a person to other people, it follows that showing your hero acting in such ways will endear him or her to the reader. The hero who lives out Mr. Spock's famous words, "The needs of the many outweigh the needs of the few, or the one," will become an instant favorite for your readers. I recommend creating such a character.

Here are several varieties of selflessness to consider for your hero.

the heroic hero

The simplest way to make your hero someone the reader wants to pull for is to show that he or she is, indeed, heroic in some way.

Portray your protagonist as courageous, especially for the benefit of someone else, and your reader will grow an instant bond of love. She stands up for her friend against a bully. He rushes out to help a woman struggling with three kids and five bags of groceries. She takes the fall for something in order to keep someone out of trouble.

Take a moment to let your mind run with the idea of how you might, given this story idea and genre, show your hero saving a little girl's kitty from the tree it's stuck in.

the compassionate hero

Most Americans believe compassion is admirable. When someone reaches out in love toward another, it is considered a virtue. Some belief systems do not value such things at all—compassion is considered a weakness that can be exploited.

It follows that your reader will most likely resonate with a compassionate hero. Show her having mercy on someone when it was within her rights to condemn, or show him going through all kinds of trouble to get a crust of bread to eat, but then show him handing it over to someone who has even less than he does (*Aladdin*), and your reader will grow an instant connection to your protagonist.

the generous hero

We also consider generosity a virtue. We love the bighearted giver. Most of us wish we were in a position to be able to give like that, to support some person or cause we believe in.

Show your hero secretly dropping a hundo into the subway musician's tip jar or leaving a fifty dollar tip for the diner waitress or anonymously buying someone's wares at auction just to be sure he has money to live on (as in the movie *The Artist*), and your reader will find her irresistibly likable. That, I don't have to tell you, is a very good thing.

the kind and gentle hero

In the same vein, we love the gentle soul who cares for orphans or shows kindness to the awkward ballerina no one else seems to notice.

A simple and effective way to connect your reader with your hero is to show your hero being gentle and kind, especially if no one else sees her do so.

the humble hero

Our final category of selflessness is humility. We despise the braggart, the person who always feels the need to draw attention to himself. Girls see it in "peacock" boys a mile away.

Psychologists tell us that the person who feels the need to point out his own greatness is actually doing so because he believes the opposite is true. He feels that everyone else is superior to him and is talking about how inferior he is, and he therefore feels compelled to give evidence to the contrary. His aim is not to show that he's better than everyone else but to feel that he's as good as everyone else. But when we look at him, thinking him a peer, and we see him aggrandizing himself all the time, it just comes across as arrogance.

Whatever the psychology of it, make sure your hero isn't a braggart. It's a real turnoff to your reader.

The corollary to that, of course, is that readers admire the humble man or woman. The person who does not crow about his abilities or accomplishments, who genuinely celebrates the successes of others—especially those not as successful as herself—who takes time for the wishes of someone not in a position to help her get ahead. Such characters become heroes your reader will agree to love.

Think about your own story: Might there be a way to depict your protagonist shunning the spotlight when it rightfully was his? It's a way to endear your hero to the reader.

the charming hero

If your protagonist can make the reader laugh, you've got her.

We all love charming, winsome people. They're fun to be around. They make life a little less burdensome. Create a hero like that, and your reader will definitely stick around to make sure she comes through it okay.

Think of Charlie Chaplin, Eliza Doolittle, Forrest Gump, Adrian Monk, and Captain Jack Sparrow. Think of WALL-E and Lucy (Sandra Bullock's character in *While You Were Sleeping*). We can't help pulling for these plucky charmers. And why wouldn't we want to?

Humor can be hard to write, so don't stress if this isn't a direction you want to go. But if you can create a protagonist who makes us smile, you'll have us in your pocket.

the principled hero

Your hero needs fifty dollars in a hurry to pay off a debt, and she sees a slick corporate guy drop a hundred dollar bill outside a Starbucks and walk away without noticing. What's she going to do?

If she snags the Benjamin and pays off her debt, tucking the other fifty dollars in her pocket and strolling off whistling, your reader will stamp a big ol' *X* over that character. Readers value honesty. Doing the right thing. Character, as they say, is who you are when no one is looking.

But have your hero pick up the money and return it to the corporate exec and then turn around and tell her debtor she'll find some way to pay by tomorrow, and the reader will silently nod. More important, she'll form a strong bond with this heroine. Even if the reader might not have done the same thing in that situation, she'll admire this person and believe her a worthy protagonist.

Show your hero as the "I cannot tell a lie: It was I who cut down the cherry tree" type of person, and we'll connect with her. You provide a glimpse into her heart, and we will know that heart can be trusted to do the right thing not only on the street but later, when the stakes are higher. In presidents like George Washington or Honest Abe, and in heroes in fiction, a high moral character is endearing.

the smart hero

Another way to get us to like your hero is to show him being smart, resourceful, and clever.

There's a reason detective shows are so popular on TV and at the movies. To many people, modern life seems confusing and foggy. We admire people who can see through the smoke and identify what's going on. This banishing of the mystery makes everything—even our lives—seem momentarily clear. We treasure the *Aha!* moment and those who can bring it to us.

Even if your novel is not about a detective, can you make your protagonist a bit of a Sherlock Holmes or Miss Marple? Your reader will connect with a smart hero.

But it's not just a piercing intelligence we admire. We also value people who can be clever in the midst of life's adversities. If your hero finds a canny solution to a problem that plagues others, the reader will begin to like that person.

In the movie *Witness*, eight-year-old Samuel, an Amish boy who has witnessed a murder, has a dilemma. His beliefs won't allow him to engage in violence, even against "bad guys"—but at the same time, he can't stand idly by and allow the bad guys to harm people he cares about. At the crucial moment, instead of picking up a gun or even running away, Samuel rings the bell that signals a fire or other emergency, thus bringing the whole village running to the scene of the struggle and ending the conflict. His brilliant solution shows his resourcefulness and makes us like him that much more.

Elle Woods (Reese Witherspoon's character in *Legally Blonde*) takes what she knows how to do and uses it to succeed in a realm she's never explored. We admire her belief in herself and her resourcefulness in the face of ridicule. Chuck Noland (Tom Hanks's character in *Cast Away*) is a FedEx employee who finds himself stranded on a deserted island. Against extreme odds, he manages to find a way to survive and even thrive, making do with what he has or can make. We admire him, and we wonder if we would be as resourceful in that situation.

When characters like this find a way to win, the reader wins, too. There's a feeling of shared glory, of being proud to be a human and to be associated with such a person.

If the hero you're thinking of creating is going to be a clever cookie, start thinking of ways that person can demonstrate his resourcefulness early in the story. Your reader will love it.

the sympathetic hero

In a sense, the chief aim of any effort to engage your reader with your hero is to cause the reader to feel sympathy. We pull for the home team and the underdog and the orphan. We hate suffering, especially in those with whom we have a connection, and we might even be willing to do something to help that person's condition.

If you can cause your reader to feel sympathetic toward your protagonist, you've won. When you show that gaping hole of pain or loss, the reader leans in, rushing forward with compassion into that person's life like air filling a vacuum.

You can generate sympathy quite easily—for instance, by revealing that the hero's parents were killed in a tragedy when she was a child. There's a reason nearly every Disney protagonist is missing one or both parents. Or you may want to illustrate the hero's aloneness in a scene. For instance, a scene that shows how the hero's great ideas are rejected by everyone around him.

When we feel your hero's loss or grieve with him as he fails once again to achieve a noble goal, we build an instant connection to him.

You need to be careful not to make your hero so sympathetic that she's actually pathetic. We want to pull for a gentle soul caught in a bad situation. But if you show us a sad sack loser, we'll be repulsed, not engaged. Make us feel like this is someone we would like who has just been dealt a terrible hand—but who nevertheless keeps trying—and you'll have us.

unlikable heroes that somehow still work

As you've read over this chapter, you may have thought of the occasional hero, probably in a movie, who was unlikable from the very beginning, and yet the story still worked. You did come to connect with that protagonist, despite how awful he or she began. And that would seem to contradict what I'm saying.

For instance, Gru (Steve Carell's character in *Despicable Me*) is, as the title indicates, despicable. The filmmakers go out of their way to show that he's mean to everyone, even a little boy. Gru knocks the boy's ice cream to the pavement. And then, as if to make up for it, he creates a balloon animal and gives it to the boy—only to pop it, driving home his villainy.

In the movie *Groundhog Day*, Phil Connors (played by Bill Murray) begins the movie as a complete jerk. He berates everyone around him, including the woman he wants to court. He's about the least likable protagonist in modern cinema. Yet the movie works, and the audience comes to love Phil Connors.

I contend that a movie—or even a novel—that succeeds despite a truly unlikable main character succeeds only because of other, outside factors. Perhaps someone else got through the book (*A Christmas Carol*, for example) and assured you that it really does get better if you can just endure the first part.

Or, and this is the explanation for the movies just mentioned, it succeeds because the audience knows this actor from other movies and understands that he often plays someone with a gruff exterior but a heart of gold. The audience expects his character to follow the same trajectory in this movie, as well. Moviegoers are willing to stick with the story in the hope that he'll become nice later.

If the director had cast some unknown actor, or someone who always plays a villain, in that unlikable role, I don't think it would've worked. The audience had to have previous positive experience with that actor in order to have a sense of baggage from his wider body of work.

When a reader comes to your novel, the chances are that she's never encountered this protagonist before. Unless you're writing a historical novel or a later book in a series, this hero will be a brand-new creation. Which means the reader will have no pre-existing fondness for her. In a book like that, if you make your hero unlikable and fail to provide strong hints that she's really a nice person under all of that dysfunction, the reader will probably put your book down and never pick it up again.

conclusion

It's hard to overstate how important your hero is to the success of your novel. Every one of your readers is hoping to find that one person in the story who can become a friend.

Imagine that you have signed up to take a cross-continental train journey with one companion. You have yet to select who that companion will be, and you have a rogues' gallery of choices before you. What are you going to look for in a cabin buddy? What would make the trip not something to be endured but rather the journey of a lifetime? I'm guessing that, at the very least, you're going to look for someone who is not an abrasive imbecile.

So it is when readers pick up this novel you're going to write. They're looking for someone who will make the long trek through your story a pleasure.

Even if you don't know *how* you're going to make your hero likable, just decide here and now *that* you're going to make your hero likable. Your reader needs it.

your hero's personality

Your story is really coming together now. You have your core idea, your awesome premise, your genre, and a sense of how to make your protagonist appeal to readers. The foundation for your novel is taking shape before your eyes.

Figuring out each of these elements at the outset will help your blitz of actual writing to progress along nicely defined channels. You'll have tons of freedom for creative discovery as you write, so don't be afraid that all of this planning is preventing spontaneity. Think of it more like preparing things downstream for the massive water release you're going to conduct at a dam upstream. Get everything set and everyone ready, and then the white water can rush through with all its power and yet manage to achieve all of your purposes. You're harnessing that energy, not letting it run wild.

If you find yourself resisting this planning stage and wanting to skip over what seems to be creativity-killing premeditation, then by all means skip it. This book is meant to be a tool that facilitates your success at this project, not something that forces you to work in a way that doesn't make sense to you. You can always fly by the seat of your pants this time, and next time see if having the rails laid down first helps you keep the train going in the right direction.

There is only one commandment in fiction, after all, and it doesn't have anything to do with planning or not planning. So long as your book engages the reader to the end, it won't matter whether you had it all figured out in advance or only stumbled upon it with the help of your muse.

In the previous Victory, we looked at how crucial your hero is to your novel. We'll continue to explore that line of thought for the next few Victories.

who is this person?

Now we're going to begin creating your hero in earnest. I hope you take all of your major and featured minor characters through this process, but if you don't, I strongly suggest you do it for your hero, at the very least.

I've written another fiction how-to book for Writer's Digest called *Plot Versus Character*. In that book, I present this character creation material in much more detail, so I encourage you to obtain a copy. I'll cover the subject here in overview fashion, which should still give you most of what you need to get going on developing your hero's personality.

If you're a character-first novelist, you may have your hero's personality already firmly established in your mind, but I've found that many of my character-first novelist friends find much value in this process, because they rely almost solely on their instincts, which can result in character inconsistencies.

If you're a plot-first novelist, I urge you to study this Victory in detail and do everything it asks of you. You may try it and not find it helpful, but I suspect it will be a godsend to you. Before I'd developed this process for myself, I was completely at a loss for how to create a realistic character that wasn't a stereotype or a clone of me. If someone had told me how crucial my main character was to the rest of the book, I would've broken out in a sweat, because I knew I didn't have a clue about how to create a great character. Read on, intrepid novelist, and I will show you the way to detailed character building.

ooh, so temperamental!

The starting place for character creation, in my system, is the person's core personality.

Many systems seek to classify all human personalities into a relatively small number of categories or types. There's one based on the four humors of Greek medicine: sanguine, melancholic, choleric, and phlegmatic. There's Benziger's brain-type theory that derives personality from the person's dominant region of the brain. There's the DISC system that draws a person's core personality from the areas of dominance, influence, steadiness, and compliance. There's one that classifies all people according to archetypes. I even found one listing the thirty-seven personality types of youth culture (crunkcore poser, neo-thrash, Williamsburg hipster, etc.).

My favorite is the Myers-Briggs temperament types, especially as articulated in David Keirsey's book *Please Understand Me II*. I recommend this book, as it tells you not only what you need to know about how each temperament thinks and acts but also how they all are as children, spouses, employees, and more.

Do some online research (try keirsey.com, personality-testing.info, etc.) and find a system that makes sense to you.

It doesn't matter which personality system you use so long as you use one (not counting the hipster one). Everything you'll do to create your main character begins with the core personality, so this isn't a step you can skip.

The Myers-Briggs system classifies every person into one of four major groupings, and each grouping has four subtypes within it, resulting in a total of sixteen possible temperaments.

Each temperament is designated by a combination of four letters (INTJ, ESFP, etc.). Each letter is a choice between two options. The first is either I or E, with I standing for introvert and E for extrovert. N or S stands for intuition or sensing. T or F stands for thinking or feeling. And J or P stands for judging or perceiving. These dyads represent how the person interacts with the world. Your four-letter designation is shorthand for describing your core temperament.

Here are the sixteen types by their letter codes. See if one of them sounds like you—and see if you can identify your friends and enemies in this list as well.

- **INFP:** Sees the world as full of wonder, as through rose-colored glasses; must have work that has a meaningful purpose; idealistic.
- **ENFJ:** Organized and decisive; works to build harmony in personal relationships; empathetic; sees potential in everyone.
- **ISFJ:** A serious observer of other people; overwhelming desire to serve others; often taken advantage of; responsible.
- **ESTP:** Tolerant and flexible; actions, not words; the doer, not the thinker; spontaneous; impulsive; competitive.
- **INFJ:** True activist for a worthy cause; good insights into other people; remembers specifics about people who are important to him.
- **ESTJ:** Self-appointed to keep everyone else in line; prefers facts to opinions; stays with the tried and true; practical.
- **ENFP:** Idea person; warm and enthusiastic; enjoys work that involves variety and experimentation.
- **ISTJ:** Quietly thorough and dependable; always seeking to clearly understand things; punctual to a fault; can seem cold; inspector.
- **ESFJ:** Generous entertainer; lover of holidays and special occasions; natural leader; good delegator; encourager; cooperative.
- **ENTP:** Ingenious; outspoken; easily bored by routine; challenges status quo; institutes change; clever; incisive.
- **INTP:** Obsessed with achieving consistency of thought; a gifted scientist; looks for the logical explanation.
- **ENTJ:** Organizes groups to meet task-oriented goals; vision-caster; always seems to find himself leading people and groups; spots inefficiencies and fixes them.
- **INTJ:** System builder; both imaginative and reliable; natural strategist; long-range planner, independent and original; mastermind.

- **ISTP:** Doesn't do something unless it's a big project into which he can throw himself utterly; great "big problem" solver.
- **ESFP:** Exuberant; outgoing; lover of life; hedonistic; serious partier; scattered; always into the new thing; Johnny on the spot; chatty.
- **ISFP:** Sensitive; caring; all about feelings—his and other people's; moody; quiet; kind; doesn't like conflict; needs his own space.

As you read over that list, did one or more of those temperaments jump out at you for the story you want to tell? Maybe not for the hero but for another character you're looking forward to bringing onstage? That's terrific! Write it all down in your notes.

Now go back over the list with your main character—and your core story idea—in mind. Your hero is going to be at the center of all the main events in your novel, so...which of the above types might be the most interesting to have in that spot?

By the way, I don't recommend that you base your main character on yourself, especially if you are, like me, a plot-first novelist. The temptation is great, of course, and if that's the only way you can imagine this story being told, then go for it. But the problem can be that, since none of us is exactly like our temperament (as defined in a book), the tendency is to deviate from the description of that type. This can cause all manner of inconsistency in your novel. Once you go off the rails, you won't have the rails to keep you, well, on track. You'll be making things up.

Which defeats the whole purpose for coming to a personality type system in the first place—to create a well-defined character who feels realistic to the reader. If you choose for your hero a temperament that isn't yours, it will be easier for you to stick with the script, and your book will be the better for it.

holding auditions

All right, the bulleted list we just saw is enough to whet your appetite, but it's not nearly enough for you to build a character on. You need to go off and do a boatload of reading about that temperament and what makes it tick. That's true whether you're using the Myers-Briggs system or another personality system.

I like to start with this list. With my story idea kernel in mind, I read over that list, giving each temperament a mental audition for the part of hero in my novel. I generally find two or three that give me some interesting ideas or angles that might work in my story. That's how I narrow my search in the great casting call for this book.

Then I open *Please Understand Me II* and read more about those two or three candidates. It's like having callbacks in theater. You select a few definite maybes from the first round of auditions and call those actors back for a more in-depth look. That's what you're doing here. Turn to the main chapter on the first of these candidates, and start reading and taking notes.

As you read and get a better sense of this temperament, you'll start having little lightbulbs come on, little inward confirmations that this is the right person to play the part of the hero of your story. *Or* you'll experience small mental blocks, thoughts of, "Ew, I really don't think this is the right person for my hero." Both reactions are wonderful, as they help you get closer to finding the perfect temperament for the role. If the temperament you're reading about doesn't give you a nice long series of affirmations, move on to the next candidate.

But if you *do* get those confirmations, pay attention. Write down or underline everything about that temperament that gives you an idea for this story.

I usually end up with a couple of pages of notes about the character just by going through the temperament chapter like this. Then, because I'm a big believer in synthesis for learning, I go over those pages several times, working on the data, writing ever shorter summaries of my notes, until I can boil it down to a couple of sentences that perfectly capture what I like about this character and what I think he would do, given the situation my story idea raises.

As an aside, it's amazing to me how different the same temperament can seem as I read its description when I have a new character and new story in mind. The notes I took for Character 1 in Story A, who was an ISTP, won't help me at all as I take notes for Character 2 in Story B, even though that person might be an ISTP as well. The needs of the story cause me to connect with different parts of that temperament description than I had connected with before. But then, I love reading through these temperaments, so it's all good.

It's time for you to select the temperament for your protagonist. Read not only the main description of that character type but also how that person will be in various life situations, which temperaments work best for that type's friends or lovers, what sorts of careers are good (and bad) fits for that temperament, and more.

The temperament is the central truth about who this person is, so you need to understand it as much as you're able. When you start writing this novel, it's best if you already know who this person is. You'll want to be able to glance back at these notes now and then to refresh your memory about what she would do in the current moment.

With one of these temperaments cast in the leading role for your book, it's time to begin adding on the layers.

only sixteen?

When I present this approach to character creation, sometimes someone raises an objection: "Wait, there are only sixteen temperaments—are you saying I can have only sixteen different characters in my novel?"

I see that logic, but it's just not true. First, for the plot-first novelists among us, all of whose characters seem exactly like the author (or, at best, stereotypes), having sixteen characters who truly feel realistic and differentiated from one another is sixteen times better than what they had before.

Second, it's not like people of the same temperament are clones of one another. That would mean that, in every random gathering of one hundred people, there would be six or seven clones of you. Unless you're living on an Earth that's different from the one I'm living on, that's not the case. You can't identify two people with the same temperament simply by how they look. Nor does everyone of the same temperament think and act exactly alike. Thousands of differences caused by upbringing, traumatic life events, intelligence level, and more play a part.

You don't have to worry that having "only" sixteen temperaments to choose from will limit you in your fiction.

Even if you do have more than one character of the same temperament in your novel, it's not a problem. You'll differentiate one from the other in the same way that real humans with the same temperament are distinguished from each other.

When I'm teaching this content in a conference setting, I poll the crowd about Myers-Briggs temperaments. Usually there are enough people in the group who know their temperaments to come up with at least two in the room who share the same type. I have the two of them stand up in front of the group, and I say, "See? They're twins, aren't they?" This usually gets a laugh, because they're obviously not twins. They're clearly different. Perhaps different gender, race, height, build, hairstyle, dress style, posture, and much more.

And those are just the visible differences. If we were to interview the two people, we'd find vast dissimilarities in their backgrounds, preferences, hobbies, relationship status, and a host of other topics.

Given enough time together, they'd probably become best friends or worst enemies because, at a much deeper level, they *are* very much the same. But the differences are vast enough that they could both populate a novel—even a whole series of novels—without ever making the reader feel as if they were interchangeable. Which is my point.

seven-layer cake

The way to make sure *your* EFTP character doesn't seem like anyone else's EFTP character—or even the other EFTP characters in your novel—is to add layers onto that temperament. The temperament is the starting place. It's the core of the character, certainly, and the whole personality arises from that. But it's not the whole of the character. That temperament will express itself differently based on all these other determiners of personality.

So after you have cast your hero as a certain temperament, begin filling in the blanks for him from these categories.

As you add to your character, keep asking yourself this question: How would this temperament express itself given this new fact about her life? If your hero is an INTP woman—a very logical person obsessed with achieving a systematized way of understanding everything—and then you determine that she is from a poor household in the Bronx, how would she look and act and become having been raised in that situation? How would this temperament express itself, given this upbringing? How would it grow, given this soil?

physical attributes

What should your hero look like? You probably get *some* mental image as you think about this person moving through the events of your story. Gender, age, and ethnicity, probably. Maybe more.

Write down all of this person's physical attributes. Things such as:

- Gender
- Age (at the time the story begins)
- Ethnicity
- Height
- Weight
- Hair color (natural)
- Eye color
- Complexion
- Teeth
- Eyesight
- Physical attractiveness
- Any deformities, handicaps, or distinctive marks

Look back at the temperament you've chosen for your protagonist. How would that personality core be affected by the physical attributes you choose?

The second question has to do less with physical attributes and more with what appearance choices *this character* has made due to her temperament. On the other hand, the first question has to do with "accidents" of birth, such as gender, stature, ethnicity, hair color, eye color, height, and how those would affect someone of this temperament. The second question has to do with how someone of this temperament would *modify* his appearance to best express that personality core.

Our INTP systematic scientist from the Bronx would dress in ways that were appropriate for her culture, but she would modify her way of dressing with distinctive choices arising from her temperament. So maybe she has only one electronic device—instead of three or more, like her friends and family have—because she's done the research and experimentation and concluded that she can achieve maximum efficiency this way. That's an example of her temperament expressing itself given specific particulars in her life.

Your character will do similar things. Physical attributes she might modify as a result of her temperament would include:

- Hair style and color
- Facial hair (for men only, hopefully)
- Clothing style (including sense of style or lack thereof)
- Accessories
- Jewelry
- Tattoos and/or piercings
- Hygiene
- Posture
- Contacts or glasses
- Type of vehicle he uses

You'll eventually need to get all of this figured out for your hero (for all of your characters, actually). But for now maybe all you do is look for a few attributes that make a connection for you and give you a spark of an idea for how they would work in your story. The more you know about your hero now, the better, and if you can get a few cool handles on this person early, it's a win.

background

Everyone is affected by the conditions of her place, time, and family of origin. Someone hailing from New Hampshire will have a whole different set of attitudes and expectations compared to someone who grew up in Zhengzhou, China. Someone born in the 1700s during the fall of the French Empire and the run-up to the Revolution will have all manner of differences as compared to someone who grew up as a U.S. army brat during the Cold War.

So it will be for your protagonist. Your hero's temperament determines a lot about his personality, but personality is also deeply affected by aspects of background, such as:

- Birth order
- Number of siblings
- Level of wealth or poverty
- Whether she lived in the city or the country (and which one or what part)
- Marital status of parents (during the character's childhood especially)
- Culture (ethnic, religious, etc.)
- Emotional climate in the home
- Education (quantity and quality)
- Relationship with parent of the same gender
- Era
- Societal backdrop (war, famine, revolution)
- Country and region
- Politics

Are any of these sparking fun ideas for your protagonist?

Given the many opportunities for things to adversely affect us as we grow, it's amazing more of us aren't more messed up. (Please ignore my facial tics; they have no bearing on my sanity, I assure you.) Indeed, an interesting little diversion with characters is to survey the many psychological disorders—phobias, manias, and such—and choose one or two that, if the "right" conditions prevailed, he could develop. Everyone has a touch of paranoia sometimes, and a bit of narcissism shows up in us all on occasion. So it is with your character. What "serious issues" does she *almost* have?

inward attributes

Speaking of conditions of the mind, let's look at the possibilities for your character's inward, psychological, and natural attributes.

Remember as you think through this list to always ask this question: How would a character with this temperament behave and appear and think given this inward attribute?

Consider your character's:

- Intelligence
- Natural gifts or talents (or deficiencies)
- Love language (see below)
- Self-esteem
- Zeal and/or religiosity

How would an extremely intelligent ESFP partier be different from an ESFP who didn't have many brain cells to burn even before the partying began? How would a mousy INFJ helper behave if she had a world-caliber singing voice? How would a rally-the-troops ENTJ behave if he had the self-esteem of Kafka's roach? What would religious fervor look like in an ISTJ who was naturally more comfortable inspecting things, clipboard in hand, than leading an evangelistic crusade in the Superdome?

love languages

Love language is a theory espoused by Gary Chapman. He proposes that all people have at least one of the five possible love languages. These are entire methods of communicating love and affection—so different from one another that they're essentially separate languages.

So you have those with the love language of gift giving, who say, "I love you" by bringing the other person little trinkets or buying knickknacks. Consequently, these people look to others to say, "I love you" in the same way—by giving gifts.

Which works fine so long as those loved ones also have gift giving as their love language. But if the other person has, for example, the love language of acts of service, she will say, "I love you," by cleaning out the other person's closet or making dinner for him.

So you have one person giving gifts like crazy and the other person doing acts of service like crazy, and each one thinks she isn't loved at all. "Why can't I get as much love as I'm giving?"

Just as with languages and cross-cultural exchange, we have to learn how to communicate in languages other than our native tongue. Realizing that the other person really is showering us with love, but in terms we don't understand, can be revolutionary—and has saved countless marriages.

The five love languages are:

- Gift giving
- Acts of service
- Quality time (spending time together in meaningful, eye-to-eye conversations of the heart)
- Physical touch (hugs, caresses, handholding, and simply sitting together on the couch, even if no conversation occurs)
- Words of affirmation (expressing words of thanks and appreciation and love)

Your characters will have love languages, too. They will have one main way of giving and wanting to receive affection. This will come out in innumerable ways—through speech, actions, dates, fights (*withholding* their language of love), birthdays, leadership style, and more.

How will someone of X temperament behave if she has Y love language?

Your character's inward attributes will color her personality, especially those who have temperaments with a rich thought life. What will it be for your hero?

other layers

As I said earlier in this Victory, in *Plot Versus Character* I go into much greater detail on how to create your characters. So for the full treatment, I refer you to that book. In this Victory's last section, I'll breeze over other important layers you should add to your character.

Consider the impact of major events in your character's life. If you look at every adult around you, each one of them is where he is today because of one or more formative events. Perhaps he became a tornado scientist because his father died in a tornado. Perhaps he became a special needs therapist because his sister was autistic. Perhaps he lives in the mountains because a flood wiped away his village when he was a child. The significant things we go through have a tendency to change the course of our lives, whether we realize it or not. So it is with your characters.

Now, don't get hung up on this or any of the elements of character in this chapter. Every one of your characters doesn't need some trauma in her life. Just think about it, especially in light of your core story idea. Maybe this will give you the handle you were looking for that would explain why this character might be the one who is involved in this story.

Also consider how your character tries to portray herself—and how others actually perceive her. Does she think she's a nobody, but everyone else keeps voting her to power? Does he think he's the Prime Human, but no one else seems to agree? Does she think she's stupid? Does he think he's God's gift to women? Do others see her the way she is, the way she wants to be seen, or in some other way altogether? It's fun to write characters who aren't fooling anyone but themselves. And it's a rare person who is perceived in exactly the way he wants to be perceived. We all wear disguises, and they're not perfect.

The final layer on any character is to create his *voice*. That includes the way he speaks and what he speaks about, but it's more than that. A character's voice is the sum total of everything that constitutes his personality.

Some aspects of a character's voice are comprised of audible characteristics such as timbre, pitch, nasality, fluidity, rate of speaking, and any speech impediments. Other aspects of voice reveal or suggest things *about* the character: accent, grammar, vocabulary, pronunciation, cliché, visual language, poetry, articulateness, precision, repetitiveness, and, of course, the topics the character chooses to speak on.

I say that voice is the final element of character creation because it is so easily abused. The plot-first novelists among us, myself included, would otherwise tend to think of a character's manner of speaking as the sum total of the character. Who needs to do all this laborious character development garbage when you can just have the guy say, "I say, dear fellow, might you direct me to the loo?" and be done with it?

Starting with a character's voice is a shortcut—that much is true. But it's a shortcut to bad writing, in my opinion. And who wants to go there—even if you can get there quickly? Starting with voice is ending with stereotype. A shortcut character who says, "Whoa, dude—that's totally awesome!" is not a real character but a cardboard cutout. Now, you can do all of your character work and still have one who says, "Whoa, dude—that's totally awesome!" but you will know *why* he speaks like that, what his temperament is, and how he will realistically behave in any situation. No shortcut will give you that.

So determine what your character says and how he says it. Write a scene or two in which you take him out for a spin. See how he acts and reacts and speaks. Keep doing these exercises—look back at your notes whenever you feel a need—until you have a firm grip on who he is. When you can drop him into any situation and write him in ways that are true to his character, your character work is done, and this person is ready for his close-up.

your hero's inner journey

The best fiction is about someone who changes. One of the reasons we come to fiction at all is to watch someone navigate a change. A hero who is grappling with something that disrupts his world and may require a radical change of direction is standing in for the entire human race. He is Everyman.

Now, some characters don't change in fiction. You've got your Indiana Joneses and your James Bonds and your [insert action hero names] who are all about surviving and battling and winning. They get the treasure and the girl and move on to the next challenge.

Another category of story, usually much better written, focuses on a hero who is out of step with the rest of the world but who eventually causes others to change around him. Thus we have *WALL-E* and *Anne of Green Gables* and *Forrest Gump* and *Mary Poppins*, brilliant character studies about main characters who do not change. And pulling off a novel about such a character requires a very high level of mastery.

But most fiction is about a protagonist who is transformed— or is at least faced with the prospect of transformation—through the events of the story. And so it should be.

In this novel you're about to write so very quickly, I would like you to consider writing about a hero who changes.

hero, we have a problem

An inner journey starts with a problem the character has. What is wrong in the character's life? In what way is she off balance? What tumor is buried inside, slowly killing this person?

Self-centeredness is often the "sin" chosen for heroes in modern stories. The hero is stuck on himself, and this selfishness causes no end of problems for him. It deprives him of the rich life he could have if he weren't so impressed with himself. So we get Ebenezer Scrooge in *A Christmas Carol* or even Lightning McQueen in *Cars*. These characters must learn the value of others and the consequences of their selfishness in order to reenter the human race as contributing members—and to begin to really live.

Other popular character problems are bitterness, ambition, pride, and a desire for vengeance and/or vindication.

But the primary well from which are drawn good, solid sins for fictional heroes is *fear*. Any from the array of fears and anxieties can propel your hero through a wonderful character arc. Fear of being hurt, of abandonment, of failure, of disappointing others, of loss, of being alone, of losing control, and of meaninglessness, not to mention neurotic fears (agoraphobia, arachnophobia, etc.), anger (which is fear in disguise), and depression (fear and anger turned inward).

I'm sure you can think of dozens more. Any of them can be a great personal poison for your hero in this story.

You don't have to be writing a horror story to give your hero a fear problem. Even light romantic comedies make use of character fears, like the pretty girl who won't go out with the handsome man because she's afraid of being hurt again. Nor does your protagonist have to be consumed with anxieties and phobias—like the hero of the TV show *Monk*—in order to have a problem big enough to drive a whole novel.

If you're going to write a story about a hero who is transformed, then you must pick a problem for him. Be sure to dig deeply to find a strong motivating flaw. "He's afraid of blue" isn't an engine strong enough to power a book. Keep digging. Keep asking, "*Why* is he afraid of blue?" *Then* ask why he's afraid of that. And so on. When you've hit the *Tell me about your mother* level of Freudian depth, you're there.

worst case ever

Now take that problem and walk it out to its logical conclusion. If nothing improved, and if she kept going in this direction, what would be the sad destination for this hero?

For example, if she's afraid of making attachments with anyone because she doesn't want to feel the hurt of someone leaving her again (i.e., that's her *problem*), what might the end of the line look like for her? Possibly that she becomes a bitter old cat lady who dies alone and no one finds her body for six weeks.

Whatever your problem is, extrapolate it to the worst end that might reasonably come about for that person if nothing changed for the better.

In terms of your hero's inner journey, this is the "or-else" point, the valley of the shadow of death. It is the doom you want to avoid for your hero. If that tumor is left untreated, this prognosis is as certain as it is awful. Write down this worst-case scenario, and keep it in mind.

the promised land

Theologians talk about God's love for humanity despite our many failures. They like to say that God loves us even with our issues but that He loves us too much to leave us stuck in them.

So it is with your dear but flawed main character. You're going to give her a problem, but, being the good story deity that you are, you're not going to leave her like that. You're going to bring about, well, the *story* to purge that problem.

It is not an overstatement to say that the whole point of your book is to give your main character the opportunity to change. To show him the error of his ways, reveal a better alternative, and force him to choose between the two.

You know now what is possible—just how unhappy the un-*happy* ending can be. So choose a happy ending for her. What is the better alternative? What is the better future into which she might step, were she to make the right choices?

Usually the positive alternative future for your hero is the opposite of the negative possible future. So if she's possibly heading to a cat lady destination, what would the opposite look like? Perhaps she would come to the end of her days surrounded by loved ones who have become such a part of her now-rich existence that she can't imagine life without them.

Take a look back at what you've chosen for your hero's tumor or problem. What would be a healthy outcome for that person? This is the future you wish for your hero. The goal of the story will be to let him choose one or the other. Write it down.

oh, it is so on

The juicy middle section of your novel will be the fight between these two alternatives: the poison and the antidote, the cobra and the mongoose, the defending champion and the upstart contender.

What does it take to make a major change in your life? For me, it usually involves pain of some kind. I like the way I am, you know? I wouldn't be this way if I didn't like it. Sure, maybe it isn't ideal in a lot of ways, but it beats all the other solutions I've found so far.

But if pain comes—hard enough and often enough—I might think about changing. It is likely that your hero will do the same.

the inciting incident

Something unwelcome is going to crash into your hero's happily dysfunctional life. (Actually, *you're* going to send something crashing into that life. Thou villain!) This unlooked-for detour, this wrench in the gears, is the inciting incident. Without it, your hero would keep plodding along toward his unhappy ending. *With* it, he'll be sent careening in exactly the direction you want him to go.

Think about your main character and her problem: What irritant might invade her life and force her to A) realize she's heading to a bad destination and B) understand that a healthier alternative exists?

I may enjoy staying on the couch all day watching *Hogan's Heroes* … but then along comes the landlady/mom/boss who tells me I have to get off my rear or find somewhere else to live. Really? I really have to do something I don't prefer? In my book such situations equal pain.

The person who lowered the boom on me brought the inciting incident—i.e., crowbar—that pried me out of my sick-but-settled ways and forced me to explore other options.

Or maybe I enjoy living alone. It's the only way I don't end up hating whoever I'm with. I do sometimes worry that I'll come to the end of my life and have no one around me. Hey, what's a body to do? But, wait, I've had an accident, and now I have to live with my son and daughter-in-law and their five annoying brats? Say it isn't so!

That accident was the inciting incident, and now it's forcing me to live with others, whether I like it or not.

Your hero won't like the inciting incident. That's a given. The patient walks into the doctor's office, and the doc says, "You're morbidly obese, you've developed diabetes, and now your heart is failing. Make these seven radical changes to your lifestyle, and you might live." That pronouncement from the doctor is the inciting incident. Think it's going to go over well with our hefty hero? Not so much.

No one gets into these desperately sick situations without a hardened pattern of decisions. So it is with your hero. Whatever dysfunction you're going to inflict upon him, he will have settled into it and have no intention of changing. The inciting event has to hurt. It has to be a punch in the nose to whatever way he's been living.

Consider one Ebenezer Scrooge. Left to himself, he would've gone to his grave a mean old miser wishing for the deaths of all those loathsome Londoners who sap society dry. He was headed toward a pathetic ending of a wasted life.

Then, *POW!* Ghosties.

Talk about a blow to his status quo. Few inciting events in literature have been as abrupt or as beautiful as this one. A ghost comes to Ebenezer and sends him staggering on a harrowing metaphysical journey through his life.

But as terrifying as the ghostly visitations are to poor old Scrooge, do you see that they are a mercy? He didn't deserve a second chance. He'd done nothing to merit this forceful but ultimately kind last effort to bring him to his senses.

That's what you're going to give your hero: tough love. A violent mercy.

Groundhog Day is a movie about Phil Connors, a self-centered man who if left to his own devices will certainly end up a sad, lonely, womanizing bachelor who dies alone. He is heading in that direction when the curtain goes up. We immediately see what an arrogant jerk he is when he makes a crude pass at a woman and denigrates his co-workers. Talk about a guy ripe for an inner journey.

Then, after living through one particular Groundhog Day, Phil wakes up the next morning and finds that it's … Groundhog Day. Again. Slightly stunned, he lives through the day again, repeating everything he'd done before, all the time experiencing a long déjà-vu. And the next morning, it's Groundhog Day again. He realizes he's living that one day over and over.

This supernatural loop is the inciting incident that kicks him off his previous unhealthy path and ultimately leads to his last chance at redemption.

Notice that with both Ebenezer Scrooge and Phil Connors, the inciting incident is huge. It's powerful. Violent, even. There's no way either hero can ignore it. It slams into them like a meteorite crashing into their house.

So it must be with your novel. Think for a minute about your hero and especially her problem, the dark alley she's tumbling down. What meteorite can you smash into her life that will divert her onto the inner journey you want her to undergo?

The inciting incident doesn't have to be a negative, although it usually is. Most of the time the wrench thrown in the gears is very unwelcome, at least in the hero's mind. Of course, later she may see it as a blessing, but not while it is happening. It's also possible that the inciting incident is something the hero does welcome—like winning the lottery—though it ends up taking her to places she didn't want to go. For it to work in the novel, an inciting incident simply needs to be 1) powerful and 2) something that sends the hero off on her inner journey.

vying for allegiance

Let's change metaphors from a meteorite to a fight for the hearts of a kingdom.

For a moment, imagine that your hero is living in an evil kingdom ruled by a cruel tyrant (as opposed to all those soft-hearted tyrants you're always hearing about). This is my way of talking about the internal problem or fear that is slowly poisoning her and leading her to an ill end. In this evil kingdom, she lives in relative peace so long as she pays her taxes and doesn't upset the status quo. She's not happy or flourishing, but things could be worse.

One day, into our hero's village rides a dashing young prince. He dismounts in the village square and proclaims that he rules a faraway kingdom based on justice and mercy and freedom and that any who wish may become citizens. They have only to follow him to their new homes.

Well, our heroine has no intention of going anywhere. She's settled here. She has a life here. No, thank you, good prince. See ya.

The prince's arrival in the village is the inciting incident. Our hero won't immediately change her mind and embrace the change, because if she did there would be no inner journey. She has to reject it at first.

So it must be with your hero. The inciting incident will come, and it will be unwelcome.

For some reason, this prince has taken a liking to our heroine. He comes to her door and pleads with her to leave this place. His kingdom is fair, and all of his people flourish. What's more, he has reason to believe things will go poorly for her if she remains.

A good "challenger" to the hero's old and toxic way of living is both compelling and persistent.

The vision cast by the prince is attractive enough for our hero to actually consider it. But she quickly stifles such crazy thoughts.

What's more, with the sound of thundering hooves, the evil king rides into town with his elite guard. He has heard that someone has infiltrated his realm and is trying to get his tax base—er, his beloved citizens—to leave for another kingdom. As punishment to the entire village for welcoming this pretender, his men are building a massive fence around the village. Now no one can leave without his express permission.

Great, things have just gotten worse for our heroine. In an effort to lessen this new persecution, she goes to the king and pledges her undying fealty. She kisses the royal ring. He is pleased, but he warns her not to have anything further to do with this alleged prince. "Believe me, O king, I won't. He's brought me nothing but trouble."

Despite the fact that she lives in an evil kingdom under a despot, our heroine is still comfortable and content. Indeed, she will choose to stay with that life indefinitely … unless something radical happens. (Which is where you come in.)

That evening, the prince comes back to our heroine when she's out gathering firewood needed to cook her gruel. He talks about how cruel her king is. Somehow the prince knows all about the king, and she can't deny the things the prince says.

Then the prince waxes eloquent about his own kingdom. He describes its meadows and lakes and delightful weather. He talks about the traditions of his people. He says he has picked out a spot for her new home, if she will come with him. He describes her neighbors and the view from her future front window. He talks about the work she'll do and the food she'll eat—all much more pleasant than what she currently has. Most compelling of all, he talks about the rich life she'll have.

Something stirs inside her as he speaks. Come to think of it, life here really isn't that great. The things he describes … could she really enjoy those? It would mean leaving all of this—but would that really be so bad?

The next day, she's in a foul mood. Now everything about her present life irritates her. The idea that a better life awaits her somewhere else gnaws at her and turns her present condition sour. The prince's depiction of a happier life elsewhere has made her discontent.

Apparently the walls have ears, because no sooner has she stepped into the village square than the evil king and his elite guard surround her, cruel looks on their faces.

"I hear you have been consorting with the enemy!" the king says, his cheeks going bright red. "I forbid it!"

"But I—"

"Guards, lock her in the dungeon!"

Despite her shock, our heroine is confused. "But our village has no dungeon."

"It does now! Mwahahaha!"

The guards clap her in leg irons and drag her to a newly constructed dungeon beneath the blacksmith's forge. They throw her in a cell and slam the metal door shut behind her.

The main piece of your hero's inner journey is this struggle between dark and light forces. The prize: the allegiance of one key citizen—the hero.

The more the new, healthy alternative shows itself as attractive, the more the old, sick way strikes back. And when the old way sinks its claws a bit deeper into the hero's heart, the new way swoops back in with an even stronger argument for change. And so it goes in an escalating battle for the hero's heart.

This battle is the core of your hero's inner journey, which makes it the core of your novel.

Try as he might, Ebenezer Scrooge could not get away from the ghosts. He didn't like what they showed him, but neither was he willing to change. The old way was too strong and too familiar. And so the new way kept pouring it on, in the form of more ghosts and more ghastly visions of Scrooge's life.

No matter how he tried, Phil Connors could not escape his *Twilight Zone* curse of reliving Groundhog Day again and again. He explored every means of avoidance—and quite a few methods of acceptance—but nothing he did could break the spell. More important, nothing he did could make him feel better about himself.

The goal of the new, healthy alternative is twofold. It is 1) to reveal to the hero that his old way is actually doing harm to himself and others and 2) to bring him to the end of himself so he will finally, authentically consider making this change.

What about your novel? At this early stage, you don't have to plot out every blow that each side is going to land as they duke it out for your hero's allegiance. But you do need to understand that the middle section—perhaps as much as 60 percent of your novel—is going to consist of these lunges and ripostes between two warring forces. Each side will win battles and suffer losses in the war raging in your hero's heart.

When the prince hears that the heroine is in the dungeon, he breaks her out. When the king hears she's been busted loose, he calls in his army. When the prince sees the enemy army, he calls his own troops. And so it goes, escalating toward an ultimate crisis.

I've been using a word picture here, but I hope you're able to make the application to your story. Earlier, I mentioned a crabby old person who prefers to live alone but, following an accident, is forced to move in with her son and daughter-in-law and grandchildren. The old, poisonous road she was on would've led her to a sorry end. She doesn't like this new road—not one bit—but it's going to present a positive alternative so powerful and persistent (those darn kids are kind of growing on me...) that she'll eventually taste the new life she could have if she let go of the toxins.

The new way—the way of the unselfish and loving father—is so strong and attractive that his old way begins to look, well, old. Stale. Outgrown.

That's exactly what you're going to do in your novel, too. What could this battle between the old and new ways look like in your hero's inner journey? That's the novel you're going to write.

backing up

Now that you know what you're going to be doing in the main middle section of your hero's inner journey, we can talk about its beginning and end.

In all the examples I've used so far in this chapter, there's been a "before" for the character about to embark on a transformational arc. We see Scrooge when he's being a scrooge. We see Phil Connors when he's being a jerk.

That before stage is important. If all we knew of Ebenezer Scrooge was what we saw of him when the Ghost of Christmas Past appears to him, we wouldn't fully understand the significance of what was happening. We need to see how the character in his state of needing transformation. We need this context or we will not feel the impact of the change.

For your story, you'll want to show your hero's before so we can appreciate the after. You'll want to show her being afraid (for instance) so we can see the amazing transformation she's gone through by the end of the story when she's unafraid.

I call this the *initial condition*. How is that toxic lifestyle—that tumor—affecting her as the story begins? Set us up. Show us what she's like and how in need of change she is. She probably won't see or admit that anything is wrong, but you will portray her "normal" in such a way that we see very clearly that something is wrong.

What might that be for your hero? Write it down in your notes.

the moment of truth

So you've determined how the story will find your hero, and you've done a lot of good thinking about what the escalating battle between good and evil will look like inside his heart. Now let's think about how it all comes to a head.

The moment of truth in your hero's life probably won't be a final physical clash between the old way and the new way. It's not the evil tyrant locked in a death grip with the young prince. No, at this point, both sides have done their utmost to win the hero's heart, but now it's time for the hero to decide. It's the moment of truth.

In the end, isn't it always about our choices?

The apex of your novel—indeed, the whole point of writing your novel—is this moment when the hero fully understands the pros and cons of both warring forces in her heart, fully understands the potential costs and benefits of siding either way, and, as the universe holds its breath, makes her choice.

In the movie *Mulan*, the heroine has been both heroic and deceptive through the course of the story. Her moment of greatest valor is spoiled when her friends discover she deceived them the whole time. They leave her behind and journey on to report to the Emperor of China that the invading general has been defeated. They are sad to leave behind the one who has been their greatest warrior, but now they see her as nothing but a woman—and a pretender, at that.

After they leave, Mulan wants to go home. Despite her intentions, she has brought dishonor to her family, and all of it so far from home. But as she's contemplating this, she sees that the enemy general is not, in fact, defeated and is planning an ambush for Mulan's friends—and the Emperor.

This is Mulan's moment of truth. What is she going to do? Her friends hate her now, so they won't believe her warnings. And certainly a "mere woman" wouldn't be allowed to cut through the crowd to whisper counsel into the Emperor's ear. No one wants her anyway—why not just go home? Let them deal with the enemy, if they're so capable without her.

And yet...

Can you taste the delicious moment here? We've seen the courage in her heart, so we know what she wants to do. But we also see her sorrow at having made a mess of everything.

It's those tests of character, those "Who are you when no one's looking?" moments, that really define us. Not for the world, but for ourselves. Mulan ultimately resolves her moment of decision by electing to at least try to warn her friends, come what may.

You will bring your hero to a moment of truth very much like this one. The outcome—not of the story perhaps but of the hero's soul—hangs in the balance. He could easily go either way. Choosing to side with his old dysfunction will be a failure, certainly, but it will be an option. If he chooses instead to grasp the new way with all of his power, doing so may not result in victory or redemption or anything else, but it will be the right thing to do.

By what he chooses here, he's deciding what is now going to be most true about himself.

I don't know about you, but I think that's pretty stinking cool. In one sense, you are orchestrating all of this. You're creating the characters and the problem and the alternative of the problem, and you're producing conditions that force a character to make a choice.

But on the other hand, you're doing something monumental. Something important. Maybe others will see it as mere entertainment, but you know better. By showing someone having to make this choice, and by having a person resolve it one way or the other, you are handling the very stuff of creation. You're saying something here—about life, about yourself, maybe even about God. And what you say here, what the hero does here, will be the most resounding word your novel utters.

final state

At the end of any journey, the traveler must rest. At the end of your hero's inner journey, she too must rest.

The end of the journey is the final state in your hero's transformational arc. Now that she faced her moment of truth, this is the result. It's the consequence and/or reward for what she chose when everything was on the line.

I'm not talking about plot things here, though they will come into play. The final state isn't whether the good guys won or lost. What I'm talking about here is the condition of the hero's soul now that her inward journey is over.

Scrooge has become a giving, joyful man. Phil Connors has become a man capable of true love. Mulan has become the hero in truth that she had only pretended to be before.

Or, if the hero chose the "wrong" way, the easy or dark way, at the moment of truth, the final state is something ugly. Characters, like people, sometimes choose poorly, even when the stakes are high. Siding with the evil king has to be a bona fide option, or it's no option at all. Readers don't like stories without happy endings, but that doesn't mean you should write one.

The final state will be good or bad for the hero no matter the outcome of the plot. The inner journey is, obviously, inner, while the plot is what happens on the outside. So a character might face his moment of truth and choose well, or poorly, even though the external result is the opposite. He might choose the dark path even as the good guys prevail. He might choose the right path and yet be externally defeated, as happened with Théoden in *The Return of the King*. He faced his moment of truth and came through it brilliantly—and as a result, he was killed in battle. That was bad externally, but internally he was at peace.

So it will be for your hero. She made a choice in her moment of truth, now how will she be?

The final state is a direct reflection of the initial condition. Go back and see what you wrote concerning the poison that affects her at the start of the story, and with that in mind, consider her final state. If she chooses poorly in her moment of truth, she'll be like she was in her initial toxic condition, only much worse. It will be as if all the safety stops have been removed, and now she's plunging to that doom as fast as she can go. If she chooses the "good" option in her moment of truth, her final state will be an exact opposite of her initial condition. She'll move freely into that Promised Land that did finally become hers.

The inner journey is like a crucible that burns out all the impurities and leaves the hero pure—purely healthy or purely poisoned. The inner journey, especially that middle escalation phase, is the fire that eliminates everything extraneous and clarifies the choice. After the moment of truth, the hero will have been purified, one way or the other.

Look over your hero's inner journey. Given his problem and the happy alternative you've picked for him, given how his problem is afflicting him as the story begins, given the brutal fight for the hero's loyalty, and given what he decides in his moment of truth, what will his final state look like?

conclusion

With that, you have completed the outline for your hero's inner journey. I like to think of the inner journey as about 75 percent of the story and the plot. Talk about your victories! We're on Victory 5, and you already have 75 percent of your story figured out.

Note that you don't have to create inner journeys for all the characters in your novel, not even all the major characters. Usually just one or maybe two characters are on a transformational arc in a novel. The reader really wants the story to be about one person, with maybe a romantic partner—or a shadowy opposite—going through a journey of his or her own. Most of the time, a novel is about one person navigating a change.

You may want to plot out smaller transformations for one or two other characters, however. The same steps apply, but you don't need to take as much page time to get these folks through the arc.

I'm covering a lot of material about your novel before you've even begun to write it. I do that with no apologies. If you don't want to think through anything before you begin writing, by all means skip all this and go to Part Two, where I give you tips for writing very quickly. However, I know that many writers like to have a lot of this stuff figured out before sitting down to write.

We've now come to the end of the character development portion of the book. Go through these chapters for each of your main characters and as many of your minor characters as you want to create before beginning the novel.

We will move from the people and the internals of your story to the events and externals. Plot time, baby.

plot particulates

The plot for this novel will consist of elements beyond characters, genre, and three-act structure. We've already come up with your book's amazing core idea. We've given some thought to your book's genre and the implications of that choice. We've looked at era, setting, and backdrop. And, of course, we've built your characters and given at least one of them a beautiful inner journey.

Before we talk about the actual framework of your plot and the things your beginning must accomplish, we have some other plot ingredients to go over. Namely: your book's villain, stakes, ticking time bomb, theme, and research.

dastardly dan (antagonist)

Your book needs an antagonist. Your antagonist doesn't have to be Dastardly Dan, evictor of poor widows, nor does he have to commit acts of terrorism while juggling hand grenades. But you do need some force to oppose the hero, or you have no story.

At its most basic, fiction is about conflict. It's about a person who wants something but is blocked from getting it by some strong force.

Consider a novel without an opposing force. The hero wants to set a world record in the high jump—but in this world there is no existing world record, nor are there any competitors, so the hero accomplishes his goal on page 1. Our heroine wants to win the heart of a certain boy, but he already loves her, so she accomplishes her goal without even trying.

Without struggle, there is no novel. As we've seen in the Victory about inner journey, the quest, the struggle, the wrestling is what the book is about. This is just as true on the external side (plot) as it is on the internal side (inner journey).

Imagine a novel that is about inner conflict alone, not at all about outer conflict. Perhaps a teenage girl sits in a shaded garden for three hundred pages, wrestling with her inner demons but facing no external challenge more serious than running out of lemonade. Yuck.

Think about your core story idea, the genre you've chosen, and the hero you've created (especially the inner journey)—given all of that, who or what would make a great villain?

Most of the time, novels focus on a human villain that opposes the hero. It's the evil overlord or the corrupt police chief or the crazed killer or the rival for the girl's affections. These are what we call Man vs. Man conflicts. Does a human antagonist seem like the best fit for your novel?

Then there is my favorite: Man vs. Monster. In these stories, the hero is up against the creature, the alien, the man-eating shark, the dragon, the poltergeist, the vampire, and the like. Feel like writing a monster story?

Or you might consider Man vs. Nature (she must climb a mountain or fight a wildfire or catch a tornado or ride out the perfect storm or escape the volcano), Man vs. Machine (the villain is a Terminator or a doomsday device or nanobots or a computer virus), Man vs. Society (the thing holding the hero back is a societal belief or rule, for example *Pride and Prejudice* or stories about slavery), Man vs. Self (*The Strange Case of Dr. Jekyll and Mr. Hyde*, plus various werewolf and vampire stories in which the "person" is trying to keep his dark side in check), or Man vs. the Supernatural (*Groundhog Day, A Christmas Carol, Oedipus Rex*).

Plus there's the ever-popular Man vs. Multifunction Remote Control. Not nearly enough of those stories being written lately.

What sort of conflict feels right for your story? Given your hero's temperament, character layers, and inner journey, who or what would best stand in the way of her getting what she wants?

You need to have the villain in mind before laying out the plot structure for this book. The antagonist provides the wall against which the hero will be banging her head. Many times it is the villain who, directly or indirectly, causes the hero to begin the inner journey. If there had been no Dark Lord Sauron, would Frodo Baggins ever have gone on the quest that transformed his soul?

For your hero's sake, make sure your villain isn't a wimp. A strong villain makes a strong hero. When a hero overcomes a weak villain—say, a red ant in his path—he's not going to seem very epic to the reader. But have him overcome a galaxy-destroying psychopath with an army of flesh-eating undead giants under his command, and you might just have yourself a hero of legend.

So what'll it be for your book? Who or what is going to be the baddie?

do it … or else (the stakes)

As I hope you're beginning to see, it is the plot, what's going on outside the character, that functions as the catalyst for the character's *inner* journey. Often it takes a low-yield nuclear weapon detonating under a character to get her moving toward her rendezvous with destiny. Often, one of those tactical strikes is the villain. Another is what the hero has to lose.

I'm talking about stakes. The OR-ELSE factor.

If the heroine doesn't tell the young man how she really feels, he's going to marry that horrible other woman—and our heroine will possibly become a lonely old maid.

If the hero doesn't get across the desert to warn the troops of the enemy salient, they will all be wiped out—and the homeland will be entirely without protection.

If the ragtag fugitive fleet of humans don't escape the Cylon invasion, humanity as a species will be wiped out.

Certainly there are inward stakes for the main character. If she doesn't deal with this fear of abandonment and learn how to love, she will lose everyone who might care for her. But it's the outward stakes I want to talk about now.

Look back over all the notes you've made about this story so far. You may have a clear idea of what the stakes are, or you may not have given it much thought before now. As you think about it now, what might be the OR-ELSE stakes you can set for this book?

The stakes can be related to a goal, a relationship, safety, or just about anything else. They can be objectively large (if the hero fails, the Earth will be destroyed) or small (if the hero fails, the team won't win the first game of the season), so long as they are subjectively important to the hero—and thus the reader.

Brainstorm some ideas. Rank your favorites. Eventually you'll need to pick one for the book, but right now it's enough to have a few candidates percolating in your mind.

tick ... tick ... tick... (time bomb)

We want your novel to generate suspense. But suspense doesn't necessarily mean car chases. It just means that you add something to the story that makes the reader a little (or a lot) worried about how things are going to end up in your story.

A novel without suspense is a boring novel. *Will* she be able to ... um ... walk across the room? That's probably not going to excite many readers—unless the person trying to walk across the room has never walked before. You create suspense by giving the reader anxiety and predisposing her to desperately hope things turn out one way and not the other.

Perhaps you already know how you're going to create suspense in your book. The OR-ELSE stakes should rev things up for you pretty well. Perhaps your villain is so powerful that there's virtually no way the hero can survive, let alone triumph—in that case, you're likely to have lots of suspense built in.

I'd like you to consider adding a sure-fire method for creating suspense in your novel: a ticking time bomb.

The villain has the hero's true love in a cell in his mountain fastness. The hero is just now arriving with his appropriated sled dog team. Unbeknownst to the princess, but known to us, the villain has planted a bomb at the base of the mountain. He intends to dispose of the hero and the princess, grab the Evil Doohickey, and fly away in his Villaincopter just before the clock ticks down to zero and the hero and his damsel are blown to smithereens.

Mwahahaha.

By its very nature, a countdown is suspenseful. We can't turn away, we must see if X happens before time runs out. So whenever you have a part of your book that is sagging and you want to make it interesting, figure out how to plant a time bomb—literally or metaphorically—in the scene and start ticking down.

It doesn't have to be an actual bomb. It just has to be a deadline, a cutoff time that the reader cares about. Can she get all the people hidden before the birthday girl gets home so they can jump out and yell *surprise*? Can the toddler make it to the bathroom before he has an accident?

Ticking time bombs work great on a small scale, for instance in a scene. But my favorite use of them occurs on a large scale. I like time bombs that tick all the way through the book.

Consider the movie *Titanic*. Chances are, when the film began you knew enough of the history to understand that that baby was going down. It wasn't a question of *if* but of *when*. And so began the ticking time bomb. With every moment that passed, I'm guessing you felt a subtle tightening of your gut. Even if you weren't consciously thinking about the looming disaster, a part of your brain knew that doom was approaching.

Suspense is a strange sort of anxiety—because we like it. Make your reader love/dread the arrival of the deadline, and she'll love your book. And when the long-awaited moment finally comes, she'll be so on edge she won't not be able to stop reading until she sees how it turns out.

Consider your story: Could you plant a time bomb in it? If your book is about an imminent battle or musical performance or due date or whatever, your time bomb is built in already. If the volcano is going to explode or the ship is going to sink or the cruise is going to end or the asteroid is going to destroy the Earth, you're golden.

But if your story doesn't have a natural countdown to lead the way, I encourage you to add one.

Let's say your book is about a young woman who wants to make it as a singer in New York. You have some fun ideas in mind for the story, and your main character's inner journey is all worked out. In this context, however, there's no deadline built in. No ticking time bomb. So how could you add one?

Take a look at the primary elements of her story and maybe something will suggest itself. Consider the setting and backdrop you've chosen, then her inner journey and her past.

Maybe she's promised her mom that if she doesn't get a paying gig by the end of the year, she'll give up this "nonsense" and come home. Mom's even got a job at the sewing store lined up for her—and Johnny Bigby, Jr., is eager to see her again. Our heroine is out of money, all of her prospects have dried up—and yesterday was Thanksgiving. Her chance to achieve her dream is about to end. Talk about your Black Fridays. What can she do in the next forty days to avoid having to go home in defeat?

See how easily we brought an element of suspense to this book? You can do the same for your book.

It works best, in my opinion, if the reader knows the details of the countdown from the beginning of the story. That way, he's feeling that delicious angst the whole time. Every page that passes increases the anxiety by a cumulative increment.

With our NYC singer, let her mother start the countdown when she's saying goodbye to her daughter at the airport. We'll know, through every audition and every mishap and every new development, that time's a-wastin', and the deadline is fast approaching. Throughout the story, we need to be reminded of the deadline—like when Mom calls to see how her daughter is doing.

It's not vital that the hero know about this ticking time bomb—at least, not at first. What matters is that the reader knows about it. Want to give your reader a stress assault she'll love you for? Show her the time bomb but don't let the hero know about it and have the hero move closer and closer to getting blown up by it. There's a reason people watching horror movies tend to shout, "Don't go in there!" at the screen. Eventually, the hero probably needs to learn that the bomb is about to go off. But there's power in this technique even when—or because—she's in the dark about it.

Not every story needs a ticking time bomb, but every story benefits from one. And why *wouldn't* you want to use a device that naturally increases suspense on every page even when you haven't mentioned it?

theme

In a philosophical sense, what do you want your novel to be about? If what you have in mind is "just" a feel-good buddy story that you've always wanted to write, and you don't really have a theme in mind, that's great. But it's also possible that you might have something to *say*.

There's a fine line between a novel with a theme or message and a novel that is driven by an agenda. Agenda-driven fiction is written with the intention of smacking readers over the head with some polemic, usually with the tone of wagging a bony finger at the reader [cough—*Avatar*—cough]. When asked to explain the idea for your novel, do you say something like, "I want to get it through people's thick skulls that X"? If so, you're probably heading toward an agenda-driven novel.

Such fiction usually fails on a couple of levels. First, readers come to fiction for escape and entertainment, not polemics, preaching, or political correctness. If you go there, readers will smell it a mile away. "Hey, this is just a screed about X. What a rip-off!" Second, agenda-driven fiction is often poorly written—mainly because the author isn't interested in learning craft or structure or character development but is concerned mainly with maximizing the whacking power.

But a novel with a theme is not only okay, it is also often one that rises above the level of mere entertainment. Is *E.T.* about an alien and a boy? Yes, but it's also about friendship and hope and family. Is *The Matrix* about humans and A.I. enemies? Yes, but it's also about the nature of truth. Is *The Truman Show* about a guy discovering he's on a reality TV show? Yes, but it's also about overcoming fear in order to truly live.

If you don't have a theme in mind right now, that's okay. Very often, a theme emerges in the story as you write it. And since you're going to be writing this thing very quickly, you have an even better chance of a theme bubbling up without any conscious effort on your part. You'll be plunging forward, chasing a word count goal for the day, making character and story choices, and going down pathways that feel right in the moment. It's a great setup for theme to arise on its own.

Don't try to force a theme onto your book. It's not like the ticking time bomb, where every novel would benefit from one. If thinking about theme makes your mind freeze up, just skip it.

Take a mental survey of what's in your heart these days. If you're feeling burdened by the plight of the poor in your city, don't be surprised if that concern shows up in your story as you're writing. If you're dealing with a terrible boss who has it in for you, don't fight a terrible boss character who tries to break into your story. Writing a novel, and especially writing a novel in a hurry, is a great self-therapy tool. It gives you the opportunity to articulate in a fictional setting what you may or may not be able to put your finger on in your life. Don't resist it. This could be your theme pushing its way into your book. Go with it.

research

Some people, even some nonfiction writers, think that writing a novel is much easier than writing a nonfiction book because, the theory goes, to write a novel you don't have to do any research. You can just make everything up.

Ha.

Those people should try writing a novel about life in the 1930s without researching it, and see how far they get. They should try writing a novel about the ISS space station without doing any research, and see what they come up with. Even speculative fiction, in which you might be making up an entirely fictional world, requires research on analogous cultures, prototype technology, and who knows what else to make it feel like a real world.

A novel written without benefit of research is a novel that won't ring completely true with the reader. Even if you know the stuff you're writing about, you'll probably need to do spot-checks to bone up on some areas you've gotten a little hazy on.

I once read an entire graduate school textbook on artificial intelligence so I could write a novel with A.I. as the core technological backdrop. I remember going back to the library day after day, slogging through that massive book, with a dictionary on one side and my notebook on the other. But I learned that material, and the novel benefitted from it.

I actually love the research phase. I do most of my research online nowadays, but I remember being delighted by the expression on a librarian's face when I simultaneously checked out books on genetic engineering, hurricanes, terrorism, and military special forces. (And yes, all of that ended up in one novel: *Fatal Defect*.)

I love the cross-pollinating that goes on when I'm reading several topics at once like that. Recently I was reading a book on a scientific topic *and* a book on cults, and I had a sudden insight that the pressure to silence questions among cult members is being used to silence questions about the prevailing scientific view on important issues. It was a realization I would probably not have had if I hadn't been doing those bits of research at the same time.

Whatever research you need to do for this novel, I urge you to do it now, before you start writing. When you have to knock out something like 1,800 words a day to hit your word count goal for the month, you won't have time to read a textbook.

The Internet is, of course, your primary source for research, but use it as a starting place. There's lots of misinformation out there, so back up what you think is true through more traditional sources of information, like scholarly books and interviews with experts.

Also become acquainted with the magical powers of *interlibrary loan* (ILL). Find a book you want to read (by browsing Amazon.com, perhaps), then search your local library system for it. Also search for it on Amazon and similar places as a free e-book (but not through piracy). If it's not available, tap into the power of ILL. Through the interlibrary loan system, which you access through your local library, you can obtain a copy of virtually any book, even if it's not in any library in your state.

As you're writing, you'll probably realize new things you need to research. That's okay, and if it's something you can answer by taking ten minutes to read an article online, go for it. But if it's something that's going to require more time than that, just write yourself a note in the text—"Learn the terms for incarceration and execution in nineteenth-century Japan"—and keep going forward. Don't stop writing.

If it's something you absolutely must know or you can't go forward with the writing, then do what you need to do, but do it fast. Try to find an active forums community online that can answer your specific question in less than a day. But try not to let anything stop you for longer than half a day, or the momentum you've started may begin to peter out.

Research is awesome, but it can become a phase in which the fear of not being 100 percent accurate causes you to get stuck. You could always read just one more book. But don't let it hold you back. Do as much as you need, but then plow forward once you begin writing.

conclusion

Your Victory this time is realizing that you have all the elements in place to begin thinking about the actual structure of your novel. Next we'll learn how to present all of these things in the story. Three-act structure is simply a way of organizing the elements you've come up with so far: premise, character, inner journey, genre, era, villain, theme, stakes, and the rest.

Take a moment to read through the notes you've generated for your story. Read them all in one sitting—out of order, maybe—to start them marinating and synthesizing in your mind. Know it so well that you can hold it all in your hand at once, so to speak.

When you know your elements that well, you're ready to arrange them according to three-act structure. And when you have a pretty good idea about how it's all going to unfold, you're ready to write it.

three-act structure

Your story will have a structure, whether you consciously choose one or not. If the idea of three-act structure makes you feel hemmed in, skip this chapter. Keep in mind, however, that most novels written by the seat of the pants end up feeling random and unfocused to readers. If randomness is not a "structure" you would prefer for this novel—and especially if you're a character-first novelist—I urge you to read this chapter.

Who knows? It might end up saving your book.

use the force

The purpose of your plot is to force your main character to go through his inner journey.

Read that sentence again.

The plot is the mechanism that you, as story deity, bring to bear on the hero's life to make her notice her issues, wrestle with her issues, and finally deal with her issues. It's the crowbar, the jackhammer, the chisel, the fire, and the healing balm of Gilead. The plot is, in short, your hero's last, best chance to change.

Said another way, the plot is the stage upon which your hero undergoes his inner journey. It's the way to make manifest what would otherwise remain inward and hidden. The plot is like an amplifier for the hero's transformational arc. Whatever the two forces battling it out inside your hero's heart are, they're probably invisible. Inward. So the plot comes along like a guitar amp and blasts that struggle to the world.

When you're thinking of plot structure, your starting point is your hero's inner journey. Whatever it is she's dealing with on the inside, that's what the whole plot will be about, thematically, on the outside.

If she's wrestling between, say, a deep bitterness that is consuming her and wrecking her relationships on one hand, and the opportunity to forgive and become part of a caring community on the other, how could you externalize that? What outside events might force her to deal with that problem? Who or what could come along and introduce the alternative? What could crash into her life that would send her in that direction? The notes you jotted down when we covered inciting incident may help you here.

As we go through this Victory, look for dozens of opportunities, large and small, to shed light on your hero's inner journey. For that bitter woman living with her grandchildren, you might create a subplot showing someone even more bitter than her, and what becomes of that other person (no one wants to be around him, etc.). Then maybe create another subplot about someone who is the extreme opposite (he's someone everybody loves and cares for). Have secondary characters, corporations, local news, and developments at the workplace speak to some aspect of that key bitterness/forgiveness issue in the protagonist's inward struggle.

Use the mechanism of the plot to force the hero's inner journey to take place.

three-act structure

Three-act structure has been around since the Greeks—or maybe longer. It's simply a way of organizing a story and making sure all the important things get included.

Some writers claim that three-act structure is outdated or that it hinders the muse. Certainly using three-act structure is not the one commandment of fiction, so don't worry if you feel that way as well. I will say, though, that most stories written without three-act structure in mind end up one of two ways: They either become directionless, seven-hundred-page messes, or they end up with a three-act structure anyway, even though the writer wasn't thinking about it.

Think about the fable of *Little Red Riding Hood*. Our sweet heroine dons her cape and heads out to bring food to Grandma, who has been feeling sick. Along the way, she meets a wolf, who tricks her into telling him where she's going. When Red gets to Grandma's house, something is strange. There's someone in Grandma's bed, but it sure doesn't seem like Grandma—unless the disease she's suffering from is lycanthropy. The false grandmother is revealed to be the wolf, who leaps out and eats Red. Along comes the Woodsman, who saves the day by cutting open the wolf and freeing both Red and Grandma.

Do you see the major phases of that story? There's some setup and introductions: We meet our heroine, we see the location where the story is going to take place, we understand her goals, and we meet the villain (though Red doesn't realize yet that he's not just a big wolf but a Big Bad Wolf). Then there's the confrontation in Grandma's room. The whole "What big eyes you have, Grandma!" exchange is the heart of the story. Then the wolf pounces, and, when we think our heroine is done for, everything turns out for the best.

Those phases—1) "Once upon a time…" 2) "What big teeth you have, Grandma!" and 3) "And they all lived happily ever after"—point to the three acts of the fable.

It's slightly too simplistic, in my opinion, to call the three acts "beginning," "middle," and "end," mainly because the climactic part of the story occurs in act three, and that isn't the "end" at all. The Woodsman's arrival is part of act three, but at that point people are not yet living happily ever after. Nevertheless, "beginning, middle, and end" is a good start for understanding the concepts.

As I mentioned, three-act structure is a means of organizing the story and making sure all the important parts are included. Character-first novelists, especially, will find this helpful, as they are not always as sure about how to build their tale as they are about creating masterful people to inhabit it.

Every story needs setup. You can't have Little Red Riding Hood wondering about Grandma's large eyes on page 1. The reader would have no clue what was going on. You first have to introduce the situation and the context and the people on the stage. Nor can you simply have Red conduct an interesting discussion with "Grandma" and then end the book there. The reader would be like, "Wait, what? That's it? What happened next? How did it turn out?"

As author, your interest in writing the story might be the middle—that wonderful tension of the innocent child unknowingly close to a ravenous wolf in disguise—but that middle can't be the whole tale. You need setup on the front end and resolution on the back end.

And that, my friend, is three-act structure.

three-act structure and inner journey

Think of three-act structure as an amazing day at Disneyland. The walk from the parking lot to the front gates … that's act one. And the fireworks at the end, followed by the walk back to the car (carrying sleeping children) … that's act three.

Call to mind your core story idea for the novel you're going to write. Go back to that amazing sentence that fired your imagination in the beginning. Read it again, but with this Disneyland metaphor in mind. What part of it would fit in that fun middle "play" phase of the time at the park? What would be required to get you there? And what would be the fireworks and contented walk back to the parking lot? This is the basic layout of your novel.

Now recall your hero's inner journey, and see how its major waypoints fall roughly into the same three phases as three-act structure.

The creamy middle of your protagonist's character arc is that escalation, that back-and-forth battle between the poisonous old way and the happy new one. Like when Red Riding Hood is struggling with uncertainty as she interviews the ersatz grandmother. That wonderful struggle on the inside roughly coincides with act two in the plot, which is the outside.

But before you can have your hero begin her journey, you have some setup to do. When the story begins, Red can't already be at Grandma's house, or readers would be confused. All that preparatory work you can do so she could get to the main thing, that escalation, roughly corresponds to act one.

And, of course, the whole point of the inner journey is to get your hero to her moment of truth, where she resolves her internal debate once and for all—or in Red's case, when she is rescued by the Woodsman. After the climactic moment is resolved, we see how the journey has left her. These two components of the character arc—moment of truth and final state—more or less sync with act three.

You can see the correspondence between the major phases of the inner journey and three-act structure illustrated in the chart below.

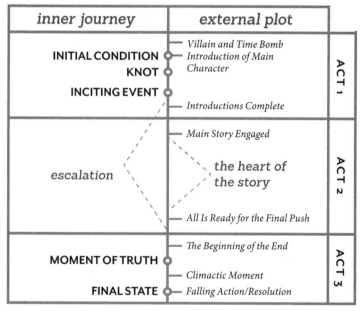

inner journey	external plot	
INITIAL CONDITION **KNOT** **INCITING EVENT**	— *Villain and Time Bomb* — *Introduction of Main Character* — *Introductions Complete*	**ACT 1**
escalation	— *Main Story Engaged* the heart of the story — *All Is Ready for the Final Push*	**ACT 2**
MOMENT OF TRUTH **FINAL STATE**	— *The Beginning of the End* — *Climactic Moment* — *Falling Action/Resolution*	**ACT 3**

act two first?

I have found that a novel's three-act structure is most easily determined (or discovered?) by starting your thinking not with act one but with act two.

Think of act two as the heart of your plot, the fun of it, the cream filling in the middle of the Twinkie.

What could that be for your novel? In that middle section, during which the heart of the inner journey is happening for your hero, what could be going on in your plot?

Act two is where you're going to have the most fun in your book. It's the great day at Disneyland. Act one is setup for this fun, and act three is how it all comes to a head and then resolves. But the middle is the heart of it all.

Act two is when Luke and Han get trapped in the Death Star, rescue a princess, and form an unbreakable bond (*Star Wars*). Act two is when Nemo is taken across the ocean far from home, and his father is transformed as he tries to find him (*Finding Nemo*). Act two is when Rose falls in love with Jack and wrestles with leaving Cal (and her responsibilities) to follow her heart (*Titanic*). Act two is when Phil Connors tries every method he knows to escape his recurring Groundhog Day and is eventually transformed in the effort.

Act two is the cat and mouse game between assassin and Secret Service agent (*In the Line of Fire*). Act two is Ebenezer Scrooge's visits from the spirits. Act two is Billy Beane's season-long gamble to transform the game of baseball by playing the numbers (*Moneyball*). Act two is WALL-E's quest to win EVE's heart and return to her side. Act two is Indiana Jones's efforts to find and secure the Ark of the Covenant.

Think of any movie you like, and pick out that glorious middle part, that extended section where the real magic of the film happens, and I'd be willing to bet you've identified its act two.

Everything else is either the setup or introductions that allow the magic to happen or the playing out of the logical ending of the magic, for good or for ill.

What could it be for your story? Given your core idea and your hero's inner journey, given your genre and theme and villain, what do you want the magical middle of your novel to be?

Write it down.

back to act one

Once you know your act two, figuring out acts one and three becomes child's play.

Before you can have Luke and Han trapped in the Death Star while trying to save the princess, what has to happen? Well, we have to meet Luke and Han—and the princess—and be introduced to the Death Star, those who operate it, and those who oppose it. We have to get the princess trapped inside the Death Star. We have to make Luke aware of the princess and somehow motivate him to leave his home to try to help her. Then we have to get Luke and Han together and inside the Death Star.

See how easy it was to create *Star Wars*'s act one when we knew its act two?

We could do that for any of the stories I just mentioned. I'll pick two more for the sake of illustration.

Before you can have Nemo trapped in the dentist's fish tank and Marlin, his father, crossing the ocean to look for him, what has to happen? Well, we need to meet both Nemo and Marlin. We need to see what their lives are like together, and we need to see their love. We also need to glimpse the strain their relationship is in and the problem (in the inner journey sense) of our heroes. We also need to see Nemo get captured and taken to the dentist's office, and we need to see Marlin vow to do whatever it takes to get his boy back again.

In other words, the act one for *Finding Nemo* is everything you need to set up before you can get busy with that incredible middle that audiences love so much. So it is with your novel.

One more. *Moneyball* is the story of a major league baseball general manager, Billy Beane, who wanted to find a way to get his team to the play-offs without having to pay the tens of millions of dollars his team simply couldn't afford. Act two is his gambit for doing so and the revolution that happened with his team in that one season.

But the filmmakers couldn't begin with that gambit, or audiences wouldn't understand what was going on or what was at stake. They had to set up certain things in order to get to that middle. Those things became the stuff of act one: establish that other teams have more money to spend and thus have an unfair advantage; show the failure of the old way of doing things; show Billy's frustration with his situation; show his discovery of a possible new approach that could be the answer he's looking for; show him seizing on the theory and deciding to roll the dice.

Think about the act two for your novel. What needs to be established before you can make it happen? Who needs to be introduced? What relationships and conditions need to be put in place? What do we need to know before we can understand act two? The answers to those questions are what will constitute your act one.

Take a minute to write those questions down and to answer them. You don't have to know yet what order they'll come in or exactly how they'll happen. Maybe just write them down as a grocery list. Whether you get the bananas first and the laundry detergent second or the other way around doesn't matter right now. What matters is that your act one is shaping up before your eyes, because even now you know you have to get all the items on the list accomplished before you can do the part of the plot where the fun is going to happen.

Take a look at the list and start jotting down some ideas for how they might work together and what sequence might be good. When you actually write the book, you'll have to decide what order to have them happen in the story, but for right now it's enough to just drop them all into the pot and let them simmer together.

your act one is finished when...

Said simply, your act one has to set up your act two. That's its only purpose. But to help you make sure you have everything you need in that act one, let me break it into five components. When you've accomplished all five of these, your act one is complete, and you can begin having your fun in act two.

First, you must introduce all of your main characters. One way to summarize act one is to call it "Introductions." Act one is not complete until we've met them all.

That's not to say you can't have new characters step onstage late in the story, because you certainly can. They just can't be major players. The reader wants to know everyone before the climax of the story. (If I were given the charge to rewrite *Little Red Riding Hood*, I'd find a way to introduce both Grandma and the Woodsman somewhere in act one.)

That's also not to say you can't conceal the identity of certain major characters, because you can do that, too. If you're writing a murder mystery, you may not want us to know who the bad guy is. But we need to see him or her, even if we don't find out until the climax who that shadowy figure really is.

So, for your story, jot down ideas for how you can introduce all of your main characters somewhere in act one. Think about how they might come onstage the first time. We'll talk more about that later.

Second, in act one you must establish the *normal* for your hero. We need to see what things were like for her before the main action of the story intruded into her life and before she embarked on her inner journey. We need to see the before so we can understand the after.

I cover establishing normal in great detail in *The First 50 Pages* (one of my other fiction how-to books for Writer's Digest), and I'll discuss it again in the next Victory, but I'll say here that ideas for introducing your hero's normal include showing her home, her place of work, and her primary relationships as the tale begins.

What might that look like in your story?

Third, your act one must introduce the main challenge of the story. If act two is going to be all about looking for the lost ark, then in act one we'd better learn about the lost ark and see that finding it is a major goal for the hero. If act two is going to be about two former strangers coming together to write a song and hopefully save a career (*Music and Lyrics*), then in act one we need to see that a career needs saving and that successfully writing a song with someone might just be the ticket for doing so.

In your story, what is the main challenge? On the plot side, what is the hero going to be trying to achieve or avoid? Whatever it is, that's one of the main things you have to introduce in act one. Brainstorm some ideas for how you might introduce that not only to the reader but also to the protagonist.

The fourth thing you need to do in act one is going to sound lame, but just go with it. In your act one you must ... introduce whatever else needs to be introduced [grin]. As you saw in some of the act two examples I gave, sometimes you have to introduce more than the characters and the main challenge. In order to properly set up act two, we have to see the strained relationship between Nemo and Marlin. We have to see how lonely WALL-E is. We have to see what a jerk Phil Connors (or Scrooge) is.

So it is with your story: In addition to introducing the main characters and showing their normal and revealing what the main challenge is going to be, what else must you set up before readers can really *feel* what you're going to be doing in act two? Jot down everything that comes to you.

Finally, and this is the pivotal point between act one and act two, you have to get the protagonist to fully engage the main challenge of the story. When all four of the other things have been done, all that's left is for the hero to strap on his sword and say, "Point me to the dragon." It's the "Let's roll" moment, the crossing of the Rubicon, the departure from the realm of safety, the *Millennium Falcon* blasting its way out of Mos Eisley Space-port, and the first step toward the main challenge of the story that ends act one and begins act two.

Most of the time, the hero decides to fully engage the main action of the story, as I've just outlined. But sometimes it's the other way around. Sometimes the main action of the story fully engages the hero. Sometimes the hero has no choice.

As in *Battle: Los Angeles*, when the aliens invade Earth. Our hero is a U.S. Marine leading a platoon in Los Angeles when E.T. phones home and starts blowing up the place. Because the writer has done his job well, we saw our hero's before condition and saw that he just wanted to retire after a great but sometimes brutal career. Then the aliens come and completely throw that plan out the window. Between him and his quiet retirement stands an alien horde trying to conquer the planet. Oh, bother.

In your story, does your hero decide to fully engage the main action of the story, or does the main action of the story fully engage her? Jot down your ideas and put them into the figurative stew to simmer with everything else.

act three

As fun as your act two is going to be, it can't last forever. Eventually Luke and Han's adventure in the Death Star has to come to an end, for better or worse. As much as we love watching Phil Connors get puréed inside his recurring Groundhog Day, eventually that part of the story has to stop. Either he gets out or he dies, but we have to see how the thing turns out. The story is not complete until the action in act two is ended and resolved.

That is the business of act three.

Act three has two main components: the climactic moment and the dénouement. Or, to use our Disneyland metaphor, the fireworks and the walk back to the car.

the climactic moment
Throughout act two, things have been building to a head. The underdog home team has come together and won impossible

games in a Cinderella story. But they still have to face … the Russians. Dunh, dunh, DUNNNH.

Luke and Han have overcome tremendous odds and have managed to gel as a team, rescue the princess, and watch as Luke grows into manhood—but now the Death Star is about to destroy the Rebels' hidden fortress. Aaagh!

Alex Fletcher and Sophie Fisher have managed to come together to write an incredible song—and fall in love. But now Alex seems to have thrown Sophie under the bus to take all the glory for himself. And tonight is the big concert!

The climactic moment is the time when the gains that have been made in act two are put to the ultimate test. During act two, the main character has been transformed in her inner journey, but what will she do when the heat is really on? It's time for the final exam.

In *Game Plan*, Joe Kingman's selfishness has been burned away by his newfound love for the daughter he never knew he had. But when he's in the championship game and the title is on the line and the clock is down to zero, will he seize the glory for himself, as he did at the outset, or will he show that he's truly changed and let someone else have the honor?

A transformation is great, but until it's tested by fire, has it really happened?

What can the climactic moment be for your story? This is the moment when the Death Star is in range and Luke is alone in the trench and Darth Vader has him in the crosshairs. This is the moment when Mulan has reunited with her friends to try to save the Emperor but the palace is on fire and the villain stands over her with his sword raised to strike. This the moment when James Bond and the evil mastermind are locked in a stranglehold beside the "Launch" button while the evil fortress collapses around them and the volcano is about to explode.

Or, if your story isn't an action story, this is the moment when the girl is furious at the boy and is leaving town on a train but her heart is breaking. Will he come for her before it's too late?

Take another look at that chart earlier in this chapter.

Do you see how close the moment of truth (on the inner journey side) is to the climactic moment (on the plot side)? That's because the hero comes to the pinnacle of her inward transformation—she decides who and what she wants to be—just before she is given the opportunity to prove it.

Marlin realizes he needs to let Nemo be strong and grow up … and then he is given the chance to put his money where his mouth is. Nemo and the other fish are trapped in a trawling net, and Nemo thinks he has come up with a way to get them all free. Marlin finds himself about to tell Nemo he can't possibly do such a thing—but then he realizes the lesson he's learned on his own journey, so he lets Nemo give it a try.

Lightning McQueen's inner journey (*Cars*) has taught him to put others ahead of himself, and then he's given the chance to prove that he's really changed. It's the last lap in the race that will decide who is the champion for the entire year, and Lightning is ahead. He sees that another car is hurt and in need of help. What will he do? Aha! A chance to show his quality. He jams on the brakes, lets another car take the championship, and goes back to help the other car. Though someone else has won the prize, the crowd cheers for Lightning's act of charity and humility. He truly has learned his lesson.

The inward moment of truth happens and then is tested shortly afterward by the climactic moment in the plot. All along, the plot's purpose has been to force the hero to go on this journey and to make it visible externally. Nowhere in the story will that be more true than in this portion of your novel.

What might that look like in your book? Look back at your protagonist's inner journey. What is his moment of truth? Now that you have a better feel for your plot, what could the climactic moment look like? And here's the crucial part: How can the climactic moment be a thoroughgoing test of the decision he made in his moment of truth?

the dénouement

After you've put your characters—and your readers—through all the angst of this story, everybody deserves a celebration.

The dénouement or "falling action" of a story is that portion of the book that comes after things have been decided in the climactic moment. It's the party, the awards ceremony, the wedding, the inauguration, the graduation, or whatever else ties everything off and puts a nice bow on the tale.

The dénouement is important for the plot and characters. We need some space to show the hero's final state, the condition he's in at the end of the inner journey. We also need time to see how things are in the world of the plot now that the fireworks are over. The hero defeated the villain, so how has that affected the landscape? The city was invaded, but the enemy was defeated, so now we need to see the citizens rebuilding. In the climax of the story, several important characters were injured, so now we need to see that they're going to be all right.

But the dénouement is also important for the reader. She went with you through the stress of this story. She pulled for the hero and stood loyally by for the events of the book. Now, psychologically, she needs a break. And a reward. I see stories that end right after the villain is defeated, but that's a mistake. Your reader has wanted so much for everything to work out well, and now that it has, she deserves to see the characters she cares about feeling relief and hope and happiness.

The Greeks called it *catharsis*. The Greek tragedies put audiences through the wringer. Ancient psychology said that you'll actually feel better if you've been through something emotional. Like after having a good cry. I think they were right. Come up with some scene that can serve as the prize for the reader.

By the way, this holds true even if your ending is not a happy one. We still need to see the hero's final state, even if he chose "wrong" in his moment of truth. And even if the good guys lost—or if this is a middle book in a series—we need to see how things are now. The evil legions march through the capital. The remaining good guys, nursing their injuries, pile into a truck and head off to regroup. Give us some glimpse of hope, and perhaps a smile and a wink, to let us know things will improve.

The dénouement is also the place to show us that danger is still out there. The villain is not dead, after all. Or someone else has arisen to take his place. Or some new menace is lurking. You may not want to do that in your story, and that's fine, but if you do, the last pages, perhaps an epilogue, are the place to do it.

What could the dénouement be for your story? I know it's crazy to be talking about how you'll end the thing when you haven't even started writing it, but it's worth consideration. Even if you change it later—because it's likely you'll think of something even better as you're actually writing—it's good to have in your mind the understanding that you'll need some scene to tie everything off at the end.

conclusion

Three-act structure takes your core story idea and your hero's inner journey and puts them in play. If your core idea and the inner journey are the theoretical physics of your novel, the plot structure is the engineering framework devised to build it in the real world.

how to begin your novel

It's time to think about how to actually begin your novel. Doing so will give you a running start at this project.

I've written an entire Writer's Digest book on this subject—*The First 50 Pages*—so I'll provide only a few key tips here. It's my hope to equip you with enough knowledge to begin your novel with a bang and to ride the inertia of that beginning all the way through to the end.

As it happens, several of the things your first fifty pages must accomplish have already appeared in this book. In your opening pages, you must begin your hero's inner journey by showing her initial condition and inciting incident. You must lay the foundation for your three-act structure, which will involve accomplishing most of the items that constitute act one. You also have to introduce the genre and story world and antagonist and stakes.

The main thing you have to do with those opening pages has also been addressed. It's the only commandment of fiction: *You must engage your reader.* Your new moral code for fiction is that anything that helps you engage your reader is Good and anything that causes your reader to become disengaged is Bad. Reader engagement is accomplished in your opening pages and is hopefully maintained throughout the manuscript.

In this part of the book I will cover how to establish normal and introduce your hero, and the four structures of a beginning.

establishing normal

Keep the Great Commandment of Fiction in mind now, because I'm going to cover something I feel strongly about—and something that other fiction teachers disagree with me strongly about.

So how do you know what to do when one teacher says one thing and another teacher says the opposite?

You remember that this topic is not the Great Commandment of Fiction.

You give my teaching a try, you give the other teaching a try, and then you decide which one you like better. Neither is right or wrong, despite what others might say. And despite how much I'd like to say that, if one way is right, the right way is mine [grin].

In the previous Victory, I introduced the idea of establishing "normal" in your novel. Now I'd like to expand on that discussion.

It is my opinion (in the nonbinding, non-right-or-wrong sense) that a novel works best when the reader is shown what the hero's life looks like before the main action of the story intrudes. I feel that the reader cannot understand how the wrench thrown in the gears of the hero's life is a massive deviation from what went before if he's not seen what her typical, undisturbed life was like.

If *A Christmas Carol* had begun with the first ghost appearing to Scrooge, we might begin to wonder if maybe this sort of thing happens to him all the time. If *Titanic* had begun with the ship hitting the iceberg, we'd be watching people we neither knew nor cared about running around on the deck.

Some fiction teachers feel that you need to get the main action started right away. Like on page 1. I agree that such a thing can work, and I certainly agree that you do need to start the book with some kind of engaging action, but I don't think it's best, for the reasons just mentioned, to allow the main action to intrude into the hero's life until after some other things have been done first.

Again, though, this isn't a hill to die on. Try both options.

It's ironic that certain artificial situations can force a novelist to begin with the main action. For instance, I sometimes serve as a judge for a fiction contest in which only the first fifteen pages of the book may be entered. Time after time, a novel that begins as I think it should—with action but not the main action, and by establishing normal for the hero—ends up being graded poorly by some of the other judges. If they don't see the main action intruding into the hero's life right away, they mark it down, and usually that entry will not win.

However, if *Star Wars* had begun with R2D2 showing the holographic message of Princess Leia saying, "Help me, Obi-Wan Kenobi. You're my only hope," and with Luke Skywalker leaping to her rescue, we might assume he was part of some rescue squad and did this sort of thing for a living. If *Music and Lyrics* had begun with Alex and Sophie already working together, we might think they'd known each other for years.

If you're willing to try what I'm describing here, figure out a way to begin your novel with action—just not with the main action of the story intruding into your hero's awareness.

That might mean showing the main danger of the story, but not in a way that causes the hero to know about it. *Mulan* opens with the Huns beginning their invasion of China. That is the main action of the story, but the hero doesn't learn about it until *after her normal has been established.*

Your book must begin with something interesting happening—so as to engage the reader, which is our only Commandment—but it can be something interesting about the hero's normal situation. If your hero is an American archaeologist who travels internationally to obtain priceless artifacts, begin by showing him going after a priceless artifact, just not *the* priceless artifact he'll be pursuing for the bulk of the story.

You can begin with action without having the *main* action impact the hero's life.

how to establish your hero's normal

Three great ways to establish your hero's normal are to show her home, her place of work, and her primary relationships as they are at the beginning of the story.

There's nothing so powerful for revealing someone's personality and situation as showing her in her natural habitat. A person's home is a reflection of who she is and what her life is like. If she lives in a penthouse apartment we can deduce several important things about her. If she lives in a little cubby under the stairs, that says something important, too. If her place is messy or Spartan or kitschy or crammed with stuffed animals or mounds of hoarded junk, it all reveals boatloads about who this person is and how she's been living.

Think about your hero: Where would he live, and what would his home look like? Jot down a few notes, and begin thinking about how you might write a scene that takes place there.

Another great way to give the reader a feel for your hero's normal is to show him in the place where he typically spends his days. If he has a job, show him at work. Show him at his desk or horse stall or gunnery station. If he doesn't have a job but is instead a student or a retiree or a slave, show him being that. Who does he work with? Who is his boss? Is *he* a boss? How does he dress when he's there? How does he behave? Is he respected or abused, powerful or at the mercy of someone else? What sort of work does he do? There is no better way to show what a person's normal is like than to show him doing what he does on an average day.

The third way to establish normal for your hero is to show her primary relationships. This is something you can do while you're showing her home and work, as we're likely to see family, friends, and significant others in those settings. Is she married or dating anyone? Who are her friends? Is she in daily contact with family? Does she have children and/or pets? Who are the people she has to interact with most at work?

Think about your own life. I'm guessing you have a few concentric circles of relationships: those closest to you, those you see regularly, those you see infrequently, and those you almost never see. Why not draw out a list of those people and put them in those circles? Your character has people in each of those circles, too. Do a similar diagram for your main characters. When you're establishing normal, be sure you show us almost everyone in the first circle and maybe a few folks from some of the other circles, as well.

After you've shown your hero's home, work, and important relationships, you've given the reader an excellent idea of who he is, what he does, what his situation is, and what sorts of things he expects tomorrow will hold. You've established his normal.

With that knowledge, when you bring in the radical departure from that normal, the reader will feel it almost as acutely as the character would.

Note that you don't have to show home, work, *and* important relationships. You can establish normal by showing just one or two of those three, or perhaps you can come up with a completely different method of doing the same thing. (Just not with backstory dumps, please. More on that in the next Victory.)

As you think about what you want to show the reader in order to set up your hero's normal, consider the particular wrench you're going to throw into the hero's gears. Jot down the aspects of her life that this detour will disrupt … and then show those aspects before you show the change she experiences.

introducing your hero

How are you going to bring your hero onstage for the first time? It's vital that you give thought to the first impression you're going to give the reader, as the reader is going to latch onto it permanently.

If you want your hero to be a gentle environmentalist who saves kitties and tries not to bend blades of grass, but you introduce her in a courtroom screaming at a witness on the stand, you can take your environmental doe image and kiss it goodbye.

To write an effective character introduction, you need to identify the main thing you want the reader to understand about that person. What's the one broad brushstroke you want the reader to see? Then construct an introductory scene that reveals that about your hero. You can do this well because you've done your character creation homework from the previous victories.

For example, let's say you want to establish for the reader that your hero is a soldier who has been drafted into the army of a repressive regime but who is, above all, a decent soul. You want that decency to shine even amidst the antihuman totalitarian system he serves. How could you bring him onstage? You'd want to show his situation—a soldier for a cruel power—but you also need to reveal his kindness.

There are hundreds of ways to do this, but one might be to have him take part in a raid on a home where some "dissidents" have been holed up. He is just as brutal as the other troops, though he is perhaps not as eager to kill as some of the others are. Then, in his search of the home, he finds a trapdoor, beneath which hide two small children, scared to death.

He hesitates, looks around, assesses what will happen to these children if he exposes them, and makes a decision. He puts his finger to his lips and shuts the trapdoor, then signals to the rest of the troops that this section has been thoroughly searched. One of the other soldiers will probably be suspicious—because all such regimes encourage their people to rat each other out— but for now our hero and the two children are safe.

Whatever else happens in this novel, the reader will remember what this character did in his introductory scene. Moreover, because of this character's actions, the reader will probably connect with him powerfully (which supports the Great Commandment of Fiction), and for the rest of the book the reader will believe in this character's innate goodness. That's the power of the right first impression.

Think about the hero in the novel you're going to write. What is the key note you want to strike about her? Brainstorm some ideas for scenes you might write to bring her onstage in such a way that 1) we'll see her situation and 2) the key note will ring out loud and clear.

How you write this introductory scene depends on whether this is your very first scene in the book or if it comes after some other opener, like a prologue. More about that in a second. But either way, the scene must be inherently interesting. It needs to begin to introduce the hero's normal, it may hint at the hero's inner journey "problem," and it certainly needs to hit that key note.

Think of this introductory scene as a short story. I think it works best when it's a stand-alone set-piece story.

Consider the scene that introduces Indiana Jones in *Raiders of the Lost Ark*. That whole jungle sequence, from opening credits to when Indy is flying away in his getaway plane, is his character introduction. Notice that the main story (searching for the Ark of the Covenant) hasn't even entered his awareness yet. Indeed, that jungle sequence could've been a short film all on its own. It works so well as a self-contained storytelling unit.

That's what I'd like to see you do to introduce your main character. Jot down some ideas for how to make that happen with your protagonist.

The Disney movie *Atlantis: The Lost Empire* has a wonderful hero introduction scene. We see a young man, Milo Thatch, making a presentation to an audience of rich patrons. He's showing how his research has led him to conclude that he knows where the fabled lost city of Atlantis can be found, and he's urging them to fund his expedition. He's passionate and articulate and obviously smart, though a little clumsy. Then we get this marvelous reveal in which we discover that he's not talking to anyone at all but is instead giving a mock presentation to mannequins and dusty skeleton models in the basement. We liked him when he was zealous and bumbling, but we love him when we see that he's still hoping to be taken seriously. It's endearing.

So the scene showed 1) his earnestness and intelligence and passion, 2) his situation (hopeful but unsung), and 3) what's likable about him.

Do something like that to introduce your hero. Create a nice little stand-alone short story that introduces him in his "normal" and before the main action of the story has yet to crash into his life.

Your other major characters—and even some of your minor characters—should be given introductory bits. You will want to give care to how you introduce your villain, for sure, and your love interest if there is to be one. Perhaps they merit their own short story-style introductory scenes as well. In the least make sure you introduce them purposefully in the scenes they first appear in, even if those scenes are not stand-alone scenes.

Think through the list of characters you've already come up with for your novel. Write down an idea or two for each one about how you might introduce him or her in the perfect way to give the reader an instant feel for who this person is.

four structures for beginning a novel

How, practically speaking, are you going to begin your novel? When a reader reads the first page, what will she find?

There are four primary structures for beginning a novel. Probably more, including some highly experimental ones, but these are the main four. Run your story idea through the filter of each of these opening methods and see if one of them feels right for your book.

the prologue beginning

A prologue is an episode that pertains to your story but does not include the hero (or includes the hero at a time well before the story proper begins, when he's a child).

The aforementioned *Atlantis: The Lost Empire* begins with a prologue. We see the final tragic moments of Atlantis at some point in ancient history. The next scene we see is Milo Thatch making his mock presentation. Our hero, Milo, is not onstage during the prologue.

Pirates of the Caribbean begins with a prologue in which two of our main heroes first meet each other as children. Our heroes are onstage, but they're not at the age they'll be for the story proper.

Mulan begins with a prologue that establishes the villain and the OR-ELSE stakes and the ticking time bomb. The action is contemporaneous with the scene that introduces our heroine, but she is not onstage, and she does not become aware of the danger until deeper into the story (after her normal has been established).

Game of Thrones (the HBO series) begins with a prologue showing less than minor characters who discover a new danger in the land. *Ghostbusters* begins with a prologue showing a nonprimary character who sees a ghost, which provides the need for the Ghostbusters to arise. *Star Trek* (2009) begins with the arrival of a terrifying new enemy vessel that can destroy whole fleets, and our heroes are not even born.

In these cases, we see some of the ways a prologue can help your story. A prologue can establish why things are as they are in the world when the main story begins. A prologue can establish why the character is as he is when the main story begins. And a prologue can establish the danger that will come to sweep over the hero's life.

the prologue debate

We're in disputed territory when we talk about prologues. Many fiction experts tell writers never to write a prologue, while others (like me) say prologues are great.

The Anti-Prologuers argue that 1) no one reads prologues, 2) prologues are just dumping grounds for backstory, and 3) prologues prevent you from getting to the main action of the story.

The Pro-Prologuers (Pro-Loguers?) contend that 1) 95 percent of fiction readers do read prologues, 2) any portion of a book that is a dumping ground for backstory should be cut—not because it has the word *prologue* at the top, but because telling is lazy writing, and 3) prologues allow you to set the right tone for your novel without having your protagonist onstage doing something heroic.

I meet with many attendees of writers conferences who tell me they've been warned that putting a prologue in a novel is a death sentence. I've seen novels rejected by editors or agents simply because they had "Prologue" written on the top of page 1.

This despite the fact that probably 45 percent of all movies and TV shows begin with prologues (in television, they're called teasers). The prologue beginning is arguably the most-used way to begin stories in our culture. This method of beginning your tale, along with the one I'm going to talk about next, comprise the beginning of what I estimate to be around 90 percent of all modern stories.

Yet you will still hear that you should never begin a novel with a prologue. Well, we're back to looking to the Great Commandment of Fiction for guidance. The Great Commandment is that you must engage your reader from beginning to end.

Can beginning with a prologue engage your reader? Yes. Can it be done so poorly that it disengages the reader? Also yes. Is having or not having a prologue part of the Greatest Commandment? No. Having or not having a prologue is not an issue of right or wrong. It's neutral. According to our fiction moral compass, if your prologue engages the reader, it's a good thing, and if your prologue disengages the reader, it's a bad thing.

However, as I said in our first Victory, standing between you and your readership may be the literary elite (agents, editors, etc.). And those people may believe beyond doubt that prologues are bad. (Some of them don't recognize what a prologue is; they're looking only for that trigger word at the top of the page—so for them you can just change "Prologue" to "Chapter

1" and be golden.) It may be that you need only cut or move (or rename) your prologue to get through their gate. But if you can, put it back later. Your readers will love it.

I say that if a prologue works best for your story, write one. Call it Chapter 1 until you get past the gatekeepers, but leave it in.

If you do write a prologue, write one that's at least eight pages long. However you begin your novel, it works best (in my opinion) to well and truly begin your story. The half-page prologues don't cut it for me. Movies don't begin with ten-second scenes, and neither should your novel. Find a place to begin where you can sit and soak in for a goodly number of pages.

A good prologue can, as we've seen, introduce your villain and the stakes and the conflict and the danger and the ticking time bomb. It can set the stage for what is to come. If you want to reveal something that happened before the main action of the story begins, I'd much rather you do it as a prologue than as a flashback that shows up later.

Just remember that it must engage your reader. Now we are in Great Commandment territory. Begin with action, even if the only action is someone running late for a meeting or trying to win a debate.

the hero action beginning

In a hero action beginning, the hero is onstage, in the same situation and age she'll be for the rest of the novel, doing something active and interesting.

So *Raiders of the Lost Ark* starts with Indiana Jones onstage doing his whip-snapping adventure archaeologist thing in a South American jungle. *Groundhog Day* begins with Phil Connors onstage giving a (sarcastic) weather report. *WALL-E* begins with WALL-E onstage doing his daily routine of garbage collecting and compacting. *Juno* begins with Juno walking through the neighborhood, drinking SunnyD, on her way to the corner store to take a pregnancy test. Nearly every James Bond movie begins with 007 onstage performing some amazing derring-do. *What About Bob?* begins with Bob onstage going through his neurotic morning rituals.

The hero action beginning is the other most common way to begin a movie or book. As I mentioned, when you add up all the modern American movies that begin with either a hero action beginning or a prologue, you've accounted for around 90 percent of them all. It's an excellent way to begin a story, and it may just be the perfect way to begin your novel.

Your book needs to begin with action. The action need not be an explosion—it just needs to be interesting to the reader. Only the rarest of story ideas can't manage a hero action beginning. Unless your hero is catatonic or incarcerated in a hole or the like, with enough creative thought, I'm certain you can come up with something interesting for him to do at the start of the novel.

The question becomes how much of a stretch is it to show that? And would a prologue (or some other form of beginning) help you more than a hero action beginning? Now you're thinking strategically about your story, an excellent thing to do.

It may be that there's a natural hero action beginning for your book. I mean, if the girl is a superhero when the story begins, start the novel by having her save the Earth. If he's a football player, show him on the field in a big game. If she's a karate champion, show her winning a tournament.

But if your hero isn't a hero yet or isn't yet in a position to show it—or if you simply prefer to establish your villain and time bomb in a prologue—perhaps the hero action beginning isn't right for your book. Both *Mulan* and *Atlantis* (can you tell that I love Disney movies?) begin with prologues because the protagonist in each story isn't yet in any kind of heroic capacity. Mulan is feeding chickens on the family farm, and Milo Thatch is a wet-behind-the-ears kid no one listens to. The writers could've invented a way for each of these heroes to be heroic at the outset—maybe in a dream sequence—but they chose not to, and I agree with their choice.

Don't force a hero action beginning. I'm sure you could come up with something fascinating for your hero to do as the book begins. But if it feels like too much of a stretch and you don't want to begin with a dream (hurray!), don't sweat it. Consider one of the other methods for beginning a novel.

the *in medias res* beginning

In medias res is a Latin phrase meaning "in the middle of things." It's one of the less common but effective ways to begin a novel.

With *in media res*, you start at a point deep in the story, show a bit of activity to intrigue the reader, and then jump back to an earlier, quieter part in the story. It's the opposite of the prologue beginnings that show an early episode from the hero's life. In this case, you show a later episode, then you hit the rewind button and spend some or all of the rest of the book catching up to that moment. Another way to say it is that, after the one early scene, the majority of the book is a flashback. But since I pretty much despise flashbacks, I won't say it that way!

Battle: Los Angeles begins with U.S. military helicopters flying over a Los Angeles under attack from alien beasties. We see the faces of some soldiers in the helicopters, but we don't know who these people are. We're just getting the uh-oh feeling about what we're seeing, and the movie skips back to twenty-four hours previously. It's a good distance into the film before we get back to that helicopter moment. And when we do, this time we know what's going on and who those people are. That's an *in media res* beginning.

Another example of *in media res* is, coincidentally, also about aliens coming to earth. The beginning of *Megamind* shows an odd blue person falling out of the sky. Obviously we don't know who this being is nor how he came to be in this predicament. Over the slow-motion sequence comes a voice, whom we take to be the voice of the blue guy, saying something like, "How did things come to this?" We jump back to his birth and growing up. Indeed, we don't catch back up to that falling-from-the-sky moment until late in the movie. In a sense, the audience feels he's been suspended throughout the interim. Nice bit of suspense, and nice use of *in media res.*

One Day is an Anne Hathaway movie that uses the *in media res* beginning. It opens with Anne's character riding a bicycle through Paris. She looks happy. (I mean, she's riding a bike through the streets of Paris, so what's not to be happy about?) She passes the camera and rides out of frame. Then we jump back like twenty years. It's a long time before we catch up with her joyride through Paris.

Why isn't *in media res* used more often? Part of the reason is because it's a gimmick, and you don't want to use those too often. Sometimes it gives readers that same ripped-off feeling they get when they read a novel that begins with a dream. I think it's also because you sacrifice suspense for that whole portion of the book until you catch up with the first moment.

Think about it: If you see the main character alive and well in what you now realize is a future moment, how nervous are you going to be when she gets into danger? I mean, you know she lives, right? So there's no tension. An *in media res* opening deflates the tension the same way a hole deflates a tire.

Over on the "plus" column, though, lies a significant advantage of using the *in media res* beginning. Once you do catch up with that opening moment, especially if it's taken a long time to get there, the reader is given an injection of fictive adrenaline. Before now, everything has been relatively safe. It's been within the protective confines of story time when you know the hero is fine. But when you get to that moment, and especially when you *surpass* it, everything changes. Dramatically.

Now that you care about that person falling from the sky, you're suddenly scared that this will be the end for him. Now that you know these soldiers and see what's been happening on the ground, all of a sudden you don't know if you want them flying in to attack. Now that you care about that Parisian bicyclist, you're very concerned about what's going to happen to her when she rounds that corner (as well you should be…).

The great payoff of the *in media res* beginning is that thrilling moment of angst you give your reader when you reach that point and go beyond it. The tension shoots through the roof.

Consider your story: Is that the sort of risk/payoff drama you'd love to send your novel and your readers on? The risk is that you may bore them if things get too slow before you catch up to that opening moment. The payoff is that breathless feeling of performing without a net that you give readers that stay with you. If your book would benefit from such a thing, go for it.

Note that my usual recommendation that you launch your novel with an eight- to eighteen-page scene doesn't apply to *in media res*. It's very hard to go for long in a scene like this without having to explain what's going on or without revealing things you'd rather keep hidden. So maybe a three- to seven-page scene would work better in this case.

the frame device

The final major way of beginning a novel is to use a frame device. In this, your story is bookended on the front and back (and usually a few instances in the middle) by a story that is outside the main story. The primary tale is *framed* by this other story.

The Princess Bride is a frame device story. The movie begins with a kid playing a video game. He's staying home from school because he's sick. His grandfather comes over and offers to read the boy a book to pass the time. Whenever he reads the book, the movie switches over to the fantasy swashbuckling adventure that is the main story. Throughout the story, we cut back to the grandfather and boy, where we get commentary on the story and see a bond developing between the two. Then it's back to the fantasy world. The movie ends in the modern day, as well.

Another example of a movie that uses the frame device is *Titanic*. The story the audience cares most about is the historical tale of Rose and Jack and Cal onboard the doomed ocean liner. But we access that story through the device of an old woman (Rose) in the present. There's a minor story going on in the modern day—they're searching for a jewel she had while on the ship—but the real drama is the historical part. Now and then during the story we cut back to Old Rose, and the movie also ends with her, but our interest is in the other set of circumstances.

Would a frame device work for your story?

One reason to consider a frame device is if you're concerned that a modern reader simply wouldn't care about your primary topic. If it's too far removed from where they are in their modern interests, you might use a frame device to show someone very much like the possibly bored reader (a kid playing a video game, for instance) coming to enjoy the main tale. Show someone much like us getting involved in the story, and maybe we'll go with you as well.

I once edited a novel in which the main story was about an ancient Babylonian priestess and her many court intrigues. Yawn, right? But the author had wisely written a frame device in which a young, idealistic American woman, an expert in ancient languages, is called to an archaeological dig to decipher the writings on an ancient Babylonian tablet. In this modern story, mysterious bad guys are trying to steal the tablet and kill anyone involved with it. Every time our modern heroine touches the tablet, she is transported into the life of ... a Babylonian priestess running for her life amidst insidious court intrigues.

The book is *Marduk's Tablet* by T. L. Higley, and it's a great example of how a frame device can draw in a reader who might not otherwise think the book has anything to offer her. If that's your situation, you might consider using a frame device for your novel.

Another great thing about the frame device is that you can use it to make large jumps in time in your inside story. If you need to jump ten years, just cut back to the frame story and have the narrator say, "It went pretty much like that for the next ten years. Until finally…" and then you go back to the historical story. The frame device can act like a DJ transitioning between scenes.

Why don't authors use a frame device more often? I think it's because it sometimes involves people who are out of danger and out of the action, which isn't especially engaging, and uses them to usher us into things that are more interesting. The instinct of most writers is to skip what's not engaging and go straight to the engaging, and I agree. But there are good reasons to use a frame device, and if you show some movement or growth in that frame story too, you can achieve something special.

The frame device can be another exception from the eight- to eighteen-page opening scene recommendation. If you want to conceal who the narrator is, as in a story with multiple women wherein we shouldn't know which one lives to tell the tale until the end, then you probably won't be able to accomplish too many pages without giving it away. It's recommended that you take eight to eighteen pages to begin your novel. Most of the time you can do so, even with a frame device, but if you have a legitimate reason not to, that's okay.

However you begin your novel, it is the very first chance you have to see to the Great Commandment. Your novel must engage the reader from *beginning* to end.

forty contiguous pages

In my opinion, it is best to stay in your main protagonist's storyline for roughly forty contiguous pages after you bring him onstage.

Let's say you start your novel with a prologue that features the antagonist setting in motion the dire events that will consume this novel. That's awesome. Try to go eight to eighteen pages in that prologue, as I've said. But as soon as you bring your hero onstage, stay with him for forty pages before cutting away to some other story line.

Now, there's nothing magical about the number 40, and violating this recommendation is not a direct violation of the Great Commandment of Fiction. But adhering to this recommendation is a direct *support* of the Great Commandment.

Here's why: Your reader wants to connect with your book. She wants to engage. Indeed, she wants to be engaged from beginning to end, or she wouldn't have picked it up in the first place. The way a reader engages with a novel is to become engaged with your protagonist, as we saw in Victory 3.

How do we become interested in someone we meet? By spending time with him. If you saw someone interesting as you rode through a station on a subway—a musician standing on the platform playing a trumpet, perhaps—you might be intrigued; you might even crane your neck to see him as long as you could. But if you rode on through and never saw him again, he would quickly fade from your memory.

Now let's say that musician was playing on the platform at your stop. You're intrigued by his style, so you stand there and listen for a while. He plays with such passion and skill that you find yourself enthralled. Between songs, he talks to you about himself, his life, his dreams, his family, his hardships. You never intended to do so, but you find yourself becoming connected to this guy. He's growing on you. You feel your heart going out to him and even beginning to become knit together with his. Something funny he says especially engages your compassion, and before you know it, this musician has made for himself a lodging place in your heart. Even if you were to mount the stairs and never see him again, you would not forget him.

How did this happen? How did you become engaged with him as a personality? You spent time with him. A good amount of time. If you'd seen him for sixty seconds every morning for a month, you wouldn't have gained the same connection you formed by spending thirty minutes with him on one day.

So it is with connecting your reader and your protagonist. If you want to have eight new main characters and eight new story lines introduced in the first eight pages of your book, you're welcome to do so. But this will feel to the reader like passing eight street musicians without even stopping at their station.

If you use a prologue beginning, an *in media res* beginning, or a frame device beginning (any kind but a hero action beginning, in other words), you're starting the book with something other than the hero onstage in the status and condition and age he'll be in at the beginning of the story. That's all fine. But when you do bring that person onstage, find a way to stay with her for thirty-five to fifty-five contiguous pages. You want your readers to grow roots into her life.

This doesn't mean it has to be an approximately forty-page chapter or scene. You can have multiple chapters and scenes across this span. It also doesn't mean you can't have other main characters onstage during that time. You certainly can. I'm simply urging you to stay in this one story line, with this one viewpoint character, long enough for us to become bound with her before you ask us to become bound with someone else.

After those forty pages, you can introduce as many story lines as you like, and readers will be fine with it. Once you give us a strong connection with your hero, we can handle meeting new characters. You'll want to keep circling back to that main character, of course, but you're fine to introduce a new one or two or three before doing so.

On the other extreme, if you are going to have more than one viewpoint character, you need to be sure you've introduced him before you've hit the approximately page 70 mark. If you stay in one character's life for a long time, the reader comes to believe that this is the only life she'll be dwelling in. If you bring in a new character too late, it's jarring. It's like the guideline for theater: If it's going to be a musical, you need to have a song in the first five minutes. In fiction, if you're going to have multiple viewpoint characters (and most novels do), you need to be sure you've introduced at least one of the others by around page 65 or the reader will think there aren't going to be any others.

So a good guide might be:

- eight to eighteen-page prologue or hero action opening
- about forty (thirty-five to fifty-five) contiguous pages with your protagonist
- eight to eighteen pages with a new viewpoint character
- eight to eighteen pages back with the main hero
- …and on from there.

Allowing your reader to build a strong connection with your protagonist right away in the novel is a good way to be sure you're following the Great Commandment of Fiction.

a word about the first line

No discussion of how to begin a novel would be complete without a look at that most hallowed spot in any work of fiction: the opening line.

However, now isn't the time to talk about it in detail. Actually, don't even worry about your opening line now. Don't worry about it even as you're writing the first draft. You're about to embark on a thirty-day blitzkrieg of frenzied fiction fanaticism, and the last thing you need is to spend two days stuck on creating the perfect first sentence.

Just write something down. Anything. Even, "This is the beginning of the novel." And move on. Later, in revisions, you can spend a whole year nailing the first line, if you want. But now, don't even let it be a speed bump.

If you've already got your perfect first line, by all means use it. Some writers get their first line and that's all they have at first. It's the seed that's going to cause the growth of the whole thing. Awesome. But most of us have no clue, so if that's you, don't fret.

Besides, the perfect first line may not even exist at the start. It will grow out of the story you create. It may occur to you halfway through writing. It may occur to you as you're writing the very last line. It may not occur to you until months after that. So you certainly don't want to worry about it now.

We'll talk about it more in Part Three, when we're covering revisions. For now, just go. Don't let anything slow you down.

conclusion

As with every Victory in Part One, my goal here is to equip you with what you need to knock out this novel in thirty days. It is my belief that knowing certain things in advance will allow you to run with endurance the race set before you.

The First 50 Pages will give you a much greater knowledge of this material, but what I've given you here is definitely enough to get a good start and move smoothly from Victory to Victory.

craft to know on the front end

Most of the instruction I'm going to give you in this book about the craft of fiction will come in Part Three. It is material that is to be applied after you've written your rough draft. I don't want you hindered during the writing phase because you're worried about craftsmanship. During these thirty days, I care less about you getting it right and more about you getting it down (on paper).

Having said that, though, there are a few things you need to know now. Mainly because being mindful of these as you write will save you lots of time later. They're topics that, if I didn't tell you about now, you'd probably say, "That's information that would've been helpful *before* I spent a month writing! Now I have to spend another month un-writing, when you could've saved me the effort." So here we go.

I'm going to cover three aspects of fiction craftsmanship in this Victory: point of view, show versus tell, and the mechanics of dialogue.

point of view

In fiction, point of view (POV) refers to whose eyes we're seeing the story through. That there even is such a thing as a viewpoint character is not immediately obvious to the nonwriter or the new writer.

In movies, our primary storytelling medium these days, most of the time we're not seeing from any one character's viewpoint. Multiple camera angles allow viewers to be privy to what's going on, and often we see things that our "hero" in the scene doesn't see—or even that no one sees except the camera.

So when we sit down to write fiction, it's no surprise that we may write it in a way that is similar to making a movie.

As you have seen in prior Victories, I refer to movies as examples of good storytelling more often than I refer to novels. On almost every level, how it's done in film is the perfect illustration of how it should be done in fiction.

Point of view is an exception.

This is another of those topics about which there is disagreement among fiction teachers. Some fiction experts say you shouldn't worry about POV. Just write it as it comes to you. Other teachers say you can use any POV style you want, including yesteryear's favorite style, omniscient, which is when you jump around from head to head, getting every character's thoughts and feelings. Still other experts say you should restrict yourself to either first-person or third-person POV (which I'll define in a second).

As in all such cases, it helps us to go back to the Great Commandment of Fiction. So, does doing POV correctly help you or hinder you in your quest to engage your reader and keep her engaged?

Not directly. There are many examples of fabulously successful novels that use every style of POV you can think of, or no consistent style at all. And I'm not just talking about the classics—I'm referring to novels published today. Books that fiction teachers would look at and say they got POV wrong are selling by the gajillions. So are books that fiction teachers say got the POV right.

How could such a thing be? Because what the reader cares about is not whether the author utilizes the contemporary preferred style of point of view, but whether she is engaged from start to finish. And you can achieve that even if you don't know POV from PB&J. The reader certainly doesn't know the difference. Or care.

So why am I even talking about it?

Four reasons. First, because I think novels written according to the principles of good POV are actually better than novels not written according to those principles. It's the pinch of intangible mystery that causes the reader to feel that this writer is a real pro. It subtly encourages the reader to trust you to know how to take her to an entertaining destination.

Second, because if you decide you want to try to get this thing published, agents and editors do usually care about POV, so getting it right would be one more thing in your book's favor. When I teach at writers conferences, I mention POV mastery as something that tells me right away whether or not a writer is ready for publishing prime time.

Third, because a novel with loose or omniscient POV is very often related to a book that tells instead of shows (I'll cover show vs. tell in a moment), and I consider both practices to be signs of laziness and a lack of self-discipline in the author. It's a shortcut that shares much in common with the Dark Side of the Force. To co-opt Master Yoda's wise words, bad POV is quicker, easier, more seductive, but to no good place does it lead. Help you, it will not.

Finally, I take the time to cover this topic because I believe good POV actually helps you achieve the Great Commandment of Fiction. Consistent, disciplined point of view in fiction results in a deeper reader experience and a more thorough engagement with your story. With disciplined POV, the reader feels a close connection with your viewpoint character or characters. Loose or omniscient POV, in my opinion, tries to engage the reader with *everyone* all at once and all the time, but it ends up leaving the reader equally disengaged with all of them.

And if you're going to care about getting POV right (well, "right" as I'm teaching it), now is the time to do it. After you've written the whole manuscript, it's ten times harder to fix point of view. If you're going to do it, learn it now and do it as correctly as you can as you're writing.

the forms of pov

Some people have identified dozens of forms of POV. Everything from third person limited to partial objective first person omniscient. Okay, I made that one up, but the lists people come up with can get a little ridiculous.

I'm going to describe five styles of point of view. Two of them are widely used and are the ones I recommend for the novel you're about to write.

FIRST-PERSON POINT OF VIEW is the style in which the writer is using *I* and *me* to refer to the viewpoint character. So a typical sentence in such a novel might be, "I couldn't wait for Jenny to leave. When she finally did, I pulled out my smartphone and checked the score of the game. My Cowboys had pulled ahead!"

First person is one of the two main styles of POV used in modern fiction, and I recommend it to you. The reader understands first person—because every human thinks in terms of *I* and *me*. We're all in first person in our own lives.

During first-person scenes, you must stay within the head of the viewpoint character. You can inform the reader of only those things the I/me character can sense, think, or know. No "Out of sight from everyone, a new danger lurked" bits when you're doing first person. If the viewpoint character doesn't see it or know about it, the reader can't see or know about it.

Think of POV as a periscope on a submarine. The person peering through the periscope can see only what the periscope can see. That's a picture of how your viewpoint character can funnel information about the story to your reader.

First person is great in that it makes the reader feel intimately connected with the viewpoint character. How much closer can you get to someone than when his thoughts are so identified with your thoughts that you are both thinking in terms of *I* and *me*?

In fact, first person can even become a bit claustrophobic—the reader may wish she could know things beyond what the viewpoint character knows. Use this to your advantage. If you're writing a detective story or you otherwise want the reader to feel as in the dark as the hero feels, consider using first person.

SECOND-PERSON POINT OF VIEW is technically available to you but almost never used. This is the "You come to a fork in the road" style of POV used for choose-your-own-adventure stories. If you were to attempt a second-person novel today, the rest of the world would certainly view it as experimental. It's hard to say how successful it could be, considering you're constantly telling the reader what she's doing and thinking! Still, if you're tempted to try it, give it a whirl.

THIRD-PERSON POINT OF VIEW is the other most-used style of POV today. It's the one I recommend you use in the novel you're about to write—if it fits. This is the he-said/he-did style that we see in most novels. To put our previous example in third person, it would go like this: "Floyd couldn't wait for Jenny to leave. When she finally did, he pulled out his smartphone and checked the score of the game. His Cowboys had pulled ahead!"

In my opinion, third person strikes the perfect balance of closeness and distance between reader and viewpoint character(s). You can hear the viewpoint character's thoughts, as in the example, but you're not so close that there's no psychological separation for the reader. Whereas first person is sometimes considered "out" or not en vogue, third person is always "in."

OMNISCIENT POINT OF VIEW is mainly the style of previous generations. In this style, also called "head hopping," you jump into every character's head and reveal everyone's thoughts and feelings. In that sense, you're godlike. You know all. And the reader gets that same level of access.

"Floyd couldn't wait for Jenny to leave. Jenny wanted to stay longer because she loved Floyd. Penny the Pug Puppy wanted to go out and do her business in the yard. She thought it was strange that Floyd and Jenny were not staying together. When Jenny finally did leave, nursing her broken heart and swearing to become a nun, Floyd pulled out his smartphone and checked the score of the game. His Cowboys had pulled ahead! Jenny thought she might never recover. Penny decided to wet the carpet."

Some novelists use omniscient POV today, and some of their novels are ridiculously successful. Again, the reader doesn't care about POV. She probably can't name a single form of POV, much less tell one from the other. As long as she's sucked into the story, nothing else matters. But for the reasons I mentioned above, it's important for you, as the writer, to know.

Head hopping, in my opinion, is lazy writing. It's related to telling in that both practices indulge the writer's temptation to explain everything to the reader. Such authors can't resist the urge to divulge everything they know to the reader. As readers, we don't have to earn the knowledge of what someone is really thinking, because the author simply tells us. We don't get the thrill of following our curiosity and being rewarded by figuring something out based on clues, because the writer serves it to us on a platter. Both omniscient POV and telling, in my opinion, put the reader to sleep.

And a novel that produces a sleeping reader is one that has violated the Great Commandment of Fiction.

Another weakness of omniscient POV is that it's much more difficult to conceal anything from the reader. If one of the people in the kitchen is the killer, it's hard to hide which one it is if you're showing everyone's thoughts. "Wow, it's a good thing they don't know I'm the killer" kind of blows the suspense for the reader! It's also hard to make the reader wonder if Person A, Person B, or Person C might be a suspect, if we're hearing how innocent they all are. (It might be fun to play with an untrustworthy narrator or a character who is lying to himself even in his overheard thoughts, but for most situations like this, omniscient is not your friend.)

The last kind of point of view I'll discuss is something we might call *CINEMATIC* or *OBJECTIVE POV*. I described it briefly in the example above regarding movies and POV. In cinematic

POV, you're not in anyone's head. Just like the cameras and microphones recording what characters do and say—but not giving us access to what any of them *thinks* or believes or feels—so you'd do in your fiction. The perspective, and thus the reader, remains a detached observer trying to infer what the characters are thinking or feeling.

I've personally never seen a novel done like this, but in our age in which almost all fiction techniques are taking cues from cinema, I suspect it's being done. My guess is that the reader would feel at arm's length from the action in such a story—which means it runs very close to violating the Great Commandment. But if your story is one in which your intention is to create a feeling of alienation or detachment, you might give it a try.

using a disciplined pov

Only first person and third person are what I call disciplined POV styles. This is because the writer must use discipline—must work *hard*—to restrict himself to that periscope metaphor. Only what the viewpoint character senses, knows, and thinks can be communicated to the reader.

This feels realistic to the reader, who is restricted to what she senses, knows, and thinks. It's so much easier for the writer to just dump all information to the reader through an undisciplined POV, but it's neither realistic nor engaging for the reader. Nevertheless, some books that do so are enormously successful.

But I suspect you are the kind of writer who is not afraid of the way of discipline, or else you wouldn't be reading a book on how to write a novel. Otherwise, you'd just sit down and start writing. Lots of people do that. Most don't finish, but that's not the point.

Or maybe it is.

When you're writing in a disciplined point of view, you need to "pick a head" to be in for the duration of the scene you're writing. You get inside one character's viewpoint, and you give us only what that person senses, thinks, or knows. That viewpoint character can try to guess what another character is thinking, but she has to be wrong at least half the time, or you're cheating. If you find yourself letting viewpoint characters somehow accurately guess what other characters are thinking, you're committing a POV error and have let your discipline slip. Pick a head and stay in it, including the realistic restrictions such a viewpoint entails.

Now, that doesn't mean you have to stay inside only one character's head for the whole book. You can have as many viewpoint characters as you'd like (though somewhere in the two to six range is typical). It just means you need to stay inside one character's head at a time and until the end of that particular scene. New scene? New viewpoint character (if you want).

It's possible to mix first- and third-person POVs in a single novel. I've done so myself. I picked one of my viewpoint characters to write in first person. This wasn't even the main character, though the reader may have felt it was. That was all right with me, because I wanted the reader to feel especially close to that one person. If you're considering mixing first and third, give the first-person POV to the person you want the reader to most identify with.

Some novels have multiple first-person viewpoint characters. There might be five characters through whose eyes we see, and they all narrate with *I* and *me*. It takes a masterful author to pull it off. I personally wouldn't attempt it, and as a reader I usually find it extremely confusing. But it's an option, should you want to try. Just be very, very sure each viewpoint character's voice is extremely distinctive.

show vs. tell

If you've hung around the fiction writing world very long, you've probably heard someone say, "Show, don't tell." Every novelist I talk to says she knows what this means. But when pressed for a definition, most just shrug.

Hey, that's okay. As we've seen, some of these issues are things that only the literary elite—folks like you and me, maybe—even care about, much less know how to define. The typical end user, the reader, wouldn't know a paragraph of telling if it stepped on his toe, and probably wouldn't care.

But it is an aspect of fiction that makes a subtle yet significant difference in your writing. Even if someone isn't able to articulate why a book with very little telling is better than a book with lots of telling, it remains one of those mysterious intangibles that make one book feel stronger and more mature than another. And, like lazy POV, telling is lazy writing, in my opinion.

What is telling? Telling is outright explanation to the reader, usually conveyed in the form of a paragraph of exposition. Consider this passage from the beginning of *Gone Girl* by Gillian Flynn:

> It had been a compromise: Amy demanded we rent, not buy, in my little Missouri hometown, in her firm hope that we wouldn't be stuck here long. But the only houses for rent were clustered in this failed development: a miniature ghost town of bank-owned, recession-busted, price-reduced mansions, a neighborhood that closed before it ever opened. It was a compromise, but Amy didn't see it that way, not in the least. To Amy, it was a punishing whim on my part, a nasty, selfish twist of the knife. I would drag her, caveman-style, to a town she had aggressively avoided, and make her live in the kind of house she used to mock. I suppose it's not a compromise if only one of you considers it such, but that was what our compromises tended to look like. One of us was always angry. Amy, usually.
>
> Do not blame me for this particular grievance, Amy. The Missouri Grievance. Blame the economy, blame bad luck, blame my parents, blame your par-

ents, blame the Internet, blame people who use the Internet. I used to be a writer. I was a writer who wrote about TV and movies and books. Back when people read things on paper, back when anyone cared about what I thought. I'd arrived in New York in the late '90s, the last gasp of the glory days, although no one knew it then. New York was packed with writers, real writers, because there were magazines, real magazines, loads of them. This was back when the Internet was still some exotic pet kept in the corner of the publishing world—throw some kibble at it, watch it dance on its little leash, oh quite cute, it definitely won't kill us in the night. Think about it: a time when newly graduated college kids could come to New York and *get paid to write*. We had no clue that we were embarking on careers that would vanish within a decade.

    I had a job for eleven years and then...

I don't know about you, but this writing does not engage me. I don't mean to pick on this book or slander Ms. Flynn. I actually find the prose well written. The problem is that it's just explanation. Nothing is happening. Readers don't come to fiction for radio narration like this. They come to "see" something happening onstage, as in a movie.

Having said that, though, I should hasten to point out that on the day I wrote this *Gone Girl* was the #4 novel for adults on Amazon.com and had been in the top one hundred books of any kind on Amazon for 155 days.

As we've seen with POV, a book full of telling may sell incredibly well. I contend that such books sell well *in spite of* all the telling, not because of it. So please don't point to some novel that is successful but loaded with telling as license to tell with abandon. You can include as much telling as you want, but telling is boring and has the tendency to disengage readers from your story, which would then be a violation of our Great Commandment.

You want everything that is in your power working toward, not against, reader engagement. This is one of those things.

A lot of telling can and will be spotted and eliminated in your revisions, after you've written the thing. But I'm telling you about it now because it's much easier to write it right the first time than to have to go back and fix it later.

Telling occurs whenever you stop the story to explain something the reader doesn't care about. Do we care that the narrator in *Gone Girl* used to be a writer in New York City? Nope. But we're made to sit there and listen to it. If you've ever been the captive audience of someone who was determined to tell you about his life despite your verbal and nonverbal cues that you're not interested, then you know what you're doing to your reader when you dump explanation on her.

In the previous Victory, I mentioned that you shouldn't include backstory in your prologue and that some teachers consider prologues to be bad things because they're usually filled with explanation/telling/backstory/information dump. I countered that prologues were not bad in and of themselves, but that what made them bad was the fact that they are often made up of telling. Cut the telling from your book, not only from the prologue but from the whole thing.

Anytime you find yourself stopping the story to explain something, you're telling. "He said it that way because..." Ack! Stop. "They had grown up in a rural village south of..." No! "She'd always hated how he..." Whoa there!

Don't tell us these things—show us.

I'm not saying you shouldn't convey information to the reader. Heavens, no. What is a novel but information conveyed to the reader? And we may actually need to know that the narrator was a writer in New York City, or that he said something a certain way because X, or that they grew up in a rural village, or that she'd always hated X about him.

So the solution isn't to try to write a novel in which no information is delivered to the reader. The solution is to find a way to deliver it that doesn't 1) stop the story or 2) explain something the reader doesn't care about. So you should give the information in a way that allows the story to advance at full speed and only when the reader has been given a reason to want to learn the information.

Our tendency is to front load a novel with information. In conversation, we say, "I'm going to tell you a story about my son, but first you need to understand that he..." whatever. We give them information in advance so they'll understand the import of the main story, which is coming next. It's no surprise, then, that when we sit down to write a novel we tend to work in the same way: tell the reader everything up front so she'll "get it" when the important stuff comes later.

The impulse is correct. Consider my lesson about the importance of establishing normal before violating normal. We absolutely do need to understand things about the hero, the world, the conditions, and more early on so we'll be able to comprehend the impact of what comes after. So it's not the impulse behind telling that's wrong (as "wrong" as things can be when we're not talking about the Great Commandment of Fiction). What's wrong is the method for delivering that information.

If given a choice of how to spend two hours in a theater, would you rather listen to a lecture or watch a mystery onstage? Depending on your interests and personality, a lecture might be thrilling for you. But most people would prefer to watch the theatrical production.

Let me ask it this way: Which would be more entertaining, engaging, and memorable for you: if someone stepped up to the microphone and told you that Gary was a two-timing jerk, or if you watched a scene in which Gary kissed his wife goodbye, left as if to go to work, then snuck to the neighbor's door, used a key to let himself in, and fell into the arms of some other woman?

There are at least four problems with outright telling in all its forms. First, it stops the story cold, which runs the risk of disengaging the reader. Go back and look at that passage from *Gone Girl*. If that were a movie, what would be happening on the screen during that passage? Nothing. Yawn.

Second, telling bores the reader by lecturing her on something she doesn't care about.

Third, telling is lazy writing. Anyone can write, "Gary was a two-timing jerk." No problem. No sweat. But it takes work to figure out a way to illustrate that Gary was a two-timing jerk. As with omniscient POV, telling is a way for the writer to indulge her urge to explain everything to the reader as quickly and easily as possible. But the path of discipline, the path of excellence, and the path that is more likely to engage the reader and get your novel published is to show instead of tell.

Fourth, telling is simply not memorable. Readers neither remember nor even believe what you merely tell them about. They remember and believe what happens onstage before their eyes, as Gary's two-timing antics illustrate. You can tell the reader that Sally is a champion swimmer, but she won't remember that or even believe it until you show Sally swimming in a race and leaving everyone in her wake. *That* is what the reader will believe and remember.

If the reader needs to know something, find a way to illustrate it onstage. Turn it into a scene. Act it out.

Don't summarize—dramatize.

Don't narrate—illustrate.

I've got a golden tool for you to use to identify whether something is showing or telling. It's a question you can ask of any passage you'd like to test for its show-or-tell quotient. Look at the passage and ask, "Can the camera see this?" If this were a movie, would this stuff be visible?

Go back and look at the excerpt from *Gone Girl* and use that tool. What, if anything, in that passage can the camera see?

That this house was a compromise? No. That Amy thought this was a punishing whim? No. (Now, that *could* be made visible by acting it out onstage. But as it is here, it's exposition.) Can the camera see that he used to be a writer? That he'd come to NYC in the late '90s? That there used to be lots of magazines back in the day? No. It's pure telling.

When you're writing a passage and you find yourself wondering if you're telling, ask, "Can the camera see this?" There are exceptions (such as internal monologue), and you'd want to include senses other than *seeing* in your question, but for the most part, if an observer can't sense something, it's probably telling.

If you spot telling in your manuscript, you should either cut it outright (my preference) or find a way to convert it to showing. Act it out. Illustrate and dramatize. Make it something the camera can see. Bring it onstage.

the mechanics of dialogue

Entire books have been written on the topic of how to write and format dialogue in fiction, so I'm not going to cover everything here. Also, much of what needs to be done to enhance dialogue is best done in revisions. However, it would behoove you to know a few things on the front end so you can get them right as you're writing.

basic dialogue formatting

Here, in an excerpt from *Hero, Second Class* by Mitchell Bonds, is an example of how the dialogue in your book should look:

> "Well fought, Dragon. Mine name is Sir Reginald Ogleby, the Crimson Slash."
>
> The dragon bent his shimmering green neck in respect. "It was an honor to fight someone as skilled as you, Crimson. I am Keeth, son of Barinol, whose sire was Kisanth the Great."

Reginald started scratching his helmet again and stopped, irritated. "Keith, you say? Odd name for a dragon."

Keeth bared his formidable fangs. "*It's Keeth!* Double vowel."

"My apologies, Keeth," Reginald said. "But how could you tell I spelled it—"

"Dragons hear vowels, Sir Ogleby," Keeth explained. "Rather a stupid ability, to tell the truth. It's a mixed blessing at best. It seems the gods couldn't think of anything truly useful to give dragons as a gift that we didn't already have, so we received magical spelling and grammar detection."

"Well, you'd make a good writer," Cyrus said, retrieving his quill and scroll. "Better you than me." He loaded Reginald's mangled breastplate opposite his spare shield on their pack mule. The mule, Cyrus noted, had been stoically ignoring the fight. "Now that proper pleasantries have been exchanged, can we get going?" Cyrus leaned against the mule's furry grey side. "I'm a bit hungry."

Keeth looked at Cyrus. "Are you certain you have no Chimera jerky?" the dragon asked. He then turned and barbecued the rabbit with a blast of flame. "It would go rather well with roast rabbit."

In terms of formatting, note that the entire spoken sentence, including punctuation, is *inside* the quotation marks. So it's, "*It's Keeth!* Double vowel." instead of "*It's Keeth!* Double vowel".

That's true even when the larger sentence continues beyond the end of the quoted speech, as in: "*Dragons hear vowels, Sir Ogleby,*" Keeth explained. It would be incorrect to have formatted it as, "*Dragons hear vowels, Sir Ogleby.*" Keeth explained. (note the period after Ogleby) or as "*Dragons hear vowels, Sir Ogleby*", Keeth explained. (note the comma outside the quotation mark after Ogleby).

Refer back to this passage to see how to format the dialogue exchanges in your novel.

dialogue silos

In dialogue scenes, keep a character's words and actions in the same paragraph. This is for reader comprehension. The reader understands that, when you change to a new paragraph, a new speaker is taking a turn and the previous speaker is done for now. Thus:

> Reginald started scratching his helmet again and stopped, irritated. "Keith, you say? Odd name for a dragon."
>
> Keeth bared his formidable fangs. "*It's Keeth!* Double vowel."
>
> "My apologies, Keeth," Reginald said. "But how could you tell I spelled it—"

The paragraphs "take turns" in line with the characters taking turns as they exchange lines of dialogue. Note that there are both actions and spoken words in the same paragraphs, each pertaining to that speaker. The paragraph can be thought of as *belonging* to the speaker.

If it had been done like this:

> Reginald started scratching his helmet again and stopped, irritated. "Keith, you say? Odd name for a dragon." Keeth bared his formidable fangs. "*It's Keeth!* Double vowel." "My apologies, Keeth," Reginald said. "But how could you tell I spelled it—"

...it would be much more confusing. Or what about this:

> Reginald started scratching his helmet again and stopped, irritated.
>
> "Keith, you say? Odd name for a dragon." Keeth bared his formidable fangs.

"*It's Keeth*! Double vowel."
"My apologies, Keeth," Reginald said.
"But how could you tell I spelled it—"

Do you see how the paragraph division indicates for the reader who is speaking? As this paragraph is rendered—"Keith, you say? Odd name for a dragon." Keeth bared his formidable fangs.—it seems that Keeth is the one who mispronounced his own name.

The last two paragraphs here are especially confusing because it appears to be Reginald speaking in the first one and someone else, we don't know who, speaking in the second. The writer intended it to be the same speaker in both paragraphs, but the paragraph break makes the reader think it is a new speaker in the latter paragraph.

Let each paragraph in a dialogue be a little character silo into which only words and actions from that character may be placed.

let your said be said

Some writing teachers say you should avoid repeating the same word over and over in your fiction. Some writing teachers say you should avoid "–ly" adverbs in your fiction. Those two teachings can cause consternation for novelists when it comes to dialogue.

The novelist might want to write:

"Are you sure?" she said brightly.
  "I think so," he said sadly.

But because she's trying to obey those dual admonitions, she ends up writing:

"Are you sure?" she queried.
  "I think so," he opined.

Tada! Mission accomplished. The dreaded *said* was not repeated, and there's not an "–ly" adverb in sight.

Except ... it's just silly. Anytime you have a *he opined, he queried, he ventured, he lectured, he growled, he lambasted, he speculated*, or an *"I'm sorry," he apologized*, you knock your reader right out of the moment. Which causes her to become disengaged from your story, a violation of our Great Commandment of Fiction.

Stick to *said* (or *asked*). *Said* is invisible to the reader, even if you use it fifty times on one page, and it therefore doesn't break the spell of a story you're weaving. I'm all about the author remaining invisible, as I'll talk about later. And as for "–ly" adverbs, I'd much rather have a *she said quietly* to a *she sibilated*.

Even if you choose to avoid repeating *said* and decide to replace each one with something clever, don't do so as you're writing the rough draft. Save the thesaurus consultations for after your thirty days of frenzied writing.

beats as speech attributions

Speech attributions are the he said/she said bits of dialogue. These are the little markers that help the reader stay oriented during a dialogue scene. I've underlined the speech attributions in the following:

> "My apologies, Keeth," <u>Reginald said.</u> "But how could you tell I spelled it—"
>
> "Dragons hear vowels, Sir Ogleby," <u>Keeth explained.</u> "Rather a stupid ability, to tell the truth. It's a mixed blessing at best. It seems the gods couldn't think of anything truly useful to give dragons as a gift that we didn't already have, so we received magical spelling and grammar detection."
>
> "Well, you'd make a good writer," <u>Cyrus said,</u> retrieving his quill and scroll. "Better you than me."

Without speech attributions, we wouldn't know who was speaking, especially in dialogues with three or more people who might be speaking, as here. I'm a fan of using the minimum number of attributions you can while still keeping the reader oriented, and many times, if there are only one or two speakers doing the talking, you can cut quite a few of them out. But when several folks are talking, you need to put in more attributions.

> "Why are you here?" Jim asked.
>
> "Isn't it obvious," Louise said, sitting at the couch. "I live here."
>
> "Not anymore."
>
> A tilt of the head. "Oh?"
>
> "You left. Moved out. Didn't call for a month. What was I supposed to think?"
>
> "That I needed time to clear my head."
>
> "Ha!"
>
> "What?" she asked. "Don't believe me?"

I was able to cut quite a few of the attributions, and you were probably able to follow who was speaking. You certainly didn't need this:

> "Why are you here?" Jim asked.
>
> "Isn't it obvious," Louise said, sitting at the couch. "I live here."
>
> "Not anymore," Jim said.
>
> A tilt of the head. "Oh?" Louise said.
>
> "You left," Jim said. "Moved out. Didn't call for a month. What was I supposed to think?"
>
> "That I needed time to clear my head," Louise said.
>
> "Ha!" Jim said.
>
> "What?" Louise asked. "Don't believe me?"

Even in such simple exchanges, every now and then you need to drop in an attribution to be sure we're still on track with who is saying what. But you should aim to leave out as many as you can and still have the reader tracking with you.

However, that's stuff to worry about in revisions. What I want to talk about here is using beats in place of attributions.

A *beat* is a bit of narration or description within dialogue. I've underlined the beats in the following:

> "Well, you'd make a good writer," Cyrus said, <u>retrieving his quill and scroll.</u> "Better you than me." <u>He loaded Reginald's mangled breastplate opposite his spare shield on their pack mule. The mule, Cyrus noted, had been stoically ignoring the fight.</u> "Now that proper pleasantries have been exchanged, can we get going?" <u>Cyrus leaned against the mule's furry grey side.</u> "I'm a bit hungry."

Notice that the beats do three things. They give us a mental image of what a character is doing, tie us down to the setting (to prevent a talking heads sensation), and they manage the pauses between the spoken sentences. We can imagine a decent space of silence between Cyrus's lines. Whereas, if the beats had been removed, it would've sounded as if it had all come out at once:

> "Well, you'd make a good writer. Better you than me. Now that proper pleasantries have been exchanged, can we get going? I'm a bit hungry."

They're the same spoken words without the nicely managed pacing we got with the beats inserted.

Beats can also function as speech attributions. They can be used instead of he said/she said. You don't need both an attribution and a beat. For instance, it would be redundant to write:

> "No," Jim said. Jim sat on the sofa.

Or even:

> "No," Jim said. He sat on the sofa.

Why not use only a beat instead of a beat and an attribution? Like this:

> "No." Jim sat on the sofa.

I've underlined the beats used in place of speech attributions in the following:

> The dragon bent his shimmering green neck in respect. "It was an honor to fight someone as skilled as you, Crimson. I am Keeth, son of Barinol, whose sire was Kisanth the Great."
>
> Reginald started scratching his helmet again and stopped, irritated. "Keith, you say? Odd name for a dragon."
>
> Keeth bared his formidable fangs. "*It's Keeth*! Double vowel."

Using beats in place of speech attributions works only if you've used the dialogue silos recommendation I made earlier in this section. If you keep a character's words and actions in the same paragraph, you can eliminate many of your speech attributions.

conclusion

All right, that's all the fiction craftsmanship I'm going to give you before you embark on your quest to write fifty thousand words in thirty days. More on the back end, but that's plenty for now.

At last we've come to the end of the preparations. Or, as Winston Churchill might say, "Now this is not the end. It is not even the beginning of the end. But it is, perhaps, the end of the beginning."

You're almost ready to begin. I hope Part One has properly equipped you to write this thing, and maybe you're even champing at the bit to get going. I'm pulling for you!

part two

writing
your
novel
[fast]

01 02 03 04 05 06 07 08 09 10 11 12 13 14 15 16 17 18 19 20 21 22 23 24 25 26 27 28 29 30

30 days of fire

The hour is upon you. The calendar leaves you with no wiggle room. Your "One day I'll write that novel" has become your "Oh, sweet pickles, it's freaking tomorrow!"

Part Two of this book, which is made up of this one Victory, gives you the tips for writing your novel quickly. If you've worked through Part One, you're ready to write. If you weren't doing this for NaNoWriMo, you could spend as long as you wanted writing it, but you'd still be prepared. The tips in this Victory are from me and other novelists who know how to zoom through this "thirty-day blitzkrieg of frenzied fiction fanaticism" and knock the thing out.

whatever you do, don't let anything stop you

The whole idea of writing a novel during NaNoWriMo or using a similar program is to light a fire under you so you can get the bulk of the book written—under your belt—in a jiffy. Once you have something on paper, even if it's terrible, you can build from there. But as long as all you have is a blinking cursor, you're stuck.

It follows, then, that you can't let anything stop you this month. You have to put blinders on, turn Facebook off, hide in your closet, and just go.

Mind you, the world will hit you hard during this month. Never will you get so many "opportunities" or "projects" or little crises or illnesses or distractions. Unless they're truly serious, don't let them stop you. Sorry, but as much as you're feeling the overwhelming urge to go cut your toenails or clean out the garage, resist, I say!

Throughout this book, I've told you that the Great Commandment of Fiction is to engage your reader from beginning to end, and that our whole moral code of fiction stems from that. All true. But for these thirty days, I'm going to give you a new Commandment: *Thou shalt not stop writing.* For this one month only, when it comes to your novel, "right" is whatever helps you slam out more words and pages in a day and "wrong" is whatever hinders you from doing so.

Explain nicely to your significant others that all of your discretionary time this month is already spoken for. Go dark on Facebook and Twitter. Disappear from Pinterest. Drop out of your fantasy football league. Make excuses for missing cousin Billy's birthday party. Become a crabby old book hermit. If you can find a Killer Rabbit of Caerbannog to guard the threshold to your writing lair, do it.

If you were embarking on an expedition to climb Mount Everest, your mother wouldn't expect you to call every night and chat. Make like you're going out of the country for a month. Actually leave home, if you can. Stay in someone's cabin in the woods somewhere. If you have to stay home, put police tape around yourself, invest in good headphones, and get ready to dig under.

You simply can't let *anything* stop you. If you lose two or three days in a row, it'll become that much harder to start again, and the month might just vanish in a puff of temporal smoke. Then you'll be left stymied and stewing. (But don't let even a few days' interruption stop you. See what you can crank out in these thirty days. Do your best to make it happen, and if you have to, do it again next month.)

As you're writing, you'll inevitably think of something you should've done in a previous chapter. You might realize on page 100 that on pages 10 through 25 you should've had your hero living in Cleveland instead of the Amazon jungle. *Don't go back to fix it now.* Just write yourself a note. Start compiling a list of things you'll fix later. Just keep moving forward.

Don't let anything paralyze you. So what if your first line is a stinker? You can fix it later. So what if you don't know whether you should double-space or single-space (double)—or whether there should be one or two spaces between sentences (one)? Just keep moving ahead. Definitely don't spend a whole day in search of just the right font. Pick any flippin' font and start writing.

You need to be like the guy running from a tsunami. You do *not* go back to get your flip-flops. You don't stop to chat. You don't admire the scenery. You don't even turn to look at the giant wall of water gaining on you from behind.

Keep moving forward. Keep moving forward. Keep moving forward.

Thou shalt not stop writing.

prepare your space

If you're going to be writing in a certain location for the next thirty days, it will help you to arrange it as you like.

If you're bothered by clutter, take an hour to clear your desk. If your desk chair isn't comfortable, consider moving the most comfortable chair you have into your writing space. If the lighting is bad, get a lamp. If you live off of Mountain Dew and beef jerky while you're writing, go to Sam's Club and lay in a pallet of each.

Two things to put up around you so you can see them while you're writing: a photo and a paragraph. Tape these to your monitor or otherwise display them where they will be visible at all times as you write.

The photo is a picture of your target reader. Maybe it's your mother. Maybe it's your teenage son. Maybe it's a homeless man. Maybe it's a single mom. I'm guessing there is one perfect reader or reader type you have in mind for this book. Someone who needs a story like this or could use some humor or whatever. Take some time (but not much) to surf the Internet or dig through your shoe box of old photos to find one of your ideal reader, and tape it to your monitor.

As you write, look at this person's face. Pretend you're reading it to him right now, with him in the room. How could you say it so he would really hear it? What joke would work on him, and what joke would fall flat? What would he think is silly? What would turn him off so much that he puts the book down?

Keeping one specific type of person in mind as you write your novel will keep it on track like a laser designator "painting" a target for a guided missile. (Not that you're launching a smart bomb at your target reader ... I know it's not a perfect metaphor. [grin])

The other thing to have on display as you write is a paragraph. *The* paragraph. Go back to Victory 1 and recall what your core story idea is for this novel. This is the glorious statement of what is cool about this idea, what is firing your emotions and burning to come out as a story.

Keeping the core story idea in front of you will make sure you're always all about that. It will keep you on purpose. Every scene you write, every sentence you write, can be evaluated against the high calling of that shining central paragraph. If you're writing along, and it's feeling less and less like the story is supporting that main goal, you'll sense it right away, and you'll be able to get back on track.

With your amazing core idea on one side and your target reader on the other, you'll have the dual guardrails that will keep you on course as you bang this thing out.

Another aspect of preparing your space is preparing the sound in that space. Can you write to music? If so, does it have to be instrumental? I personally can't write if there are words (well, English words) in the music I'm listening to. It ends up engaging my brain to process the words I'm hearing, and my concentration is split. What about you? Perhaps you can find some white noise or a CD of nature sounds to help you focus.

I know a writer who keeps a little battery-powered trickling fountain on her desk and uses that to mask other sounds. You can find YouTube videos in which each one is six hours of ocean surf sounds.

I like to find a movie soundtrack to write by. I prefer to find a new one for each book, a soundtrack that puts me in just the right mood for *this* novel. In a way, I'm hoping that the mood of the soundtrack will somehow infuse my writing and become the mood for the book I'm writing. Back in the days of CDs, I'd purchase a new CD for a new book project. Today, I'd just compile a playlist from YouTube or Pandora or iTunes.

What else could you do to make your space the perfect one for this huge project? If it's in your power and budget and schedule to do it, why not make it happen?

Once you start writing, you want everything as conducive to concentration and productivity as you can make it. The temptation to rearrange your bookshelves will come upon you hard as you're writing. Make the changes now, before you begin, and your resistance will be stronger during the thirty days.

the tips

The following are suggestions from me or other novelists for writing a novel quickly. Read them as a checklist of ideas. Some of them repeat—or even contradict—things I've recommended elsewhere in the book. Not to worry. Apply the ones that make sense to you and jettison the ones that don't. Above all else, just keep moving forward.

word count goal

Have a word count goal per day. If you're going to hit the fifty-thousand-word mark in thirty days, you have to average 1,666.67 words per day.

That sounds like a lot, but once you hit your stride, you'll be able to do it easily. My average is 4,500 words/day. That includes time for thinking and strategizing and note taking. Microsoft Word and similar programs have a word count feature, so you can see your total word count with a click of the mouse.

Also, you probably won't be writing every day for thirty days, so you may need to raise your average to make up for those days when you're not able to write much or at all.

use a character sketch

One writer said, "I do a basic character sketch to get to know my characters a little. Obviously I learn more about them as I go." I've recommended much more than just a sketch, but maybe doing it this way will work better for you. Maybe use it for secondary characters only.

kill a character

One writer said, "I have a pretty good idea of the beginning and end of the book. The middle usually surprises me. If I get SMS (Sagging Middle Syndrome) I just kill someone off, and the story keeps moving." She can do that in her genre. Maybe you can, too.

write wherever you go

One writer said, "I write scenes wherever I am … the doctor's office, the drive-through line, waiting at the bank … I'm always jotting something down. Then all I have to do is come home and put it in the computer."

Having a netbook or iPad or other means of writing when you have to leave the house (but not while driving!) is a terrific idea. Only when you're in a hurry do you realize how much time you spend waiting around for things. The line at the bank or while sitting in a PTA meeting or while in the dentist's office waiting to be called back are all terrific times to keep that word count mounting up.

Another writer said, "I'm always thinking about scenes. And yes, killing off people works. I take notes in my iPhone when I'm away from home, or I can dictate them onto my phone and e-mail them to myself. Then I cut and paste when I get home."

make multiple backups

Your hard drive may crash. Your computer may die. Your flash drive may go belly up.

You must make multiple backups of the document you're creating. I don't mean that every time you write you must save it every two minutes, though of course you should save save save (use Word's auto-save feature). I mean that you save it on your hard drive, you save it on an external drive, you save it to a flash drive, and you save it at some other location, either on the Internet (use Mozy or a similar service) or you e-mail it every day to your mother in Idaho.

I recommend at least three backups—with one of them being somewhere far away. So if your city gets nuked, at least one copy of your novel thus far will remain extant. To help the people of Earth rebuild, of course...

Make your remote backups after every day of writing. At worst, you'd lose one day of writing. That sure beats losing the entire manuscript on day 29.

Do not neglect this! [wags bony finger]

use your critique group

If you have a writing critique group already in place, see if you can use them now in a new way. Use them for real-time brainstorming or to get quick feedback on scenes or ideas.

Do this only if they're helpful and knowledgeable and an emotionally healthy group. Antagonistic feedback during these thirty days could be harmful, so use your crit partners only if they're going to be a boon for your confidence.

create a schedule for yourself

One writer said, "One of my strategies is to make a timeline, similar to cooking Thanksgiving dinner. In the same way you put the brown-and-serve rolls into the oven at the same time as you take out the turkey, I plan a timeline, with self-made deadlines, to get the entire book 'on the table' at the right moment. I try to set my deadlines for earlier than they would seem to need to be—because something, from flu to Oscar parades, can draw me off course for a day or more. Not being down to the wire on a manuscript is such a stress reliever."

use a timer

One writer said, "I use a kitchen timer, set for an hour, and track how many hours I actually write—as opposed to answering e-mails or FB'ing. About a year ago, I started a separate calendar to track my written words each day. That was so revealing."

use dr. wicked

Another tool to use that is a combination of the word count goal tip and the timer tip is "Dr. Wicked's Write or Die" (www.write-ordie.com). It's a for-purchase program or app now, but when I discovered it, it was a free utility on the Web. You enter your word count goal and hit start. A blank window appears, allowing you to begin typing.

Every time you pause for more than ten seconds, the screen changes. It starts to go red or scary music begins to play. When you start typing again, it goes back to normal. You can even set it so that if you pause for X seconds, it will begin erasing what you've written! Talk about motivating you to go-go-go!

If you find yourself needing a jump start, consider using Dr. Wicked. After you get hopping with that, you might be revved up for the rest of the day (and be able to write as productively in your regular word processing program).

For a slightly less dramatic version of this, you can do as one writer suggested: "Set a timer and do thirty-minute speed writing exercises. The words will come if you just keep writing and don't stop."

develop your main characters before you write

One writer said, "I think developing your main characters up front is very helpful to write more quickly. I've interviewed my characters, had them write letters to me, and done personality profiles on them. Next I want to try taking the Myers-Briggs profile test for them. I like that idea. In my opinion, the better a writer knows his/her characters, the more easily the character will reveal his/her actions when it's time to write."

If you've worked through Part One of this book, you have a great idea of who your characters are. It's fun to see that other authors explore the Myers-Briggs idea with fictional characters. (And you thought I was crazy...)

Another writer said, "It really helps me to start out with strong character sketches/archetypes that let me know what the hero/heroine will and won't do."

say no to time drains

One writer said, "When writing, look at what drains your energy and what gives you energy. Build in time for the things that give you energy. Get rid of the drains. Don't procrastinate. Procrastination is an energy drainer.

"Say no to certain things in order to say yes to writing. You can't do everything. Keep a good to-do list in one spot (I use black, spiral, lined notebooks I buy at B&N) to capture the wayward 'I ought to be...' to-dos while I'm writing. Jot 'em down and move on."

stop cooking

One writer said, "Stop cooking. Do carry-in, delivery, Schwan's, finger food. It's actually healthier if you just eat raw vegetables for the month. This way, you can combine writing with a colon cleanse and restoring your health. Works best if you can also write while walking the treadmill. I can't, so I don't worry so much about the health while I'm writing my novel in thirty days."

Another writer said, "Go on one of those diets—just for thirty days—where the meals are delivered to you, like Jenny Craig. That's a win-win if you're wanting to lose weight, too! Or if you live with other people, knight them and have them cook for you for a change."

stop cleaning
One writer said, "Stop cleaning. The dirt will wait. Trust me. And 'attack dust bunnies' is only a cute phrase. They don't really attack. They lie in wait."

pretend you're away
One writer agreed with what I said before. "Pretend you are on a trip. Friends and family wouldn't need you if you were in Paris. Pretend you are—without the baguette, cafés, museums, theater, chic neighborhoods, and flea markets to die for."

Another writer said, "The *only* thing that has worked for me is to go away to write. I've written at a B&B a mile from our home, where I hauled my big lime green iMac back and forth every day. I've written at a condo in Branson, Missouri; I've written in my parents' basement while they were in Florida for the winter; I've written at coffee shops and in hotel rooms and in my car at a park.

"Sadly, the hardest place in the world for me to pile up words is at home in my wonderful office. (That's doubly true now that my hubby's office is just downstairs from mine.) Our back deck is a close second to going away, but weather in Kansas doesn't allow for that on very many days. Maybe the bottom line of all the above is that new places inspire me and help me avoid the distractions of home so I can focus, and thus write faster."

stock up on necessities

One writer agreed with me about laying in your favorite stuff: "Stock up on chocolate, coffee, and paper products."

reward yourself

If you're like me, you have to be shooting for something on a daily basis. Not just the larger goal of having a completed draft to brag about, but little rewards along the way.

I once had to write a novel very quickly. I stayed for two weeks in a relative's summer home to knock out as much of it as I could. There was no cable TV and no nightlife in the area. But I had a DVD player and a TV monitor to watch it on. If I hit my word count goal for the day, I would reward myself by watching a movie that night. Actually, I would just keep writing until I hit my word count goal, even if that meant no movie—or no movie until late at night. And each Friday night, if I'd hit my weekly goal, I rewarded myself with a movie at the local bijou.

Another writer said, "Reward yourself when you meet your word count each day by opening your e-mail in-box. Open your e-mail in-box only when the word count goal has been met."

Set little carrots in front of yourself so you can get some relief and joy when you reach your milestones along the way.

Also consider promising yourself a big reward if and when you hit your month's goal. When you hit fifty thousand words (or whatever your personal goal is), treat yourself to something amazing. It has to be really good to keep you motivated. Of course, completing a manuscript is its own reward, but tangible prizes can be very motivating for large projects like this.

lose your cell phone

…At least temporarily. Maybe you reward yourself at the end of the day, after you've hit your word count goal, by checking your messages and returning a few texts.

sleep beside the desk

One writer said, "Inflate a mattress, and set up a cot in the office."

turn off your internal editor

One writer said, "For the most part, I turn off the internal editor to get words on the page. I can't edit, and I allow myself to adjust 'nothing' on the page. Better to write something imperfect than to write the perfect nothing."

This is terrific advice. It goes back to, "Thou shalt not stop writing." Few things can paralyze a writer like the fear that what she writes won't be perfect. Well, yeah, it's not going to be perfect. So what? No one's going to crucify you for writing something imperfect. It's impossible to do otherwise. "It'll do for now," should be your new motto. Don't let anything stop you. Just keep moving forward.

abort a scene that isn't working

One writer said, "If I'm bored or grinding through a scene and I get the feeling that it's not working or that something's off, that's my cue to either cut it or cut a good chunk (right back to the spot where the grinding started)."

If you've gotten down the road a ways in a scene, and it's just not working, don't keep at it. Doing so could lead to frustration and tempt you to quit entirely. Instead, go back to where it was interesting, and start again from there.

If there's not much left to write in that scene, you might not even go back and fix it now. You might write yourself a note, "Finish this scene so that Johann tells Julius about the baby," and move on to the next scene. You can't do that too often, or you'll end up with only notes and no scenes! But if it's something you think you know how to fix or you know what needs to happen but you don't want to kill your momentum to address it right now, more power to ya.

Above all else, just keep moving forward. You'll have plenty of time for revisions and fixes later.

ruminate and improve

Whether you mean to or not, your mind is going to constantly work on this story while you're writing it. Inevitably you'll think of something tomorrow, you should've written in yesterday's scene. No worries. Either add it to the list of things to be fixed in revisions or put it into that previous scene—either in full or in note form: "Add the revelation that Pedro is really Julio."

One writer said, "While cooking, cleaning, driving, I am thinking through scenes and figuring out to make them *more* compelling. I do one read-through of the last chapter I wrote and try to weave those ideas in."

figure out how to best start today's writing

Some novelists like to begin their day's writing by picking up where they left off the day before. Others like to go back and read something from several chapters ago, trusting that they'll be more objective and see things now that they didn't see before.

I personally like to read over all or part of what I wrote yesterday as my warm-up for today. I do a quick polish as I go, but the main thing I do is get back into the rhythm and mind-set I had yesterday.

figure out how to best finish today to help yourself tomorrow

Likewise, you need to figure out how you can end today's writing to give yourself a good start tomorrow.

I have found, paradoxically, that reaching a great finishing point today sometimes actually hurts me in my efforts to get started tomorrow. It's that interval, that brutal inertia of unmoving, that can be so difficult to overcome when you combine a natural break in the story with a natural break in time.

I always try to get over that interval before stopping for the day. Either I leave myself some bit to finish off in the scene I'm currently writing, or I sit there until I've written a paragraph or two of the scene that will follow (and maybe some notes for what I was thinking to write next).

One writer said, "Getting started each time I begin a new day takes me a long time. If I start a new scene before I quit for the day, I have an instant jumping-off point that helps me get going. Otherwise, I waste a lot of time trying to get into the zone."

The interval is a cruel and bottomless pit. Don't leave yourself a yawning abyss to face the next time you sit down to write. Allow yourself to hit the ground running, and you'll be able to leap the canyon in a single bound.

make character trading cards

One writer said, "I make a cheat card for each character. Rather than a lengthy profile, I use an index card for basic stats, appearance, job, company's title, family relationships, horse/dog name and sex and breed, car color and model, gun make, etc. This helps me find info quickly during the writing process without going to another computer file or place in the manuscript file. All I have to do is reach for the card stack.

"And it helps me avoid using names that are too much alike. If I need to name a new character, a three-second flip through the cards tells me I already have used three last names starting with C and two with T, but no S or D or R, so I pick one of those."

use a calendar for chronology in the story

One writer said, "If my story takes place over less than one month, I print a calendar sheet for that month/year. This even works with historical novels (consult a site called www. timeanddate.com). On each square of the calendar sheet, I jot down what main events happen that day, and in the corner of the box I put the chapter numbers. If it takes longer than one month, I generally make a timeline of the story in a computer file instead."

Another writer agrees: "Filling in a calendar ensures that there are no timeline issues—which are so time-consuming to find and fix otherwise."

use a synopsis as you write

One writer said, "I create a detailed synopsis of the story and put it in a Word document. As I complete a scene or chapter, I read that part of the synopsis again to be sure I didn't omit anything crucial, or I make a note if I need to rearrange some events or revisit something later.

"Then *I delete that part of the synopsis*, so the next scene I have to write is always on top. I put xxxx in the synopsis at the place I left off writing for the day. When I start writing each session, I go to xxxx, and there's my synopsis of what to write next."

Great idea!

try scrivener

Scrivener is a software tool designed especially for writers. You can try it for free by visiting www.literatureandlatte.com.

One writer said, "The best time-saver I've found for writing is Scrivener. It has all my outline/synopsis/character sketches/setting descriptions and pictures to go with everything. All my research is neatly stored on corkboard notes inside the program. And the program offers many more features that I don't use but that other writers find helpful. It's a fantastic tool."

track your subplots

One writer said, "What I do ahead of time is to figure out my subplots, then I sit down and brainstorm long lists of things that could/should happen in each subplot. I weed out the crazy stuff and put the ideas in a long typed list in semilogical order. As I'm writing, I then have a host of possibilities to use. Some things I don't use, some I do—but it all helps spur other ideas as I go.

"With my subplot tracker, I keep a record of everything that happens in every chapter and scene as I finish each scene. With this chart, I can instantly go back to find any point I need to tweak, and at a glance I can see which subplot columns are starting to look too empty—and therefore I can make corrections/additions before I've gone too far.

"I also use Kathy Lloyd's Conflict Grid. It helps a lot." *Google it.*

Another writer uses note cards in a similar way: "On my last book, I took index cards and wrote ideas for scenes—sometimes even with dialogue—as they came to me. Then I put them in order and wrote the scenes on my computer one by one. Once I was finished with a scene, I tossed the card to the side. I'd done that using Scrivener, but for some reason having the actual cards in hand made the process move along faster and made me more productive. I chalk it up to my being partly a kinesthetic learner. I was able to knock out half a book of publishable material in two weeks. Of course having a deadline looming helped, too."

print it out as you go

Here's an idea that goes along with my suggestion that you never pause in your movement forward, but rather create a list of things to go back and change. This author actually prints out what she's written and writes the notes on the appropriate pages of the draft.

"As I finish each chapter, I first paste a copy into my master doc where all the chapters are adding up. The original I format into an 11-point font with columns/single space, and I put it into a three-ring notebook kept open by my keyboard. I use that as a constant reference. I'll highlight and circle things, add all sorts of Post-It notes/reminders/corrections ... so if there's something I know I need to add or change, I don't have to waste time doing it now, but I can go to The End and then go back and work on all the edits when they'll make more sense.

"To get started after a few days off, I can skim this notebook and see my whole story, which also helps me catch inconsistencies and repetitions."

take breaks

Most of the writers whose advice I'm passing on to you will remain nameless, although their comments are terrific. But the following is so entertaining that I just have to reveal who said it. This is from Christian novelist Jenny B. Jones.

"I am not a plotter, so I often get stuck and use the thinking time to contemplate jumping off tall buildings or stepping in front of extra-large Arkansas chicken trucks. Between lack of ideas (that don't involve my death and feathers) and the clock furiously ticking, I can work myself into a completely uncreative panic.

"My advice: Even though you have no time to lose, don't be afraid to take a break if you need to. Step away from the computer and go do something mindless. For me, it's going to the movies. For two different books, I was just miserable—unsolvable plot hole, brain-dead, running out of time. I somehow ended up at the movies with friends anyway. And each time, for each book, without even trying, I came up with a book-saving idea while sitting there in the dark, eating trans fats, and letting my brain be on autopilot.

"I think there's value in *not* thinking. It's like when I gave my brain a much-needed rest, it did the work while I wasn't trying so hard. That time you think you don't have? Use some of it to just go have fun."

Another author adds: "Washing dishes and taking a shower help get me through roadblocks in my writing. Or ten segments of *Doctor Who*, back to back. That'll drive you back to the keyboard."

stop and think

Nonwriters may not understand that a writer can be writing even when he's just sitting there. It's not all about pounding out words on the keyboard. It *is* that, of course, but if you haven't stopped to think about what you need to do next, you could forge ahead with words, but they'd be words you'd have to cut later. That doesn't help you.

I know I said you shouldn't let anything stop you. "Thou shalt not stop writing," I said. But what I mean is to not let anything sway you from your task of writing the novel. I don't mean you shouldn't take time to think about your next scene or the ramifications of what you've just had a character do. Those things, you must do.

Journalist Burton Rascoe said it this way, "What no wife of a writer can ever understand is that a writer is working when he's staring out the window." That goes for husbands of writers, too.

block off your date book

If you're going to do one thing long and hard for thirty days, you need to *not* do as many other things as possible. It also helps, as we've done in this book, to do as much prework on the story as possible so that the writing time can go more quickly.

One writer said, "Sure, since I can write ten to fifteen pages a day when things are flowing well, I can write a novel in thirty days—provided I have already spent a year or two thinking through the plot and the characters. I usually have a file 2" or 3" thick with the plot, descriptions of characters, fully worked out scenes, bits of dialogue, etc., before I start writing the actual book. Writing fifteen pages a day is pretty exhausting, so it is important to not have any other work to do in that time."

write the last chapter first

Here's an interesting experiment. If it sounds good to you, give it a try. If it doesn't, don't.

One writer said, "Make a rough map of your novel's three-act structure. Don't call it an outline if the O word gives you hives. Know what your major plot pivots are and all the points of no return.

"Then write the last chapter first, just to give yourself a target to shoot for. You will probably change 80 percent of it when you finally catch back up to the last chapter, but it's amazing how visualizing that last chapter helps you quickly craft a journey of transformation for your main character."

find accountability partners

Having people in your life who will hold your feet to the fire can really help, especially if you're the type of person who knows you need that sort of help.

One writer said, "Have people in your life who will hold you accountable to your word count. Empower them with prods that will cause you discomfort."

I have repeatedly offered a service to writers. I invite them to send me any amount of money—over one thousand dollars is preferable, and the bigger the better—for me to hold in a savings account for them. If they don't make their deadline, I get to keep the money.

So far, no takers. [scratches head]

track your progress

When you're trying to reach a goal that is achieved incrementally—like steps toward the summit of a mountain—it helps to chart your progress toward your objective.

One writer uses a visual aid to track her progress and earn psychological rewards: "I use a page progress temperature graph (like the United Way thermometer, but with ten-page increments). This is so motivating to me that I'll often push ahead to be able to fill in another square as a reward. Silly, maybe, but still a marker of achievement—and I can also see exactly where I am in the page count of the book, which helps me judge plot development steps."

Another writer said, "I have been using a countdown spreadsheet since my first contracted deadline. I enter date countdowns.

Page countdowns. Word count countdowns. I have formulas that automatically add the words completed daily and subtract the daily pages from the total pages needed. It also spits out an average of how many pages a day I need to get it finished on time. It is a huge help for me."

prepare for rest after you're done

Whenever you force yourself to do a major sustained project like this, you need to plan for some major downtime after you're done. You can squeeze your brain to work long and hard, like squeezing the last bit of toothpaste from the tube. But after that, you need a serious rest.

For at least four days after you finish this thing, plan to be something more or less like a vegetable. Tell your family about this at the outset, or they'll expect you to write "The End" and then hop up and be Mr. or Ms. Everything and start making up for the time you've been "away." You've got to have some couch potato time. No, let me say it this way: You will be a couch potato/vegetable for four days after you finish, whether you've warned anyone about it or not. Best to have them expect it from the outset. Besides, if you hit your objective, you deserve a party! Some major celebration is in order, even if that celebration looks more like sleeping or vegging out than dancing.

conclusion

Well, there you have it. Best practices from dozens of multipublished novelists on how to write fiction fast. I suspect some of their ideas sounded terrific to you and others left you shrugging. That's fine. I don't expect you to use all of them. I'm just hoping that one or maybe several of them will significantly help as you write.

And write is what you're ready to do. I've prepared you as best I know how. Now it's up to you. I'm sort of like the Olympic coach working with a gifted athlete. We have lots of time together to prepare for the big moment, but when it finally comes, no one is out there but the Olympian.

Don't let fear hold you back. Right around the 75 percent mark, you may hit a wall. In my experience, that's just fear.

Pay it no mind. Blow right past it. Wave to it as you roll by. You *don't* have to show it to anyone. Tell them you'll still have weeks (months? years?) of revision to do before you'll let people read it. That may not be true. You may have someone—spouse, critique partner, neighbor—read it in its rough draft form. But *telling* people it's not ready yet will get them off your back and give you some psychological breathing room.

You're going to find your rhythm as you're writing this novel, trust me. You're going to hit your stride and find your groove and get into the zone and all the other clichés. I'm telling you, it will happen.

You can do this. You can. Lots of people not as smart as you have done it. Not only can you do this, you can do it well.

Every novel that gets published has to first be written. Duh, right? But it's true. Every novel that sells a jillion copies has to first be written.

You can do this, my friend. Crank the music, get a drink of your favorite go-juice, shut the door, and start putting down some words.

part three

publishing

your

novel

01 02 03 04 05 06 07 08 09 10 11 12 13 14 15 16 17 18 19 20 21 22 23 24 25 26 27 28 29 30

revising your novel

Well, how did it go?

If you're reading this chapter, I can only hope it means you finished your novel. Writing under a tight deadline, either one imposed by a publisher or an artificial one like NaNoWriMo, can be a blessing and a curse. A curse, because it's so merciless. There's a reason we call it the tyranny of the urgent. But a blessing because, if you can survive it, you can pump out a lot of work in a short time.

Writing a novel is one of those things that everyone wants to have done but very few want to actually do.

If you've succeeded in your quest, take a minute to bask in your accomplishment. Writing a novel, like I said in the opening words of this book, is on many people's bucket lists, but most will never do it. You, my friend, have turned "One of these days, I'm going to sit down and write that novel" into "Yeah, I remember that day when I actually finished writing my novel." That's a huge accomplishment, and I'm very proud of you for doing it.

what now?

So, what are you going to do with it now? You have a rough draft. You probably already know it's not ready to show to agents or editors yet, but you may not know what your next steps are.

Never fear! That's what Part Three is all about.

The first thing to do is get the book as "finished" as you can. Here are some steps to make that happen.

look at your list

Hopefully as you blew through the thirty days of writing you kept a list of things you'd need to go back and fix. You realized, maybe, that Fred needed to be Frieda, so you went forward as-

suming you'd make that change later. That was the right decision. But now poor ol' Fred needs to undergo a gender switch.

Go back through the manuscript and take care of everything
on your fix list.

Some of those items will be easily accomplished, like adding the revelation that Susie is left-handed or changing a scene
from afternoon to nighttime. Others may be more significant,
like writing new scenes or adding a subplot or combining two
characters into one.

That's all right. You have something to work from now, which
sure beats the alternative. And unless you're still under a deadline of some kind, the heat is off, and you can make these changes at a more leisurely pace.

This phase is how you create a finished rough draft—which
is an oxymoron of sorts. I mean, a rough draft is *rough*, as in not
the completed version of the book. So how can you finish something that is by definition unfinished?

I liken it to how George Lucas kept tinkering with the *Star
Wars* movies. Every release contained changes—some major and
some very minor—that the movies obviously did quite nicely
without. But these were his ways of trying to make the movie
the way he intended it originally but didn't have the budget or
technology to achieve in 1977.

So your first step is to get it as done as best you know how.
Make all the changes on your radar, and then consider your
rough draft done.

save it everywhere

This is a good time to make a whole new set of saves. Save it in all
of your locations, plus maybe a few new ones. Until you get this
book published, you want to hang onto that rough draft. And,
frankly, you might want to hold onto the rough draft indefinitely. Who knows when you might want to go back to it and release
the "author's preferred version" or whatever? Plus, sometimes you

end up not liking the revised version as much as the rough draft, so it's nice to always have it there to go back to when you liked it.

Now that I've had several novels published, I'm not as sentimental (or is it paranoid?) about keeping the rough draft. I usually just hang onto the typeset version that went to print. But until you get there, a healthy dose of paranoia (or is it sentimentality?) would serve you well.

Do a "Save As…" of your rough draft and call the new file "First Draft" or something. From now on, you'll be working from the first draft document. Your rough draft is safely put away. Now let's take it to the next level.

show it to someone … if you dare

Gut check time. Are you ready to show your rough draft to someone?

This may or may not be a good move for you at this moment, so do a little self-evaluation first. Understand that this is your baby. In some ways, it might be more difficult to show this to someone than to show off your own child. If this is your first novel, it's more like doing your first painting project for a college art class or performing a dance of your own creation. It is so utterly personal that it almost takes more courage to show it than it did to write it.

Earlier, I said you wouldn't have to show it to anyone until after you'd done tons of revision. That's true, but not mandatory. If you're pretty sure that one discouraging word would send you leaping off the nearest bridge (and I'm only half kidding), don't show it yet.

Because, guess what, not everyone else is going to love it. Sorry. Some people just don't like books, some don't like novels or they don't like this *kind* of novel, or they are jealous that you wrote a novel and they didn't, or they are hiding the fact that they can't read … or whatever. No matter, you can be pretty sure you are going to hear discouraging words. Hopefully some encouraging words as well, but the former is guaranteed and the latter is only hoped for.

A less than overjoyed response to your book doesn't necessarily say anything about the book. It certainly doesn't say anything about the *worth* of the book or its author. The worth of those things are unchanging (unchangingly positive) and removed beyond the reach of mere mortals. If you wrote it, it's important. Now, a negative response to your book may say something about the reviewer, or it may mean that you indeed have things you can improve in the manuscript. No matter what, don't let it crush you.

So if you think it's possible for you to receive someone's reaction to your book as something besides a value judgment on you as a human, then maybe it's okay to show it to a small number of folks. Perhaps show just a sample (the first fifty pages) to test their reactions before handing over the whole thing. Maybe show it only to other writers or those qualified to give you good feedback and that you trust to want to help you succeed.

The great thing about first readers is that they give you something you lost when you wrote the first word of the book: objectivity. You can't see your book clearly anymore. Too much of your own identity and your own intentions are wrapped in it now. A good reader can help you see it again. Maybe not objectively, but at least not hopelessly subjectively.

I used to ask six to eight friends and family members to read my rough draft and take notes. I'd have them all over for dessert, and we'd go through the manuscript page by page. They caught some terrific things and identified places where I'd left something out or contradicted myself or made them think X when I'd meant for them to think Y. It was wonderful.

Except that it was awful. It was two hours of torture. Item after item of what I did wrong and how I forgot something else and how my spelling was terrible. Sometimes it almost felt like they would gang up on me to say how laughably bad my book was. This, despite the fact that I knew how deeply they all cared about me and wanted me to do well—and the fact that I was pretty confident in my self-image. I thought, "And I fed them dessert? I should've put arsenic in it!" Okay, not really, but you get my drift.

I finally laid down one ground rule for them: You cannot say anything negative or "constructive" about my book without first telling me one thing you liked about the book. One for one.

I recommend you do that, too. That way, you'll get all the bennies of their objective input but without the wounds such "helpfulness" can sometimes inflict.

Once you've received input from your reader(s), start applying all the items that make sense to you. Certainly correct the true errors they catch. On the more serious or sizable items, take a long, hard look at them before implementing them. Don't make changes just to please one person's set of preferences. Be sure you're making the changes that make the book better. That's another benefit of keeping a rough draft saved. You can always go back to that pristine version if you try out someone's suggestions and you end up not liking what you've done.

conclusion

The next major step in revising your book is to apply the principles of excellent fiction craftsmanship to it. That's what is coming up in the next Victory.

But before moving on, take one more minute to grasp the significance of what you've achieved by writing a book-length manuscript.

There's a reason I didn't use *chapter* to designate the different parts of this book. It's because when you do something like what you've done, it is truly a victory.

craftsmanship revisited

Now that you have a rough draft to work from, the hard part is behind you. From here on out, we're just refining and tweaking and strengthening.

To use a sculpting metaphor, writing a novel is the process of starting with a block of granite and chipping away until you have something that looks pretty durn close to what you had in mind. It may be a bit rough-hewn, but people can certainly tell what it is you're working toward.

Revising a work of fiction, then, is like finishing the sculpture. Here's where you step back and look at it and decide what still needs to be done. For the most part, the large-scale cutting and hammering is done. What's left is to smooth it out and refine the edges and add embellishment, detail, and artistry.

The great advantage we have with a novel over the sculptor with her block of stone is that we can completely rework the thing if we need to, whereas if the required changes to the granite are too severe, the sculptor has to set it aside and start over. Not that we'll need to make such sweeping changes, but we can if we must.

Maybe it's better to think of yourself as a surgeon and your novel as your patient. You'll be doing procedures on it for as long as you need to. If you spot something new that needs your attention, you can open her up again and go back in.

In this Victory, I address the craft topics introduced previously, and in the next Victory I'll cover some I haven't introduced before. With rough draft in hand—with the patient in the O. R. and ready for the surgeon—we can do some amazing work.

revisiting point of view

How'd you do with this as you were writing? POV is deceptively difficult to master. Unless you had a strong grasp of this at the outset, I'm willing to guess you might have done some head hopping.

Because POV errors are so hard to see in your own writing, I recommend you enlist some help here. You need to find yourself one or more point of view specialists and ask (or pay) this person or group to go through your manuscript looking for nothing but POV errors. They must have the following qualifications: 1) They must read English (or whatever language you wrote the book in), 2) they must understand what it is to stay inside one character's head, even if they don't personally think a disciplined POV is important, and 3) they must provide a price and turnaround time to your liking.

Critique groups are great for this sort of thing. Even if you've written a mutant zombie robot mystery and your crit partners write only prairie romances and don't even understand what you've written, they can still skim through in search of head hopping. (Unless, of course, creatures in your book actually hop between human heads, but I digress.)

Read over the discussion of POV in Victory 9 and see if you can apply those points to your rough draft. Here is some further advice for succeeding with point of view.

establish your pov right away

Unless you flag it for the reader, she will assume that the head you're in (the viewpoint character) for this new scene is the same head you were in for the previous scene.

There are times when you want to conceal from the reader whose eyes we're looking through in a particular scene. But most of the time, you want the reader to feel oriented, understanding that she's in the mind of the character you want her to be with.

The best way to do this is to signal the change by establishing right away in the new scene—in the first sentence, preferably, but certainly in the first three lines—the name of the viewpoint character you've switched to.

So instead of beginning a scene like this:

> *Of course they're closed.*
>
> He jiggled the door handle just to be sure. This was the last pharmacy in town, and now he knew they were all closed. What kind of town shuts down at 6:00 p.m.?
>
> He wandered down the street, his stomach grumbling, wondering if any restaurants would be open.
>
> "Hey, Steve! Great to see you."

The writing isn't bad, but you don't know whose head you're in until you're deep in the scene. (And, actually, you still don't know if Steve is the viewpoint character or if the unnamed viewpoint character has just seen someone named Steve.) And if the previous scene had been in the head of a male character (Robert, maybe), you'll assume that you're still in Robert's head in this new scene.

The simple fix is to establish right away whose head you're in:

> *Of course they're closed.*
>
> Steve jiggled the door handle just to be sure. This was the last pharmacy in town, and now he knew they were all closed. What kind of town shuts down at 6:00 p.m.?
>
> He wandered down the street, his stomach grumbling, wondering if any restaurants would be open.
>
> "Hey, Steve! Great to see you."

Just one word change and the reader is oriented into the new viewpoint character's perspective. Few things are as jarring as reading along thinking you're in one character's mind and then realizing halfway through that you're actually in someone else's mind. You have to reread the whole scene up to there and re-understand it from the other person's point of view.

Sometimes the reader can miss the change of heads even if you've written the new name early on, as I did above. This happens when two or more viewpoint characters are very similar; for instance, they're both cheerleaders or sailors or whatever. Without being too heavy-handed ("Yes," said Steve who is not the same guy as Robert), you can wave the flag a bit more noticeably.

For instance, if the previous scene in Steve's POV had him needing some medicine for bad hay fever, perhaps you could begin the new scene with a sneeze and a reference to hay fever. The keywords will help connect the reader back to the previous scene.

Also, watch out for confusing the reader by making an unintentional connection between the previous scene, in Robert's POV, and this scene, in Steve's. For example, if Robert's scene ends with him heading to a home improvement store in search of a PVC pipe and hoping he can get there before they close, and then this new scene begins with *Of course they're closed* and a male character trying the door and finding it locked, the reader could miss the "Steve" because she's assuming she's still with home improvement store guy.

This is something you don't need to worry about while writing. But when you're in revisions, check through each scene ending and beginning, especially the ones in which you change viewpoint characters at the scene/chapter break, and be sure the change is clearly marked, established right away, and disambiguated from what came before.

viewpoint character as narrator

I contemplated putting this in Victory 9 so you'd be thinking about it as you wrote your rough draft. But I decided against it because I didn't want to mess you up with what some people consider an advanced technique. The higher goal was to equip you to finish the draft in a hurry. Though it may be a bit of a pain to add such changes now, this technique can certainly be applied after the fact.

I'd like to talk to you about using your viewpoint character as narrator. First, let me show you what I mean about a narrator. In the following, I've underlined the narrator's input.

> Show yourself, foul creature.
> Fabian walked the mall, looking into everyone's eyes. Could he see the preternatural gaze, the glint of malignant intelligence, in the glance of any of these people— or was that something he could see in Marsha only?
> The mall was already decorated for Christmas, though Thanksgiving was still ten days in the future. For retailers, Christmas seemed to come earlier each year.
> He squinted at a woman pushing a stroller but could see nothing unusual. He traded sneers with a teen boy in a letter jacket, and he looked so deeply into the eyes of a frail old woman that he almost ran her over. In no one's eyes could he see what he was searching for.
> Where are you, beastie?

Do you see how Fabian's direct thoughts are rather epic in tone, while the other writing in the scene—the accounts of what he's doing and looking at—are fairly workaday?

I call that stale, generic tone "Narrator Voice." It's more or less the author's own voice, and it's not meant to be noticed. It's a utilitarian means of conveying information that is neither thought nor dialogue. Narrator Voice sounds the same across all scenes and viewpoint characters in the book.

In theater, actors are taught to "stay in character" no matter what they're doing. This applies mainly to when the actors are onstage, but some actors get into character when standing in the wings and stay in character not only while onstage but also until they're back in the wings. And the purists get into character in the dressing room (or before) and stay in character until leaving the theater (or after).

In the same way, most novelists get into their viewpoint character's minds and personalities in order to write dialogue and internal monologue, but that's it. They climb into that costume, say the lines, then climb back out and stand there in Narrator Voice's costume until it's time to put a costume on again.

I contend that no Narrator Voice should appear in your entire novel.

Once you decide whose head you're going to be in for this scene, you should be in that head *for everything that happens* in that scene. You should stay in character for everything, even the description of events, people, and locations.

Here's the mall scene again, done in character.

> Show yourself, foul creature.
>
> Fabian stalked the corrupt corridors of materialism called Lake Aire Mall like a witch-hunter at a cemetery. He winnowed the gaze of each member of capitalism's cult—those possessed by possessions—searching for the red glint of his quarry. Perhaps, lurking behind the dull look of peasants pursuing their bucolic desires, he would perceive the same malevolence he'd glimpsed in Marsha's glare.
>
> Everywhere the mall—how fitting: the *maul*—was festooned with the accoutrements of Saturnalia: Green boughs of ersatz evergreen and large brass bells to sound the unheeded alarm of debtors sinking deeper into debt. Why, with the celebration of the abuse of First Americans still ten days away, bring out these trappings? Soon there would be an unbroken span between All Hallows Eve and Saturnalia. From pagan festival to pagan festival. Why not?
>
> Fabian espied a female cultist pushing a pram with a tiny future cultist inside. He pressed his eyes upon her but did not find his quarry. A lad of sixteen winters locked eyes with him with a vigor that would one day serve him well as a warrior. Aha! An old hag with furtive glance! Surely the evil resided there. He came at her like a bear but, alas, did not sight the object of his hunt.
>
> Where are you, beastie?

Okay, maybe I had a bit too much fun with that, but I hope it illustrates my point. The first version gave us the flavor of Fabian's personality, but only in the dialogue. In the second version, we experience the Fabian flavor throughout.

Some people call this "deep POV." I think it's the way novels should be written.

It's the logical extension of what POV is, anyway. You get inside a viewpoint character's head and stay there for a full scene. But if you're in a person's head, doesn't that mean you're perceiving the story through that person's mind, senses, attitudes, and personality? Wouldn't one "periscope" see things differently than another periscope would? Fabian might notice the ersatz evergreen, while another viewpoint character walking through the same mall might not see the boughs at all but would instead focus on the tiles in the floor or the jewelry worn by passersby or the smells wafting from every shop.

Take a look at a scene from the book you've just written, and see if you can spot Narrator Voice. Now rewrite that scene, staying in your viewpoint character's personality for the whole thing. Point out what the character would see, notice, and have an opinion about. Color her descriptions of events, people, and locations with her own attitudes and mood. Let the whole thing be a product of her mind.

If you like what you come up with, consider doing it for the rest of the book.

revisiting show vs. tell

As you were writing, did you feel the siren call of telling? Did you feel the temptation to simply explain why certain things are the way they are, instead of going to all the effort of writing everything out in scene form? Did the "Can the camera see it?" tool help you? Did it even occur to you to use it?

Telling is something else that is almost impossible to spot in your own fiction. I mean, you know what you were thinking when you wrote it, so it becomes invisible to you. Here's another great opportunity to enlist critique partners. Explain to them that telling is something a camera cannot see, a microphone cannot "hear." It's anything that cannot be otherwise sensed by an observer. It's invisible. Though there are exceptions to this rule (discussed below), you need to have your critique partners mark every questionable passage—not only sentences and paragraphs, but phrases and words. Then you can scrutinize them all for telling.

You may have noticed that I'm pretty much 100 percent against telling. I simply can't imagine a time when a novel is helped by killing its momentum to lecture the reader. However, not telling—or telling only sometimes—isn't the Great Commandment of Fiction. And, as I said before, plenty of novels that are full of telling succeed in the marketplace.

exceptions to "can the camera see it?"

The "Can the camera see it?" question is a great little tool for getting a handle on show vs. tell. However, it's not foolproof. There are things that an observer cannot see that are nonetheless not examples of telling.

Interior monologue, for example. One of the great advantages that a novel has over a movie is that you can get the reader deeply into the mind of the viewpoint character. As we've already seen, cinema can give viewers the feeling of a detached observer who's on the outside of everyone.

When you describe the viewpoint character's thoughts, you are not necessarily telling. If you write, "Penny stopped at the park. Where were they?" you haven't *told* us anything. You haven't cheated. But our camera question would tell us it is telling. So internal monologue is an exception.

But watch out! It's a short walk from "Penny stopped at the park. Where were they?" to "Penny stopped at the park. Where were they? They were always doing things like this. It irked her to no end that they would call her out here and then not show up. The last time, she swore she would never again fall for..."

You see how it could go? With interior monologue, it's very easy to hop the fence and go from showing to telling. Or, as the saying goes, to go from preachin' to meddlin'.

The exercise below will help you realize that you're telling and keep you from doing it in your internal monologues.

the silent film

If you were restricted to the only tool of the silent film era—the camera—how would you reveal something to the audience?

Let's start with a softball: How could you reveal that a character was left-handed?

Well, duh, by showing her pick up a pen with her left hand and start writing. Easy peasy.

Okay, here's a harder one: How could you reveal that a character was a terrific baseball player?

The easy solution would be to show him out on the baseball field stealing a base or hitting a homer or making a diving catch in the outfield. But let's make it harder and say you have to reveal this information but you can't have him at a baseball field at all.

Ooh, that's harder. Remember, you can use only the camera. No fair having someone come up to him and say, "Wow, Dave, I'm so glad to meet such a terrific baseball player as you." (Also no fair using those text placards that silent films used.) Using only a camera, and depicting him away from the baseball diamond, how could you show his talent?

Brainstorm a few ideas before reading on. I want you to develop an area of your brain that you may not have used very often when it comes to fiction. Go on, write down some ideas for how you could do this. Don't read farther until you've done it.

Okay, welcome back. One idea would be to show him at home, surrounded by pennants and trophies and framed magazine covers showing him hitting a baseball. Another idea would be for him to arrive somewhere in a limo, whereupon he is swarmed by adoring fans, one of whom hands him a baseball, which he signs.

Are you beginning to get a feel for this? You want to reveal things to the reader in a cinematic way, with clues and hints that make the reader ask the right questions. That's what showing is.

Now for a hard one: How could you reveal that a woman has desperately wanted a baby for a long time but has just suffered a miscarriage? Camera only.

Keep on your cerebral cortex until the ideas flow. Why not go ahead and write that scene, using visuals only?

Here's one that's expert-level difficulty: How could you show that a man's pancreatic cancer has been in remission for five years but has come back with such a vengeance that he has only a month to live?

Stretch your creativity. Flex that brain muscle. Jot down several ideas, even if each one reveals only a portion of the whole.

What you'll find when you're trying to show complex, multilayered things like this is that you can't do it all in one chunk. The best you can do at first is to get us in the ballpark, to get us asking the right questions. Then in a subsequent scene you can get us a bit closer, and so on.

For instance, in one scene you show a woman sitting against the back wall of the swimming pool, dressed in street clothes and looking anxious. That's enough for round one. In a later scene, you show her going to a new hotel with friends and taking a wrong door, which leads her to the indoor pool area—she drops her things and backs away so quickly she knocks someone over.

"Hmm, interesting," says the reader. "What's this about?"

In a later scene, you show the same woman being forced to go poolside with an important cell phone call for someone out there. She all but hugs the rear wall and calls the person over to her, rather than going out to the pool.

You get the idea. Eventually, someone asks what's up with this woman and pools, and you can reveal that her older brother drowned trying to save his sister, our heroine, in the family pool, and she's been terrified of pools ever since.

It would've been cheesy to communicate all of that at once. Besides, the reader wouldn't have cared to hear about it at first. Bigger and more complex pieces of information deserve to be revealed in phases. Reel the reader in. Treat the information with respect. (It would've been so easy to simply spell this out in exposition, but that's telling, which is lazy.)

Okay, so pick some mildly difficult information to be revealed in a silent film. Then write out the scene in which it is all revealed Charlie Chaplin-style. No pantomime, and nothing but the camera allowed. Figure out ways to *illustrate* the information you want conveyed.

Remember the rule for showing: Don't narrate—illustrate; don't summarize—dramatize.

After you've written the scene and conveyed the important information graphically, in a way that a moviegoer would "get" if watching it as a silent film, then you know you can add in other elements without resorting to telling. You can add dialogue, for instance, and rest assured you won't be adding in telling. Why? Because you've already done the hard work. You've figured out how to illustrate the information visually, so you won't feel a compulsion to explain it another way. You won't need someone to come up and conveniently speak the information you want to convey.

Then you can go through the scene again, this time adding internal monologue. You'll restrict your viewpoint character's thoughts to perceptions, reactions, and direct thoughts—and you won't hop the fence to telling—because you won't feel the need to. You'll be confident that the reader will get what you want to express through what you've shown, so you won't be tempted to tell.

When you've done this exercise, perhaps more than once, you can turn to your rough draft. If you identify a passage where you've engaged in telling, now you know what to do about it. You'll take that paragraph of explanation and make it into a movie.

Or you'll decide it's not important enough to write a whole scene about in order to convey it graphically. And if that's the case, may I suggest that it's probably not important enough for the reader to know about—so cut it.

converting telling to showing

Here are some techniques to help you convert those passages of telling into scenes of showing. But first, three ways *not* to make that conversion.

First, don't use what I call telling in quotation marks. That's when you have someone just up and say the information you need conveyed. This is the dreaded, "As you know, Bob…" syndrome. "As you know, Bob, Jennifer and Carlisle were once madly in love but they had a falling out in which …" Putting quotation marks around a paragraph of explanation (i.e., telling) is not the way to go. You must do it visually.

Second, don't use what I call sneaky telling. That's when you toss in a line of explanation but you don't give a whole paragraph of telling.

> "Hello," said the former steamboat captain.
>
> "Hi," said the woman who had just washed out of dance school after three failed relationships. "How are you?"
>
> The man who had recently stopped smoking tilted his head. "Fair, I guess."

You laugh, but I've seen this more times than I can count. If you find yourself making use of every opportunity to explain something or sneak in some bit of backstory, you are telling.

The third method that is *not* a good way to convert telling into showing is to interrupt the story with a flashback. I'm not 100 percent against the use of flashback. It's a legitimate literary device, and some novels really should use them. But many times, especially in unpublished novels, flashback is used not to advance the story but as a way to indulge the author's temptation to explain everything.

My definition of telling is when you stop the story to explain something the reader doesn't care about. Most of the time flashbacks fit the bill. The "Can the camera see it?" tool may deem a flashback as good to go, but because flashbacks stop the main story to explain something the reader doesn't care about, I deem them as devices of telling.

Okay, here are two techniques that will help you convert telling to show. Most of the time you should simply act out the information. Find a way to bring it onstage, to illustrate it graphically. But you can—very sparingly—use these two other techniques.

The first is what I call the "Dumb Puppet Trick." I used to write puppet scripts for children, and it was always useful to have a dumb (or at least uninformed) puppet who had a reason to ask what was going on. Since Flopsie and Mopsie knew that all of these bicycles had been gathered for the big Ride for a Cure race, it would've been silly for them to talk about it to each other. "As you know, Flopsie, all these bicycles have been gathered for the big Ride for a Cure race." Instead, you bring on Goober, who does not know why there are so many bikes here. "Guhuh, is there a fifty-legged man coming to town?" "No, Goober, these bikes are for the big race…"

Bring in someone who doesn't know what's going on and has a reason to ask, and you can reveal information in a believable way. Got some complicated steampunk device you need explained? Bring on a city inspector responding to a complaint of a dangerous device and have the chief engineer spell it out. Want to have the reader understand something … anything? Simply find a way to summon the powers of the dumb puppet.

The other technique for converting telling to showing is "the argument." Have two characters argue about something and suddenly all kinds of information gets out there. The characters are throwing things in each other's faces or defending themselves or clarifying what the boss actually meant, or whatever, and meanwhile the reader is learning all manner of useful information.

revisiting dialogue

You can ask an objective test reader to look at dialogue for you. You want to know if the spoken exchanges between characters in your novel sound realistic. You also want to know if you got everything formatted correctly. Critique groups can help you here, even if they don't "get" what you're doing with you novel.

Now that you have your dialogue passages written in rough draft form, you can begin improving them. One way to do so is to read your dialogue aloud. Better yet: Have someone else read it aloud in your presence. Best of all, get a group together, assign roles, hand out scripts, and have them speak these scenes aloud in your presence.

It's amazing how good dialogue can sound in your head when you're the only one reading it—and how awful it can sound when someone else reads it. Maybe it's because that person is a lousy actor, or maybe it's because the dialogue needs to be improved.

If you can, videotape your helpers reading through the lines. At the least, take notes as they read. Whatever changes you wish they had made, make those changes in your manuscript.

verisimilitude

When it comes to dialogue in fiction, we're not shooting for absolute accuracy and realism. If you've ever read transcripts of exactly what people say in an unscripted conversation, you know it's loose and incomplete and even incomprehensible. Without access to the gestures, body language, facial expressions, and tone and volume and rate of speech, you would likely find the words themselves nonsensical—though, in the moment, everyone in the conversation understood its meaning.

Nor do we want to write dialogue that is so perfectly grammatical and complete that it sounds like it should be in a first-grade textbook. "Why, yes, that is a wonderful plant, James. I feel I shall love to place it beside this window, where sunlight may reach it with ease." Blech.

What we're after is something between the two extremes. We're shooting for *verisimilitude*. It sounds realistic and it is comprehensible, but it's neither overly realistic (like a transcript) nor overly comprehensible (like a book for new readers).

There are a number of techniques by which you can achieve dialogue with verisimilitude, but I'll limit myself to the one I think is best: Let your characters speak meaning to meaning.

Poor dialogue has characters speaking *word to word*, as if the other person's words contain his or her precise meaning. So it looks like this:

> "Hi, Julie. It is good to see you."
>
> "Why, thank you, Bob. I am glad to be here. It has been too long since I've been to a Broncos game."
>
> "Yes, it has been too long. I believe the last time was in September, when we were still winning. That was just before you started acting strange, and I began to suspect you were experimenting with amphetamines."
>
> "Ah, yes, now I recall. I should not have experimented with amphetamines. They are bad for me. I'm so glad I stopped."

Ick. It's all right there on the surface. They say what they mean, and they mean what they say. But real people don't talk like that very often.

Spoken language is meant not simply to convey the words we choose. Language is meant to communicate the meaning behind the words. When we hear someone say something, we're listening to his words, but we're also trying to discern what he *meant* by those words. Let's go back to Julie and Bob:

> "Hi, Julie. It is good to see you."
>
> "Huh. Sure."
>
> "No, really. It's been a long time. I haven't seen you at a Broncos game since…"
>
> "Look, I made some bad choices, okay? I don't see how it's any of your business."
>
> "I was just talking about football, Julie."
>
> "Sure, Bob. Look, if you want to hassle me about drugs, write it on a note, and I'll tell you where you can file it."
>
> "Whatever, Jewels. So, are you still … you know?"
>
> "Just watch the game."

Okay, it could've used some beats to manage the rhythm of the dialogue, but it's much better than before. Do you see how Julie inferred that Bob wasn't interested in football at all? Maybe he wanted to deride her about her choices. Maybe he wanted some of her drugs. Who knows? Even Julie didn't know what he was driving at, but she had a guess, and her responses were based not on what he actually said but on what she thought he meant.

That's how to achieve verisimilitude in dialogue.

Go back through your dialogue scenes and make your characters speak meaning to meaning, not word to word.

conclusion

Is it strange to have thought about show vs. tell—or POV or dialogue—before you wrote the book and to think about it again now that you're on the other side? Especially if this is your first novel, you may have thought you understood those rules before you actually started writing, but when you got into it, you realized you didn't understand them at all.

These issues are hard to see in your own writing at any time, especially when you're trying to find them in your first manuscript. If you don't already have a critique partner or critique group, now is a good time to find one.

Next, we turn to more craft issues.

craft to know on the back end

The Victory you are going to experience now is that you can continue refining your manuscript with fiction craftsmanship even though the main work—the writing—is largely over.

In this Victory, we'll talk more about issues of craft.

your first line

In Victory Eight, I said not to worry about the first line of your novel and that we'd come back to the topic later. Well, now is later.

Look at the opening line of your rough draft. Did you come up with a good one or just put in a placeholder? Better question: Now that you know the story of your whole novel, is the first sentence you wrote the right one?

In my opinion, a great first line for a novel has three characteristics. It will be simple, engaging, and appropriate for the tone of your book.

First, it has to be simple. Those paragraph-length opening sentences with multiple commas and phrases just don't skip off the tongue. A first sentence that seems difficult or awkward will make the reader think the whole book will be difficult and awkward. Because she's not engaged with your book at all yet, you've just made it very easy for her to keep looking for a good book to read. Which would be a shame, considering all the work you've put into making this novel amazing.

Think of your novel as a skyscraper in Manhattan. Your reader has heard that there are wonders inside, so she arrives at the building. But instead of an automatic door or a revolving door or even a door that is simply unlocked, sandbags, barbed wire, and armed guards barricade the entrance. No one is getting in. The guards look at the reader with suspicion, daring her to approach.

That's what a complicated first line does to the reader (although perhaps not with as much drama).

By "simple," I mean grammatically simple. One that is straightforward enough not to need commas. You don't want it to be convoluted.

Instead of a barricade across the entrance to your novel, you need the literary equivalent of a red carpet, with paparazzi and cheering fans and doors wide open to welcome the reader and usher her quickly inside. Maybe replace the red carpet with a Slip 'n Slide. You want her inside and enjoying those wonders as quickly and painlessly as possible.

> Simple: "Barry Fairbrother did not want to go out to dinner." (*The Casual Vacancy* by J.K. Rowling)

> Not simple: "Amid the noises of the night in downtown Oslo—the regular drone of cars outside the window, the distant siren that rose and fell and the church bells that had begun to chime nearby—a rat went on the hunt for food." (*Phantom* by Jo Nesbo)

> Simple: "We should go to a bar and celebrate." (*Bared to You* by Sylvia Day)

> Not simple: "Located in Griffith Park, a four-thousand-acre stretch of land featuring two eighteen-hole golf courses, the Autry National Center, and the HOLLYWOOD sign, the Los Angeles Zoo and Botanical Gardens is more of a run-down tourist attraction than a wildlife conservation facility." (*Zoo* by James Patterson and Michael Ledwidge)

All of these first lines are from best-selling novels, so it's clear that having a first line of the sort I'm suggesting is not a prerequisite for having a successful book, nor is having a first line unlike what I'm suggesting going to necessarily doom your book to obscurity. But once again, I think it's a case of a book doing well in spite of—not because of—a writing choice I wouldn't recommend.

Look at your opening line. Is it simple? Can it be simplified? If you haven't written one yet, or if you're wanting a new one, begin thinking in little bursts of words. Keeping it short will help you keep it simple.

Second, a great first line should be engaging. The Great Commandment of Fiction is that you must engage your reader from beginning to end. Well, the first line of your novel is the beginning. It's your first opportunity to engage. If you fail to engage with your opening line, some readers will put the book down and look for one that grabs them from the very first words.

To be engaging, an opening line has to be interesting. It has to arrest the reader's mind in some way. None of the first sentences just quoted—not even the simple ones—were especially engaging, in my opinion.

Here's one that isn't simple but is fairly engaging: "Jimmy Sharp stepped back from the curb and impatiently waved the car by, waved it by like a big shot, like he couldn't be bothered to assert his rights to a pedestrian crosswalk." (*Mad River* by John Sandford) It's longer than I would prefer, but I'm drawn in by the taste of characterization I'm given of Jimmy Sharp. It's engaging.

Here's one that is both simple and engaging: "The eyewitness said he didn't actually see it happen." (*A Wanted Man* by Lee Child) Wow, that's a great opening line. I'm not tripped up by an overlong sentence, and I'm intrigued. I mean, how can an eyewitness be an eyewitness if he didn't see the crime happen? I'm engaged. I will definitely keep reading.

And, in the end, that's what it means for a first line to be engaging: It keeps the reader reading.

Also, a great first line is one that is *appropriate for the tone of your book.*

"All of them are dead," is simple and possibly engaging, but if this is going to be a light romantic comedy, it's setting the wrong tone for the book.

Now that you've written your rough draft, you know what sort of tone your book will have. (Or, possibly, you don't. Have someone else read it and describe the mood or tone of it—you might be surprised to learn that you didn't set the tone you thought you did.) With that knowledge in hand, you can craft a first line that sounds the right note for a book that's going to feel like that.

That line above, "All of them are dead," is actually the first line from one of my own novels. A North Korean family has discovered that the relatives they've come to visit have killed themselves rather than starve under their country's crushing food-rationing policies. This is a serious drama about unpleasant conditions, so in this case the first line does strike the right tone.

Here are four opening lines that meet all three criteria:

> "I didn't set out to be the town luminary." (*Operation Bonnet* by Kimberly Stuart)

> "The magician's underwear has just been found in a cardboard suitcase floating in a stagnant pond on the outskirts of Miami." (*Another Roadside Attraction* by Tom Robbins)

> "Today I am going to kill a man in cold blood." (*Operation: Firebrand* by Jefferson Scott)

> "It was the first time anyone could remember a shark falling from the sky at the golf course."

Believe it or not, that last one is not a line from a novel—though it should be. It's a line from a news report in 2012 about a small shark near the California coast that had been picked up by an eagle (or something) and then dropped as the bird flew over a golf course.

But just look at that line. It's simple and highly engaging. I mean, wouldn't you read at least one more page of that book? And if the tone of the novel matched the tone of that line, the third criterion (*sets the tone for the rest of the book*) would be met as well.

Now that you've written your book, you have the luxury of messing around with your opening line. Don't stress about it, but if you can push it in the direction of these three criteria, you'll begin engaging your reader on page 1.

circularity

Another cool thing you can do with your opening line is to employ circularity. In this context, I mean that you can, at the end of the book, refer back to the beginning.

For instance, if we were applying circularity to *Moby Dick*, we'd leave the awesome first line, "Call me Ishmael," but then we'd go to the very last line of the novel and try to hearken back to it. So maybe we'd change the last line to something like, "Now you know the troubles I have endured and why I insist that you call me Ishmael." Or whatever. Chances are good that the reader will remember your opening line, especially with a nice little reminder like that, and see that you have circled back to the beginning.

Circularity gives a book a feeling of completeness and intentionality that makes its author seem like a genius, like she had the ending all planned out even before she wrote that first line. Of course, you and I know that she probably didn't have it perfectly planned out before she began, but there's no need for the reader to know that!

Maybe, though, it doesn't work when you try to tie the first and last lines together. Maybe it just feels awkward to you. That's okay. You can still use circularity in scenes or locations or conversations that are repeated—but with a twist, for instance. And I've already explained how the main character's initial condition and final state are connected. The scene you create for the final state will be either the direct opposite of that initial condition or it will be that initial condition scene on steroids. If you do this, you're already creating a nice feeling of circularity for the reader.

Give some thought to the novel you've just written. In what way (or ways) might you create some circularity?

It's not vital that you do this, of course. But when done well, it strikes agents and editors and readers as a little touch of mastery they weren't looking for but appreciate when they find.

beats

In Victory Nine, I introduced the idea of beats, but mainly as a tool for eliminating speech attributions in dialogue. But beats are more than that. You can use them as tools to manage the pacing of your scenes and to tether the scene to the setting.

The term *beats* comes from the world of theater. In the script for a play, if the playwright wanted the actor to insert a pause in his delivery of a line, he'd write, "a beat," in the script at the spot where the pause should fall.

Novelists have adopted this concept and brought it to fiction. But we can't simply say, "a beat," and have the reader understand what in the world we mean. Can you imagine:

> "Jimmy, time for dinner." A beat. "And don't tell me you're not hungry."

Actually, you can occasionally get away with that or a form of it by writing, "He paused a beat" or the like. But most of the time you'd replace "a beat" with a description of an action or of a thought or of something in the setting. As in:

> "Jimmy, time for dinner." She sighed deeply. "And don't tell me you're not hungry."

The sigh between the lines of dialogue is a beat, even if it isn't called one.

Beats are terrific tools for inserting pauses in fiction. You'll use them mainly in dialogue scenes, but in other moments as well. Use a short beat to imply a short pause and a long beat to imply a long pause. For instance:

> "Susie Mae, I have something to tell you." He blinked. "I'm leaving you."

...vs...

> "Susie Mae, I have something to tell you." He wouldn't meet her eyes. Instead, he stared at the brass rabbit on the coffee table as if it held the secret of life. He went over to the couch and sat down, still staring at the figurine. This couldn't be good. He opened his mouth to speak, but nothing came out. He sighed. He bit his lip. He tied his shoe. Then, still not looking at me, he found his words. "I'm leaving you."

Okay, not great prose, but you see the point. The pause between spoken lines seemed lesser in the first example and greater in the second. Not just because I had the character doing things in the second example that took longer than a blink. It was simply because *there were more words* between the two spoken lines. The reader experienced a longer gap in actual time—because it took longer to read all of those words in the second example—and this simulated a longer pause in story time.

Go through your manuscript looking primarily at the dialogue scenes. You can't simply imagine pauses where you want the reader to read them. Just as you have to include rests in music, so you have to write beats into your novel, and you have to use beats of varying lengths to create those pauses for the reader.

Conversely, when you want something to proceed without a pause, take out all the words that come first. For instance, which sequence feels like it happens more speedily?

"Dude, you need to back off."

Then, without a moment's hesitation, Jasper immediately summoned his courage and instantly replied:
"No, you back off."

...or...

"Dude, you need to back off."
"No, you back off."

Sometimes a novelist can pack a sentence with words that imply
immediacy but that end up causing more of a delay. A beat—
a group of words that delay the "arrival" of spoken dialogue—
causes a pause. If you don't want a pause in a specific spot, take
out the intervening words. They slow the reader's eye.

Use beats as your primary tool for maintaining control of
the pacing of your dialogue scenes.

Beats should also be used to give the reader a feel for what
the characters are doing and to tie the reader to the setting. If a
dialogue exchange extends for a page or longer, the writer has
to work hard to keep the scene tethered to the earth.

"Yes," Petunia said.
"Ah, good." Oscar smiled. "I'll come up then."
Petunia held up her hand. "No, don't."
"Well, one of us has to move."
"I think you should go."
Oscar's smile faded. "Petunia, we have to discuss
the matter of the horse."
She nodded. "I know. You really think it's stolen?"
"Stolen, found, appeared in a ball of fire—who
can say?"
"I think it's stolen." Petunia tilted her head. "Odd,
really, considering Julianne's dream."

You can picture the characters' expressions and body language
fairly easily, but where is this dialogue taking place? One is

"up" and the other is "down," but as the conversation continues, you lose even that tenuous grasp on setting. See if this is any better:

> "Yes." Petunia stuck her head over the edge of the roof. A sturdy ladder rested against the side of the house.
>
> "Ah, good." Oscar walked to the ladder and took hold of the sides. "I'll come up then."
>
> Petunia held up her hand. "No, don't."
>
> "Well," he said, looking up at just the top of her head, "one of us has to move."
>
> "I think you should go."
>
> Oscar's smile faded. The metal of the ladder was cool and rough in his grip. "Petunia, we have to discuss the matter of the horse."
>
> She nodded. "I know. You really think it's stolen?"
>
> "Stolen, found, appeared in a ball of fire—who can say?" He walked back around to the front of the house.
>
> "I think it's stolen." Petunia tilted her head. "Odd, really, considering Julianne's dream."

Did you feel more *grounded* this time? The beats not only managed the rhythm of the dialogue, they also kept the scene (and the reader) affixed to the setting. Without little reminders of where we are, little tie-downs to the story world, dialogue scenes float up and away like hot air balloons.

Keeping your reader oriented in the scene is a way to keep her engaged in the moment. And that is a way to get the power of the Great Commandment of Fiction working in your favor.

Beats can contain description, action, "stage business" (things the characters do), and thoughts.

description

So far we haven't discussed description. It's one of my favorite topics in fiction. Passages of well-written description are powerful. They magically transport the reader from wherever she is to the place you've described, which is the main reason some readers turn to fiction in the first place.

Description is another of those topics about which fiction experts disagree. Indeed, along with prologues and show vs. tell, it's one of the issues about which there is more argument than any other.

It comes down to your philosophy of fiction. If, as a reader, you prefer not to be told what a person, place, or thing in a novel looks like, then you probably won't want to include descriptions in your own fiction. If you find yourself skipping over even a sentence or paragraph of description, that preference will show up in the novels you write. That's fine.

If, however, you *like* description in the novels you read, and if you want a more cinematic presentation of the people, places, and things in the fiction you read, your fiction will reflect that preference.

Neither stance is correct or better than the other. Both philosophies have fans and haters. Both sides will attract some readers and repel others.

Whether or not to include description and how much is not the Great Commandment of Fiction. It could certainly be argued that passages of description that a reader does *not* want to see and over which she skips are areas that cause her to disengage with the story. But it also could be argued that not including description might cause a reader who wants to more fully envision what's going on to fail at doing so and thus knock her out of the story. Both situations put us in the region of violating the Great Commandment.

Since there's nothing you can do about which sort of reader you'll get, I urge you to not worry about it and just write it the way you feel is best. Some gatekeeper may prefer that you had more or less description than you include, and you can always adjust the amount you have in order to get through that particular gate. But until you reach that gate, just go with your instincts.

As you wrote your rough draft, my guess is that you didn't include much description. Most unpublished novels I read have very little description of settings, especially, but also of characters. Sometimes that's because the writer doesn't want description. More often it's because he didn't think to add it.

If you're going to include description, then it's my experience that you haven't included enough. You'll probably need to add about five times the amount you included as you wrote it. (If you're not going to include much description, you may still wish to read on, as there are elements of good description writing that will empower other areas of your novel.)

Happily, description is something that can easily be added in revisions, which is why we're talking about it now. Ideally, you had the setting firmly in mind—preferably by going there or looking at an image of it as you wrote—while you were writing. That will reduce the difficulty of your task now, because all you have to do is actually describe the location you had assumed it was in.

If you didn't have a setting in mind as you wrote, and you decide to incorporate one now, you may have some rewriting to do. For instance, if you said she ran up the stairs to her room but then later decide it's a single-story dwelling, you'll have to rewrite that part.

Every time your viewpoint character enters a location other than what he was in during the previous scene, we need you to describe that setting to some degree. More, if this character has not been here before now or if something is significantly different from other times; less, if he or she has been here before.

If you can physically go to the location you're writing about, that's ideal. Second best is to see and hear it on video. Third best is to see (or create) a picture of it. Least best is to simply make up a setting completely in your mind without any visual guide whatsoever. Locations imagined like that lack authenticity and are subject to change from scene to scene as the author's memory wiggles around.

Go through your manuscript and write in more description of your locations (and characters).

A good guideline is to begin describing the setting on the first page of a scene that takes place in that new location. You don't have to begin the scene with a description. Indeed, it's usually best not to, as those opening lines should be spent on things that will reengage the reader, like a bit of arresting dialogue or action. But once the reader is on the hook, she's going to begin wondering what this place looks like, who is there, and so forth. By the end of the first page in that new setting, she wants description.

I recommend giving readers a paragraph of description. I don't think it's best to throw out little crumbs of description here and there so that by the end of the scene the reader finally has a clear picture of the place. By that time, she's already formed a picture in her own mind, and it's very likely not the one you wanted her to have.

Authors often avoid writing a paragraph or two of description because they fear they're telling instead of showing. They're not, but more on that in a moment.

Having said that, it is sometimes a good idea to give description in phases. For instance, if a woman walks into a sporting goods store, you'd want to give a good description of what she sees, hears, smells; an idea of how many people are there; and that sort of thing. But if, a moment later, there's a commotion in the baseball department and her attention is drawn there, you'd want to give more description, this time focusing on that particular part of the store.

Before the viewpoint character's attention is on something specific, there's no need to describe it in detail. But when the character's attention goes there, the reader wants to know more about it. Think of it as the camera zooming in to focus on something closely.

That's the guideline, by the way: Whether you're describing a character or a location or anything else, as soon as the viewpoint character notices it, that's when the reader wants to know about it.

plant and payoff

This is a principle for all of your fiction, but it fits best to talk about it while we're on the subject of description. I call it plant and payoff.

If you want your hero to save the day at the climactic moment by climbing into a construction crane and using it to pull the damsel's car to safety, you had better have shown the reader beforehand that he knows how to use construction equipment.

If you want the hero to solve a crime because of her expert knowledge of beauty products and practices (*Legally Blonde*), you jolly well better have shown us before the crucial moment occurs.

Even if your hero is going to pull out some yet-to-be-introduced secret gadget that he uses to defeat the villain and save the day, we need to have learned before then that he has various secret gadgets … including some we haven't seen yet.

This is the principle of *planting* something in the reader's mind that you'll call upon later in the story (the *payoff*). You can't be calling upon it if you haven't introduced it, or it will seem like you're pulling rabbits out of a hat. The reader will be mad at you if the hero suddenly has or can do something that solves the problem instantly. Such a solution makes the reader feel dumb for having worried about how things were going to turn out. That's payoff without plant.

Plant without payoff, on the other hand, occurs when you introduce something prominently enough for the reader to take notice, but then you don't use it later. For example, if you take pains to show that the hero knows how to fly a helicopter but then never have her fly a helicopter, we'll be like, "Why did you make me waste brain cells remembering that if you weren't going to use it?"

Go through your manuscript and make sure you've introduced early in the story all the main tools, abilities, attributes, and otherwise that you'll use later—especially in the climactic moments of the book. Likewise, be sure you haven't made the reader notice something that you're not going to use later. (Now, if you're writing a mystery and you want to have lots of red herrings, you can make us notice things that throw us off—but you still need to address or tie off each of those things later.)

Plant and payoff are important not only in a large sense, as I've outlined here, but also in the small sense: in description.

I read an unpublished manuscript once in which two characters were having a long conversation "outside" (the author hadn't added enough description, in my opinion), when suddenly, at the end of the scene, the cheerleading squad got up and left. I was like, "What cheerleading squad?"

The cheerleading squad in the scene was a payoff but the writer had failed to establish that it existed in the first place (a plant), so the girls and their pom-poms seemed to appear in a puff of smoke just in time to get up and leave.

Anything important you're going to use in your scene needs to be planted early on ... in your description ... so that when the character draws his sword, the reader already knows he had his sword and won't be assuming the sword magically appeared just when the character needed it.

The introduction of the item you're going to use later doesn't have to be heavy-handed. In this case, you could describe the setting—a castle bailey in which the men-at-arms are conducting drills—and you could say that the key character has to back against the stone wall of the castle to let the men-at-arms through and at one point pulled his sword and scabbard aside to keep it from scraping. Or whatever. You can be subtle about introducing that he had a sword early in the scene. Later, when he draws his sword, we'll be like, "Oh, right, I remember he had that sword on." That's what you're after.

Incidentally, it's okay to think up things that need to be in the setting halfway through the writing of a scene. You may not have known he was going to need his sword when you started writing the scene, but then you got a great idea for an action bit in which he'd draw Excalibur and do battle. Hey, that's awesome. No problem. You just need to go back to an earlier place in the scene and mention that he had Excalibur with him.

That's a good principle for your whole book, actually. You're always going to think of cool things later that logically would've been there the whole time. You get new and cool ideas as you write, of course. But then you have to go back and plant those things in earlier parts of the manuscript.

I edited a science fiction novel once about primitive villagers who had been brought into a futuristic city. About halfway through, the author realized she needed surveillance cameras throughout the city. Cool. Good idea. She'd written the second half of the story with those cameras everywhere. Problem was, she hadn't gone back and added those cameras to the first half of the manuscript. So they seemed to magically appear, as if installed overnight by futuristic elves. Once she went through and added them, the story read realistically to the reader.

I'm guessing you have one or more similar issues in your novel. It's okay—encouraged, even—to come up with great ideas later in the writing process. But then you have to implement those ideas throughout the manuscript so you appear to have had that great idea in mind all along.

Back to description: Payoff without plant causes things to magically appear and will irk your reader in the same way that plant without payoff will. If you make her notice something unusual in the environment—or even if you take pains to make her notice something mundane—you'd better use it or refer to it later in the scene. There's an adage in theater that if you bring a revolver onstage, you must have it go off at some point. If it's not going to be used, then don't bring it onstage.

description is not telling

As I mentioned, some writers don't include description because they don't like to see it in the fiction they read.

I once heard a novelist tell a crowd of aspiring writers, "I shall never dictate to my reader what she must think." It sounded very lofty and noble, but I muttered, "Then don't write a novel." I mean, what is a novel but a scene by scene and line by line dictation of what the reader should think? If you didn't want to tell the reader what to think, you should've left her alone with her thoughts instead of trampling her free will by telling her that this character did these things and said these words in *this* setting.

The only *real* way to avoid dictating what the reader should think is to *not write anything at all.* Grr.

Sorry. Okay, I'm feeling calmer now. Must … move … on…

Back to description. If you don't want to describe what the locations or people in your story look like, that's fine. But some novelists leave out description not because they're poetically disinclined to do so, nor even because they didn't want to slow down their writing while they were pushing through the rough draft, but because they're concerned that description is telling.

Novelists who want to cut down on their telling but who haven't yet mastered where showing stops and telling begins are likely to stumble when it comes to description. They look at a passage of dialogue in their manuscript and think, "Okay, *that's* not telling. And I have no 'As you know, Bob…' passages, so I'm good." And then they look at passages of action, in which people are moving and things are happening, and they go, "Okay, these parts are fine too because the camera can certainly see these things happening."

They're not sure what to do with paragraphs of internal monologue. And they're *definitely* not sure about paragraphs of description. Either they haven't written any such passages at all or they're pretty sure they should cut them. After all, if it's not dialogue or action, doesn't it have to be telling? Isn't that the only other option?

No.

Let's go back to our two helps for show vs. tell: the definition and the test question.

My definition of telling is when you stop the story to explain something the reader doesn't care about. Now, if someone who doesn't like description reads your novel, then yes, your passage of description will stop the story for him. He'll skip over it. But, as we've seen, just as many readers want description (actually, I think there are many more). For them, a paragraph of description isn't stopping the story at all. Indeed, for these people, the story can't move forward without description. So, for at least half the readers out there, description is not telling, according to my definition.

Now let's look at the testing tool for whether or not something is telling: Can the camera see it?

Can the camera see that, thirty years ago, these two used to be best friends? No. Can the camera see that the pavilion had been chosen because of last year's debacle with the rain? No. Can the camera see that the bookshelf reached to the ceiling and the library was lit by only a nightlight plugged into an outlet?

Did I trick you on that one? Yes, the camera can see that. Our test question in this case reveals that yes, indeed, the camera can see description.

So by both our definition and our test question, description is not telling.

Be ye empowered to go through your manuscript adding gobs of description. Be aware, however, that it's possible to overdo description (I once read a book with four pages of what the clouds looked like), but I'm guessing you're more likely to do too little than too much. You can always scale it back later if you need to.

the full work-up

When novelists sit down to write a description of a location or a character (I'm mostly thinking of locations in this section), they can sometimes write lots of text and still end up failing to communicate an adequate sense of what the place looks like.

So I'll get a half page on the hooks used to hang clothing, the metal shelves with shoes on them, and the box of white powder on the floor, but I'll still have no idea that this was supposed to be a locker room.

To help make sure you have all of your bases covered when it comes to describing a location, I've created the following list, which I call "the full work-up." Give a setting the full work-up, and you will have satisfactorily described it.

First, be sure to provide the establishing shot, which includes the generic descriptor. The "establishing shot" is a term from cinema. It gives the context for what is about to take place. So if you show an office building and then cut to a scene in an office, we assume that this office is inside that office building. The image of the office building was the establishing shot that provided the context for what comes next.

The generic descriptor is the word or term that explains what this place is in a general sense: locker room, office, garage, hangar, cockpit, elevator, bathroom, city park. You'd be surprised how many times the writer leaves it out. So the reader gets the feeling that this is the "space" in which hooks, shelves, and powder reside, but he has no knowledge that this is a locker room.

In fiction, the establishing shot and generic descriptor combine to give the reader a quick handle on what this space is like. Examples: a conference room big enough to hold thirty people, a subway tunnel wide enough for two trains to pass, a scientific laboratory barely large enough for two people to squeeze into.

Even if you gave only the establishing shot with a generic descriptor, the reader would be oriented into the setting. I'd gladly keep one sentence like this in exchange for a paragraph of details that don't tell me where I am or how big it is. Go through the descriptions in your manuscript and add a sentence like this to each one, as necessary.

The next element in a full work-up of a setting is a comparison or word picture. The so-called "lake" was hardly larger than a backyard swimming pool. The device on the worktable was as spherical as a basketball. The vehicle reminded him of a cross between a Corvette and a dump truck.

The brain works in comparisons. It takes the store of images and memories it has, and it compares those against what it's evaluating now. Your characters think that way, and your readers think that way, so include comparisons in your descriptions. Plus, word pictures can be fun. A comparison in your description is the quickest way to give the reader the right feeling for a location or thing. Go through your descriptions looking for opportunities to use comparisons.

Third, be sure to include the atmosphere of the setting. That's my umbrella word that includes whether this location is inside or outside, whether it's day or night, what the weather is (if visible to the viewpoint character), whether it's hot or cold, and most important, how it's lit. The eyes depend on light, and a setting feels drastically different if it's flooded with light or lit by just one birthday candle.

These aspects of atmosphere are essential in communicating the setting to the reader. Another adage from theater is, "If it ain't on the page, it ain't on the stage." In other words, if the playwright imagined the scene in a classroom but didn't say so in the script, it won't be in a classroom when the play is produced. In fiction, if you don't describe what exists in the setting— or whether that setting is inside or outside—it won't be on the "stage" of the reader's imagination. If you're picturing the scene inside a warehouse lit by extremely blue fluorescent lights but you don't say so, the reader won't get it.

Fourth, give a full sensory sweep of the location. We need to know not only what the place looks like but also what it sounds like, feels like (temperature, wind, and such), smells like, and tastes like (like grit in your teeth because you're at a beach).

Nothing transports a reader into a setting like sensory information. And the senses of smell and feeling/touch are your secret weapons. If you want to be sure your reader experiences a particular setting, find a smell or texture or temperature to describe.

This doesn't mean you have to mechanically give a listing of something from each of the five senses in every description. But you should at least survey all five for that location, looking for the ones the viewpoint character would realistically perceive in that location.

Fifth, place the players on the stage. How many people are there? Where are they in relation to one another? What are they doing? Is there a cheerleading squad on the premises? If a person were to walk into this setting and look around, one of the things she would notice right away would be whether or not she were alone. If not, she'd pay attention to the folks with whom she shared the space. Yet it is surprising how rare it is for a novelist to think to include that information in a description of a setting, and so we get cheerleaders who magically appear. Go through your manuscript and be sure you mention this obvious bit of data in every description of setting.

The last part of the full work-up is the detail of the setting. Details are not the least important, but I mention them last because they're often the first and only things novelists think to include. Details are important, but they're not the whole story.

After you're sure you've given the reader a great feeling for a place, then you can tell her about the hooks for shoulder pads, the steel shelves in the lockers, and the boxes of athlete's foot powder on the floor. Once we have the former, the latter is great icing. But if all we find out about is the icing, we have no idea what kind of cake it is, or if it's even a cake at all.

Note that you don't have to include every element of the full work-up in each of your descriptions. If the characters are just walking through a hallway, there's no need to describe the hallway in detail. But the more important the location, the more detail you should include. I don't consider a setting fully described until you've included something from each of the categories.

So choose the details carefully. Describe those details that 1) will be important later and/or 2) help you establish the mood you want the reader to be in when she reads through a scene in this place—which brings me to the next topic.

use description to set mood

An advantage enjoyed by novelists who include description over novelists who do not is the ability to set mood through description.

Part of good fiction writing is putting the reader in exactly the right state of mind to receive what you're about to deliver in exactly the right way and with exactly the right impact. If you want her to laugh but you've set her up to cry, you may not get what you're after. If you want her to be nervous about what is soon to happen but you've bungled it and have instead set her at ease, she won't feel the moment the way you meant it to be felt.

One of your primary tools for setting reader mood is description.

What would you expect to be set up for in the following passage of description?

> A shadow lay over the yard like a grave cloth. The grass was long and unkempt. Against the bole of a withered oak lay a child's ball, shrouded by the creeping Bermuda. The features of the house shimmered in the blaze of the afternoon, blurred beyond recognition to the unwary passerby.

If this description were followed by a whimsical scene in which a child received a puppy at a birthday party, you would feel a little disoriented. Why? Because you'd been led to believe that something scary was afoot.

Same location, different mood:

> Zinnias blossomed against the cherry tree beside the front porch, their sun-kissed inner circles wreathed in bashful pink. At the base of the grand oak, a mother rabbit led her furry litter out from the shade of a rhododendron's lacy leaves. She sniffed the breeze with delicate nostrils, brushed her eye with a paw, and bounded into the sun.

Now you can have your puppy.
Same location, third mood:

> The dirt showed through the grass in brown scars. The grass that remained was brittle and sharp, like a smoker's eyebrows. Signs remained of the home's luxuriant past—the garden path, the children's toys, the "Home of the Week" sign out front—but they lay wasted. An American flag still fluttered on its pole, but the sun had washed it out to a milky translucence and its trailing edge was shredded. It hung from only one tether, twisting in the wind like a castaway's last cry for rescue.

After this, the reader is set up for something depressing.

See how powerful description is? Notice the word pictures and comparisons. Notice the word choice and vocabulary. Notice how no word or image undercuts the mood I'm going for. If I had inserted "grave cloth" into the description that talked about bunnies, it would've sent a mixed message, and the impact would've been dulled.

Go through the descriptions in your book and be sure they are setting the mood you want your reader to be in at that spot in the story.

description through the eyes of the narrator

I covered the idea of using your viewpoint character as narrator in an earlier Victory, so I'll just touch on it here.

Description is a key element of how the reader understands what's happening in the story. And if you're staying in character and giving all the details through the mind and perceptions and personality of the viewpoint character, then you must be double sure that all of your descriptions are done the way that person would do them.

Also make sure she notices everything that character would notice—and doesn't notice the things she wouldn't notice. If she wouldn't normally notice something you need the reader to know about, find a way to force the viewpoint character to take notice. Like if she would typically overlook the flora here, you could have some other character run up and try to sell her flowers that had been picked nearby. A male character might not notice specific flowers, but maybe he spies a set of tracks through the garden.

You can see by the number of pages I've spent on this topic that I believe description is one of the most powerful tools in your kit for creating strong fiction that transports the reader into the world of your story.

conclusion

Your opening line, the beats in your novel, and your passages of description are all terrific elements of fiction craftsmanship that will elevate your novel. Happily, they can all be added in revisions.

Next up: my last tips and techniques for revising your novel.

final touches

Whole libraries of fiction how-to books have been and will continue to be published, and most of them can be used to revise a novel you've already written. Indeed, whole books have been written on individual topics such as dialogue and show vs. tell and point of view.

In spite of the presence of so many terrific resources, I'm going to offer just one more Victory on craft.

The following are techniques that I've found to contribute to a more excellent fiction manuscript. None of them are the Great Commandment of Fiction, but each of them *supports* it, as you will see.

paragraph length

It's going to sound odd, but the length of your paragraphs actually has an impact on the quality of your novel. Here are three ways to improve your manuscript at the paragraph level.

monster paragraphs

Even if you don't write horror, you're capable of writing monster paragraphs.

You know what I mean: those massive, page-length monoliths of text without break or relief, those solid walls of words with neither foothold nor crenellation, that defy the reader to even attempt to read them.

[ahem]

I once had to read a philosophy of religion textbook that, I kid you not, had paragraphs that would go for five pages at a time. It was like trying to wedge your way into a concert that was already packed to the walls.

Few things better say, "Put this book down immediately—you're not wanted here," than pages that look dense, unfriendly, and intimidating. Readers come to fiction for escape, not eye strain. They want to be ushered to the front row, not made to feel that they can't penetrate the outer perimeter.

Even if readers aren't aware they're doing this, they're looking at paragraph length as an indication of how enjoyable it's going to be to read your novel.

Monster paragraphs = no fun to read.

Reading long paragraphs feels too much like work. Shorter paragraphs suggest that this will be a brisk read, entertaining and easy to digest. That's not to say you need to break your paragraphs apart so each one is only one line long. There's room for variety of paragraph length and, as we'll see in a second, there's good reason for using that variety. But if your paragraphs tend to go long, you'll need to get out your splitter/splicer gun and divide them into smaller chunks.

This is purely subjective, but I have found that paragraphs of one to seven lines (as they fall in the Microsoft Word document when formatted in 12 point Times New Roman with 1" to 1.25" margins) are ideal. Go to eight lines and beyond, and paragraphs start to look like philosophy of religion textbooks—and (almost) nobody wants that, certainly not the typical reader of fiction.

Now, will an eight-line paragraph kill your novel? No. And will keeping all of your paragraphs between one and seven lines long guarantee that it will be a bestseller? No.

I will say that this subject does pertain to the Great Commandment. If the only true rule of fiction is to engage your reader from beginning to end, and if long paragraphs make the book appear difficult to read, you can see how keeping the paragraphs shorter helps you adhere to the Great Commandment.

You don't have to cut out any content to keep your paragraphs short. Rather, find good places to divide what you already have. Forget what your high school English teach taught you about avoiding one-sentence (or even one-word) paragraphs. Divide them up as you please.

Even if you do it as an experiment but have no intention of carrying it through your manuscript, I think it's an interesting exercise. Show someone two versions of the same text, but with one all-in-one paragraph and the other cut up, and see which one he finds easier to read. Take the opening paragraph of *The Twelve* by Justin Cronin:

> Later, after supper and evening prayer, and bath if it was bath night, and then the final negotiations to conclude the day (*Please, Sister, can't we stay up a little longer? Please, one more story?*), when the children had fallen asleep at last and everything was very still, Amy watched them. There was no rule against this; the sisters had all grown accustomed to her nighttime wanderings. Like an apparition she moved from quiet room to quiet room, sidling up and down the rows of beds where the children lay, their sleeping faces and bodies in trusting repose. The oldest was thirteen, poised at the edge of adulthood, the youngest just babies. Each came with a story, always sad. Many were thirdlings left at the orphanage by parents unable to pay the tax, others the victim of even crueler circumstances: mothers dead in childbirth, or else unwed and unable to bear the shame; fathers disappeared into the dark undercurrents of the city or taken outside the wall. The children's origins varied, yet their fates would be the same. The girls would enter the Order, giving their days to prayer and contemplation and caring for the children they themselves had been, while the boys would become soldiers, members of the Expeditionary, taking an oath of a different but no less binding nature.

Now, I don't mean to pick on Mr. Cronin, but if I had been his editor, I wouldn't have let him get away with a paragraph like this. First, it's packed with telling. Apply our "Can the camera see it?" question to every sentence of that paragraph and cut out everything that the camera can't see. You'll be surprised how little is left. It didn't seem to hinder the popularity of his book, though, as when I wrote this Victory *The Twelve* was on *The New York Times* bestseller list.

But the thing I want to look at in this monster paragraph is how dense it is and how hard it is on the eyes. You won't find another paragraph in this book nearly as long as that one. Let's take a look at the passage again, but this time with some creative paragraph splitting:

> Later, after supper and evening prayer, and bath if it was bath night, and then the final negotiations to conclude the day (*Please, Sister, can't we stay up a little longer? Please, one more story?*), when the children had fallen asleep at last and everything was very still, Amy watched them.
>
> There was no rule against this; the sisters had all grown accustomed to her nighttime wanderings.
>
> Like an apparition she moved from quiet room to quiet room, sidling up and down the rows of beds where the children lay, their sleeping faces and bodies in trusting repose. The oldest was thirteen, poised at the edge of adulthood, the youngest just babies.
>
> Each came with a story, always sad. Many were thirdlings left at the orphanage by parents unable to pay the tax, others the victim of even crueler circumstances: mothers dead in childbirth, or else unwed and unable to bear the shame; fathers disappeared into the dark undercurrents of the city or taken outside the wall.
>
> The children's origins varied, yet their fates would be the same. The girls would enter the Order, giving their days to prayer and contemplation and caring for the children they themselves had been, while the boys would become soldiers, members of the Expeditionary, taking an oath of a different but no less binding nature.

Isn't that easier on the eyes? Now, I arbitrarily cut this apart. There was no real reason to make the "There was no rule against this" sentence stand alone in its own paragraph, but I liked the variety of paragraph length it gave the page. (Plus, the sentences are so long that they're almost paragraph length all by themselves—something else I would've addressed in the edit.)

Notice also that the shorter paragraph, nestled as it is between two longer paragraphs, has greater dramatic impact. It seems to be standing in the spotlight. Use this phenomenon intentionally as you manage the paragraph lengths in your manuscript.

Which brings me to my second recommendation about paragraph length.

using paragraph length for impact

Use shorter and longer paragraphs for impact, emphasis, and pacing—and to set up your reader for something big.

Long paragraphs, as we've seen, can be intimidating to the reader. They imply seriousness. They also imply a long pause. It takes a lot longer to read a long paragraph, after all, than a short one. It actually delays the eye in one general location on the page and causes the reader to feel suspended in that moment for an extended time.

Use this to your advantage. When you want the reader to feel relaxed and to settle back, use longer paragraphs (in the six- to seven-line range). Long paragraphs are like a lazy summer afternoon or an hour of meditation. They're like deep breathing exercises.

A great use of long paragraphs is to include one right before you're going to have a very short paragraph, maybe even a one-word paragraph. Here's an excerpt from *The Tenth Crusader* by Kirk Outerbridge:

He lost sight of her, her crimson hijab flashing in a multicolored burst of light. One of the palms near the jungle swayed as if hit by something, then another some distance away. The process repeated itself, disappearing up the mountain slope and into the shadows of the retreating night. Tariq struggled to breathe despite the thundering in his chest. The stories were true. This Houri was no woman. Smacking his head again, he removed whatever was left of his hair. He felt for the device in his pocket and took off running for camp. Whatever this thing was, he wanted no part of it.

Not when it came from a djinn of a woman like that.

The one-line paragraph has greater impact because it comes after a longer paragraph. Had the previous paragraph been split into one- and two-line paragraphs, the final one-liner would've seemed like just one more of those.

When you have something you want to emphasize in a passage, try putting it in a very short paragraph—especially if you can have it fall after a longer one—or between two longer ones.

paragraph length in action scenes

Who knew you could talk so long about something as mundane as paragraph length, right? But I'm telling you, it makes a subtle but important contribution to the feeling that your manuscript has been written by someone with a mature fiction skill set.

Some novelists, when they come to writing action scenes, write longer and longer paragraphs. Their feeling, I suspect, is that the paragraph will be like a long-held breath, and the longer they make it, the more suspense the reader will feel.

Unfortunately, in my opinion, long paragraphs have the opposite effect on readers. A long paragraph says, "I'm slow; I'm sleepy; take a nap." Which, when it comes to moments of frenetic action in your book, is pretty much not what you're going for.

Consider:

> And then time stopped. In perfect clarity, like a paused DVD, Jason saw the moment the final battle began.
>
> Five tanks fired their main guns. The shells were silver gleams in the cloudy light, frozen in a bizarre *Matrix* still-frame that Jason could walk around inside. On the other side, three RPGs hung on smoke ropes tied to the launchers on men's shoulders. To the west the first Baggara rider's sword was stuck as if bronzed into a man's shoulder. To the east an orderly flight of bullets sprayed across the battlefield like a high-speed photo of a man watering his lawn with a hose.
>
> Overhead a bomb rolled off an Antonov's cargo ramp. He could see the foot of the man who'd kicked it out. Two Mig-29s stood on their wings as if mounted there by a modeler. On the hillside to the north three of the howitzers expunged smoke from their muzzles.
>
> Then time switched to fast-scan. Two screaming men ran over Jason's head. One tripped and fell, where he was crushed beneath a Baggara stallion. Treads reared up before him. Sucking everything into the crusher. He dove out of the way. Fire burning in the grass. Get away from it. Shadow passing over me. Shockwave throwing a horse and rider to the ground. Shoot that one with pepper. Two tanks colliding. Rachel firing her gun. Looking deadly and beautiful. A gap. Run for it. *Whump-whump-whump* Men fighting hand-to-hand. Stay low.
>
> Another tank coming. The size of it! No, it's hit by a rocket. Trieu and Lewis dodging horsemen. Chris tossing a smoke grenade. Screaming man lunging at me with bayonet. Sweep point away. Grip the rifle stock. Punch in face. Kick in solar plexus. Stab with bayonet. No, don't stab. Throw gun down and move. The earth rippling like water? Men climbing on a muddy tank. Trying to get in. Opening the hatch. Grenade. Tank

swerves. Men falling off. *Grenade!* Am I hurt? Where is my team? Arm with no man. Not my arm. Garth pulling a man off a horse. Good, go there.

A nice rain shower. Pushed from behind. Roll over. Baggara cutting down with his sword. Arms up! Baggara bayoneted. Pushed off me. His blood's on my face. Trampled by my rescuer. Roll up. Move toward the hill. More tanks. Who is that screaming? Is that rocket turning to chase that MiG? So many bodies. Look, most of the tanks are past me now. Chris in front of me, motioning me to him. The others are there. They're yelling at me but I can only see their lips move. Trieu is pulling Garth's boot off. There's no blood but his leg is bending where he's not supposed to have a knee. Is Lewis crying? I need to go back to them now. They need me.

Wow, lots of action here huh? The short sentences give a staccato feel to the event. But they're in such long paragraphs, the impact is dulled. At first, in the paragraph when things are standing still, it makes sense to have it all packed into one long paragraph, because everything's moving as if in slow motion. But when "time switched to fast-scan," it no longer makes sense to have long paragraphs, as you see above.

This is taken from my novel *Operation: Firebrand—Crusade*, by the way.

Now here it is as it was published. Note the use of both longer and shorter paragraphs to imply not only the apparent speed of the events but also the mental state of the viewpoint character.

And then time stopped. In perfect clarity, like a paused DVD, Jason saw the moment the final battle began.

Five tanks fired their main guns. The shells were silver gleams in the cloudy light, frozen in a bizarre *Matrix* still-frame that Jason could walk around inside. On the other side, three RPGs hung on smoke ropes tied to the launchers on men's shoulders. To the west the first Baggara rider's sword was stuck as if bronzed into a man's shoulder. To the east an orderly flight of bullets sprayed across the battlefield like a high-speed photo of a man watering his lawn with a hose.

Overhead a bomb rolled off an Antonov's cargo ramp. He could see the foot of the man who'd kicked it out. Two Mig-29s stood on their wings as if mounted there by a modeler. On the hillside to the north three of the howitzers expunged smoke from their muzzles.

Then time switched to fast-scan.

Two screaming men ran over Jason's head.

One tripped and fell, where he was crushed beneath a Baggara stallion.

Treads reared up before him. Sucking everything into the crusher.

He dove out of the way.

Fire burning in the grass. Get away from it.

Shadow passing over me.

Shockwave throwing a horse and rider to the ground.

Shoot that one with pepper.

Two tanks colliding.

Rachel firing her gun. Looking deadly and beautiful.

A gap. Run for it.

Whump-whump-whump

Men fighting hand-to-hand. Stay low.

Another tank coming. The size of it!

No, it's hit by a rocket.

Trieu and Lewis dodging horsemen.

Chris tossing a smoke grenade.

Screaming man lunging at me with bayonet.

Sweep point away.

Grip the rifle stock.

Punch in face. Kick in solar plexus. Stab with bayonet.

No, don't stab.

Throw gun down and move.

The earth rippling like water?
Men climbing on a muddy tank. Trying to get in.
Opening the hatch. Grenade.
Tank swerves. Men falling off.
Grenade!
Am I hurt?
Where is my team?
Arm with no man.
Not my arm.
Garth pulling a man off a horse. Good, go there.
A nice rain shower.
Pushed from behind. Roll over.
Baggara cutting down with his sword.
Arms up!
Baggara bayoneted. Pushed off me. His blood's on my face.
Trampled by my rescuer.
Roll up. Move toward the hill.
More tanks.
Who is that screaming?
Is that rocket turning to chase that MiG?
So many bodies.
Look, most of the tanks are past me now.
Chris in front of me, motioning me to him.
The others are there.
They're yelling at me but I can only see their lips move.
Trieu is pulling Garth's boot off. There's no blood but his leg is bending where he's not supposed to have a knee.
Is Lewis crying?
I need to go back to them now. They need me.

It's actually hard to read the extended section of one-line paragraphs, isn't it? Sort of like drinking two cans of Monster energy drink and then going to a party. I've never again written a passage like this, and I'm not necessarily recommending it for you.

But I think it's a good example of how paragraph length contributes to the perceived speed of the moment.

Long paragraphs, as we have seen, physically slow the eye down. It takes longer to get through a page when there's very little white space. Conversely, shorter paragraphs allow the eye to race down the page. It takes slightly less time to read over a whole page like that, as you may have experienced in the example above. When you're progressing more quickly down a page and more quickly flipping to the next page, your book has quite literally become a page-turner.

When you want the reader to feel breathless, as if things are speeding up in the story, start creating shorter paragraphs. Go shorter and shorter until you reach the most frenzied portion of the scene, at which point you'd go to one-line and one-word paragraphs. Then, if you're easing out of the panic and things are slowing down again, consciously move to longer sentences and paragraphs.

This is subtle but übereffective.

Paragraph length: It is your friend. It is a powerful tool. Use it to your advantage.

the hop-over-and-recap error

I've seen the following practice so many times from so many authors that I now understand it to be a widespread and apparently "natural" error. Years ago, when I first started seeing it, I thought it was so odd that it must've been simply the proclivity of one or two authors. But now I know otherwise.

I'm referring to the practice of hopping over some important event in the story and then giving a recap of it later.

Thus:

> "No, really: What do you see up there?"
>
> While they had been talking, John had been constructing a strange device, which he now used to shoot down the invading aircraft. "Nothing now."

Let me explain: We've been reading this scene in which two or more characters on the ground have been harassed by an aircraft. The tension is high, the enemy airplane is bent on murderous intent, the characters may die ... but then we find out that John had been constructing a weapon all along.

Really? When? I mean, we were there the whole time, sitting on the front row of the story, and we never saw any stinking "device."

Grr.

Another example. For many chapters of a novel we've been looking forward to some event—a championship football game, let's say. It's the key moment in the character's life, when all of his dreams will be either fulfilled or dashed. We stay by his side through practices and qualifying games and team morale variations and scary injuries. We pull for him with his studies and his girlfriend and his leadership on the team. Finally, the day arrives. He suits up and steps onto the field. And ... the scene ends.

The next chapter is him on the phone with a friend:

> "Yeah, it was great. Winning the championship was awesome. What? No, I threw four touchdowns, not three. Huh? Oh, yeah, she kissed me after the game. Hmm? Yes, I did talk to college scouts. It's looking good for UCLA!"

If you do that, your reader will be ticked. She paid her dues with you. She slogged through scenes she maybe didn't care all that much about. She dutifully read every page. All because she was connected to this character and wanted to see how things turned out for him.

And you reward her by skipping over the main event and recapping it after the fact?

Your reader will feel cheated, and rightfully so. Might as well cut the attack on the Death Star and just have C-3P0 summarize later how the battle went.

I'm not sure why writers skip over important things and then try to make up for it by giving a summary of events later, but I've seen it enough to know it's a fairly common error.

Please don't.

Remember our beloved Commandment: You must engage your reader from beginning to end. One way of violating that rule is to deprive her of the opportunity to witness things she cares about in your story. An angry reader is not an engaged reader.

> When Fred and Irene had refused to take the medicine,
> their enforcers had held them down and made them take
> it. "You will take it!" they had said. "And you will like it."

The "had refused," "had held" and "had said" bits tip us off to the fact that this isn't a scene we're watching but a scene we missed. But how could we have missed it? We didn't go anywhere. We've been reading every word, but somehow we missed it? Next you'll tell us that the wedding happened offstage too and someone will come in and recap it for us.

The skipping over and recapping later can come in small ways too:

> Wilfred walked down the passageway toward the com-
> mand bridge, stepping aside so Iggy and Ug could pass.

This one may not bother you at first, but notice that Iggy and Ug are gone before we even knew they were there. It would've been less irritating to the reader if he had seen Iggy and Ug coming down the passageway—with, perhaps, some description of them—and had then seen Wilfred step aside to let them pass. By not establishing that they were there and by telling us about them only after their time on stage is over, the writer has hopped over the event.

Do enough of these skips, even if they're all small like this one, and your reader will give up on your book. She may not realize what's happening to her or why, but she'll find herself feeling more and more frustrated with your book. A frustrated reader is not an engaged reader.

When you cause things to happen outside of the reader's vision, despite her every effort to witness those things, you make her feel left out. Staved off. Pushed away. Shouldered out of the in crowd. Such a feeling does not help her remain engaged in your story from beginning to end.

Now, I'm not saying you have to show the reader every single thing your characters do. We don't want to see them in the bathroom, for instance, or picking their nose or doing mundane things that don't advance the story or reveal character. Of course you can have things happen offstage in your book.

But when it comes to the events of greatest import to the main characters (and thus the reader), they must happen onstage. Nor can the reader be made to feel that her powers of observation are defective because something was happening right in front of her but she didn't notice. To paraphrase Robbie Hart from *The Wedding Singer*, "That's information that would've been useful *yesterday!*" Don't deprive the reader of what she wants to witness (unless you're doing so to conceal the murderer's identity or something else that's imperative to the story).

She's earned the right to watch it happen.

> "Oh, didn't I tell you? Last night the aliens came and took the president away. Sorry ... should've told you earlier, I guess."
>
> "Dear me," he had said, after having discovered the aliens and scaring them away. "Yes, that would've been nice to know."
>
> As they talked, she had created a UFO-finding device right there in the Oval Office, which he had then used to find and retrieve the president. "There," he had said, "that's better."
>
> The president left after telling them everything that had happened to him.

"Whew," she had said, "what a story!"

"I know!" he had answered. "Glad I didn't miss *that!*"

One thing about skipping over major events and merely summarizing them later is that it's a lot easier on the writer. Why go to all the trouble of writing out a huge scene when it's much quicker and simpler to just get a recap from someone who was there?

Why? Well, because it's lazy writing, and because it leaves the reader feeling cheated, excluded, and disengaged.

If you find you have skipped over anything the reader should've seen or would've noticed had he actually been there, I urge you to cut the recap and replace it with a full dramatization of the event.

the invisible novelist

In the Victory about description, I mentioned philosophies of fiction, but I didn't go into the idea. Let's do so now.

Whether you realize it or not, you have a philosophy of fiction. It's a whole worldview, a constellation of opinions and preferences that determines what you feel a novel should and shouldn't be like. You've arrived at this philosophy by reading novels and watching movies over the years. Maybe even from writing fiction, studying fiction craftsmanship, and/or critiquing other people's fiction.

The fiction that arises from your philosophy will resonate most with people who share your philosophy. For instance, if you feel a novel ought to be a formula-free tale of open-ended exploration without commentary or theme that ends with the death of the "hero," that's what you're going to write ... and the people who will love it most will be those who feel the same way about what a novel ought to be.

For the most part, you don't have control over what sort of people read your novel or what philosophy they may have. You just have to know that part of why a novel succeeds or fails is to what degree it connects with readers who feel the same way about fiction as the author does. There are many other factors, as well, but this is one.

One decision you have already made, even if you're not aware of doing so, is whether or not you believe that the novelist should be visible to the reader.

By that, I mean whether it is the story and characters or the language and sentence structure that the reader most notices. Is your goal to make your own presence disappear so as to create the illusion that the reader has been transported into the story, or is your goal to rejoice with the reader in shared revelry of beautiful, sensual language?

When you come to fiction, what are you most drawn to: amazing story and characters or incredible artistry of the written word? Whichever you like best in the fiction you read is what you're going to want to create in the fiction you write. You're going to try to create for your reader the same pleasure you receive when you read the sort of fiction you love best.

Here's a passage from *The Beautiful Room Is Empty* by Edmund White:

> She was talking to a young man who seemed all hair, a haystack of hair; his shoulder-length hair merged into a russet-highlighted beard, which in turn seemed to grow into his brown poncho, to be its father. Maria was wielding a cigarette unconvincingly, sipping wine, and squinting. But when I glanced back a moment later, she was wide-eyed and laughing. Her smile looked so clean, as white as the whites of her eyes. She was really laughing in an almost soundless quake, but her eyes were blind with tears of amusement. When Ivan introduced us, she wiped away the tears and dialed down the brilliance of her smile.

I actually quite like this passage. Fans admire White's beautiful prose and the texture of his language. Can't you just feel words like *russet* and *quake* and *poncho*?

But I've seen books that go beyond this into a realm we might call purple prose. In those cases, it is obviously the language itself that is the star of the show. Plot and character are secondary to the words chosen to convey them. I suspect it takes at least two to three times longer to *craft* a sentence than it does to just *write* one. But the payoff can be large … when you find a reader who desires prose that calls attention to itself.

To a reader who prefers not to be forced to notice the language of a novel, "painted prose" can seem like it was written by an insecure author saying, "Look at me! I'm smart! I use fancy words!"

That reader would prefer that the novelist render herself invisible. That reader wants the mechanism of the story—the vocabulary and the way the words are strung together—to vanish, leaving the reader in the world of the story. The words are utilities, vehicles, in service to something else, not things to be admired in their own right.

The invisible novelist does everything she can to be unobtrusive. It is the characters and their plight, not the words on the page, that she wants the reader to notice. She actually wants the reader to be so utterly transported into the story that he forgets he's reading a book at all. She certainly doesn't want to seem to be waving a flag to draw attention to herself. Therefore, anything, including an odd word choice, that knocks the reader out of that illusion is to be *eschewed* (if I might go purple myself a moment).

Which philosophy of fiction is right? Both, of course.

Imagine two people gazing at a work of art in a museum. One is struck by the image and the overall impact of the painting. The other may not even notice or care what the painting's subject is but moves up as close as the security guards will allow in order to discern the individual brushstrokes and heaping up of pigment. The former wants to be wowed by the painting; the latter wants to be wowed by the painter. One wants the brushstrokes to disappear; the other wants the hand of the artist to be clearly on display.

You probably know which kind of writer you are, or at least in which direction you lean. The Great Commandment of Fiction works for you either way, but you come at it differently. If you're writing to the reader who appreciates astute alliteration, erudite vocabulary, luscious texture, and the brilliant turn of phrase, you keep your reader engaged from beginning to end by providing that on every page and in every paragraph. I don't envy you!

If you're writing to the more numerous, if more plebian, readers who prefer to escape into a story rather than the celebration of phraseology, you keep such a reader engaged from beginning to end by doing everything you can to make her forget she's reading a book. Your goal is immersion and transport.

Perhaps it is the difference between art and entertainment. Not that art can't be entertaining and entertainment can't be art. In any event, the Great Commandment applies. No matter your philosophy of fiction, and no matter how you go about it, if you keep your targeted reader engaged from beginning to end, you win.

conclusion

Eventually you need to start thinking about moving from the workshop into the showroom. The remainder of this book will be about taking your book into that place and bringing you Victory.

seeking publication

You have reached the part of the book that tells you what to do with this novel you've written in thirty days. Many people want to write a novel someday, but most of those who actually accomplish that feat are interested in more than just the accomplishment.

They'd really like to see their book on the shelf.

So anyone can read it. Even Aunt Betty, who said you'd never amount to much. Even your ex. Even your kids. Even your boss. Even people you've never heard of. *Especially* people you've never heard of.

As long as you've gone to all the work to write this thing, why not see if you can get it in print?

Let's explore how you might go about that.

the phases of "ready"

Some novelists are so eager to get published that they rush their rough draft right out to agents, editors, and friends of cousins whose neighbor's cat's veterinarian knows a guy who used to be in publishing.

I get this sort of e-mail on a regular basis. It has an undisclosed recipient list, begins with "To Whom It May Concern," and proceeds to gush about the sender's awesome manuscript, which is certain to be a bestseller, revolutionize publishing, and reinstate Pluto as a planet (Go, Team Pluto!).

The sender has obviously sent out a mass e-mail to everyone he could find. He certainly hasn't bothered to research any of the publishers he's contacting—obvious because the book he's pushing is a nonfiction book about snails, and I publish only speculative fiction with a supernatural edge.

In his eagerness to reach out to anyone who might possibly be interested, the only thing he has hastened to do is get his e-mail deleted. And, if the publisher has a good memory, to get himself put on a black list forever.

I don't know what helped you slog through the long, hard work of writing this novel. Possibly it was the thought of publication that kept you going. If that's true, even in part, I would urge you to apply the brakes and shift into park for a while.

If your book is amazing, it will get published. In truth, anything can get published, especially in today's publishing environment, and this will certainly be true of books of a higher quality. So there's no rush. It's not like today is the last day publishers will ever want to look at unpublished fiction, so you'd better hurry! We passed Y2K and the Mayan Doomsday pretty well, so until the real Apocalypse happens, fiction publishers will continue to need fiction manuscripts.

It's also not as though publishers have a dearth of excellent manuscripts to evaluate, so you'd better get yours in today. Nor is it (probably) the case that your idea is so breathtakingly original that 1) your book will be fabulously published even if it's not really ready and 2) you'd better copyright and trademark and bronze-plate it so everyone will know it's yours, your own … your Precious.

Let's just wait a bit, all right? It's much better to go slow, do your research, polish your novel, learn the biz, survey the landscape, and then send it off intelligently than it is to rush it out the door and think you can just sit back and wait for the fat royalty checks to start rolling in.

There are phases of readiness that every fiction manuscript, and every novelist, goes through. Or, rather, that every manuscript and novelist *should* go through. Today, it's possible for a book to be published long before it's ready, and that doesn't do anyone any favors, especially the author.

Here's the path an unpublished manuscript often takes:

- The author writes the novel.
- The author sends it (the full manuscript or just a proposal or query) to agents and publishers.
- The manuscript is rejected by everyone and his parrot.
- The author feels she wasn't cut out to be a novelist after all.
- The author gets mad/gets a second wind and starts trying to figure out why the book was so soundly rejected.
- The author learns to improve her fiction skills.
- The author learns the publishing landscape.
- The author meets lots of people in the industry.
- The author learns a better approach for sending out her much-improved manuscript and a better person or set of people to send it to.
- The author sends it out a second time (hoping no one remembers her first attempt) and either gets published or gets much closer to that goal.

Here's the path I'm urging you to take:

- You write your novel.
- You resist the urge to send it to everyone and his parrot.
- You go through this book and other teaching/critiquing aids to improve it to the highest level you're able to take it.
- You survey the publishing landscape and meet people in the industry.
- You research your publishing options.
- You start working on your marketing plan and platform
- You decide whether or not you want to attempt to procure a literary agent.
- You shop the book around in an intelligent manner and take charge of your publishing career.

Sound better? Let's talk about this path one step at a time.

improving your novel

You've already jogged down this particular road a fair distance, simply by applying the things you've learned in this book. But, as we've seen, there are always more books and articles to read!

Book learning is great, if you're someone who can learn from a book. I am that kind of person, and since you're reading this, I can assume you are. But other people learn in other ways. That's neither good nor bad, but simply how things are.

Your goal is to get your manuscript to the highest level of quality you can achieve. We know that the end user may not care about quality, but you should. Agents and editors certainly do (most say they do, at least). I'm hoping you'll take it upon yourself to learn the skills and techniques of excellent fiction, rather than simply paying someone else to take it beyond your level of capability or interest. I suspect you want to bring these skills onboard yourself or, again, you wouldn't have bothered to make it so far in this book.

So here are the tools and services that can elevate your novel and your fiction craftsmanship. Most serious writers will eventually use all the items on the list.

- **WRITE:** Simply writing lots of fiction will improve your writing on some levels. Certain things—not least the mastery of your word processor—will become second nature for you. Of course, if you're starting with bad habits, writing more and more might just solidify them; best to keep moving down this list.
- **READ GOOD FICTION:** Few things inspire you to perform at your utmost potential than examples you admire.
- **READ BOOKS AND ARTICLES ON CRAFT:** If you're a book learner, by all means avail yourself of the many books on the craft of fiction writing. Writer's Digest has a wonderful selection of winners, as do other publishers. But book learning may not be your style, and in any case a book

can take you only so far; sometimes it's very difficult to take what the book advocates and discern whether you're doing it or not doing it in your own writing. That's where objective eyes help.

- **USE CRITIQUE PARTNERS:** If you don't have a crit partner yet or aren't already a member of a (healthy) critique group, consider doing something about that posthaste. A good crit partner/group can be hugely valuable not only in helping you see what has become invisible to you and in giving you constructive feedback about how to improve your manuscript, but also in giving you access to people who have perhaps been studying publishing longer than you have and may be able to help you understand what's going on in that world.

- **GO TO WRITERS CONFERENCES:** Unless you live far out in the sticks, the chances are good that there is an annual writers conference within driving distance of your home, and many across the United States are worth flying out to. The three great things about writers conferences are 1) you meet other crazy people like yourself (including folks who might be future critique partners for you), 2) you get advice about craft and the industry from experts in the field (the larger conferences are more likely to have a world-class faculty than the locals, but sometimes the little ones can surprise you), and 3) you get direct access to literary agents and editors from publishing houses and can pitch your manuscript directly to them. The latter reason is the best benefit for going to these events. How better to learn the industry and get "in" with pros than to meet them face to face? Invest in yourself and go to a writers conference this year.

- **JOIN AN ONLINE FICTION TRAINING SERVICE:** A phenomenon of the 21st century is the rise of online training services for pretty much anything you want to get trained in. I operate Fiction Academy (at www.BestsellerSociety. com), which contains streaming video of all of my teaching plus access to myself and other industry professionals, fellow novelists, marketing experts, and live events. There are several services like this popping up all the time now. Nothing like having the writers conference experience without shelling out hundreds or thousands of dollars or having to leave home or even take off your fuzzy slippers. The other benefit of these is that, if you can find one with a good teacher, your level of instruction will be consistently high (while the quality of teaching you get at writers conferences is hit or miss), plus you can watch the videos over and over rather than having to rely on the notes you took when you heard it live.

- **HIRE A FREELANCE EDITOR:** This one will require us to break out of our lovely bulleted list and go back to paragraph form. Read on.

working with a freelance editor

In my mind, there is nothing more valuable you can do to improve your novel—and your own writing skill—than to work with a freelance editor. Editors are, after all, professionals at taking a promising manuscript and turning it into the sort of excellence we expect from major publishing houses. They can take a C+ manuscript and turn it into an A manuscript. And, since most of the aforementioned major publishing houses have fired their editors and dumped them onto the freelance market, you have access to virtuosos who you'd not be able to so much as meet, unless you were under contract at that house.

The problem is that there are also exactly one bajillion lousy freelance editors out there, and you probably have no way of knowing which is which.

You can't rely on the fact that someone calls herself a professional editor, because you could call yourself that. You could even have business cards printed up saying so, whether it's true or not. You can't rely on the fact that the person previously worked as an editor at a publishing house, because some publishing houses employ lousy editors.

Even if you find a bona fide professional editor who has experience with fiction, you can't know that she's any good. Perhaps everything she'll say about your manuscript is exactly wrong—or wrong for you. How would you know? Well, you might have a little knowledge of what's what if you've done the other items on the bulleted list you just read, but as we've seen many times in this book, even writers of fiction how-to books and articles don't agree with one another.

It's enough to boggle the mind and tempt you to skip this phase altogether. But I urge you to persist. If you can find an editor who is truly helpful, you will have found a gold mine. Nothing is more beneficial to you and your career than a terrific fiction editor.

finding a great freelance editor

First, ask around. Have your writing friends worked with a freelancer they found especially helpful? Why not start there?

Second, do your homework. When you get a name, check out the person's webpage, blog, or Facebook presence. See if you connect with his personality and style as expressed there. See also if you can find his rates.

Most people new to writing get sticker shock when they learn how much freelance editors cost. Of course you can pay much less and much more, but to receive a full enchilada edit on a 100,000-word manuscript, you can expect to pay $2,500–$5,000. And upwards of $8,000–$12,000 or more for the award winners and very best editors in the industry. You can pay less than this, but sometimes you get what you pay for. Other times, you pay a lot and *don't* get what you pay for. Which brings us back to our question of how not to get burned.

Check Preditors & Editors (pred-ed.com) for that person's name. The site lists people who have been identified as scam artists. Granted, some people are unfairly placed on that list, so don't take it as gospel. But if you find that person's name on the preditors side, apply caution. Ask the editor for references, then actually communicate with the references.

In the end, there's no better way to find out if an editor is going to be a good fit for you than to have her edit your fiction. Some editors will do sample edits for you (two to ten double-spaced pages is common) for free. Others will charge you a small fee to do so. Find out how much it would cost for that person to do a full edit on the opening ten to twenty pages of your manuscript. Chances are it would be a lot more affordable to do this— between fifty and two hundred dollars, probably—than to go for the full edit without first taking this step.

Then, if you like what the person did on the sample edit, and if you believe it will truly improve your book and your writing, go for it. Maybe take the plunge and pay for the full edit or have her do another segment of your book. You're the boss here, so you can work within your budget. At worst, if you don't like what the editor has done, or maybe she did almost nothing to the pages but happily took your two Benjamins, you can just keep looking for the right editor.

Editors have been known to take novels that would otherwise quickly fall upon the literary trash heap and turn them into award winners and/or bestsellers.

I can't tell you how many novelists have come to me, in my role as freelance editor and book doctor, wondering what in the world is going on with all of these rejections. They've struck out, and they want to know why. Abandoning their notion that they could just write it, send it out, and get famous, they're finally willing to get serious about improving it.

That's another thing you want to look for in an editor: Can he diagnose what's working and what's not working in your manuscript? Perhaps instead of paying two hundred dollars to have him do a trial edit, instead pay whatever he charges to simply read through the whole manuscript and give you a brief write-up of what he sees as the strengths, weaknesses, and the way forward for your book (this is sometimes called an editorial review).

understanding publishing today

Getting your novel up to snuff may take you a while—up to a year or even longer. Don't be in a hurry. Before the aforementioned Apocalypse, publishers will continue to need new fiction manuscripts to publish.

The next two items on our big bulleted list above are to survey the publishing landscape and meet people in the industry and to research your publishing options. I'll address those together.

First, let's talk about understanding the publishing landscape. By which I mean exploring whether you're hoping to be traditionally published, to self-publish, or to try a new publishing option.

going traditional or nontraditional

In general, it is more blessed to be paid than to pay. When it comes to having your novel published, it's always ideal to have someone other than you shell out the cash for bringing it to market. Thus the traditional publishing avenue is the one most people would prefer to take.

In that scenario, the writer receives an advance (some amount of money, usually between $1,500 and $12,000 for first-time novelists), takes the manuscript through a professional edit, receives a professionally produced cover, and sees his novel released nationally in bookstores and online. If the book ever breaks even ("earns out"), the author will begin receiving royalty payments periodically.

For generations, this has been the primary publishing model in America. It's still what people think of when they think of getting published. Their imaginings also usually include multi-city book tours, champagne parties in Manhattan, and movies based on the book.

As you might guess, this didn't happen very often, even in the heyday of publishing.

We are no longer in said heyday. The downturn in the economy, the rise of electronic publishing, and a shift in the mood of the day has brought about the slow collapse of that model. It will hang around for a while in much smaller form, but for the most part, the Golden Age is long gone.

Novelist Athol Dickson sums it up nicely:

> "Authors no longer need traditional publishers (or their contracts) for editing, cover design, interior design, bulk printing discounts, warehousing, distribution, marketing, promotion, or sales. The only thing left is management (i.e., oversight of the above so the author doesn't have to think about it) and the advance, which means the industry has been reduced to offering nothing authors can't do themselves except for providing venture capital.
>
> I can't think of any other industry that survived after becoming irrelevant in nine out of ten of the key services it offered—unless the players made massive structural changes to their way of doing business, and we've seen none of that."

In the place of the traditional publishing model has come a panoply of new publishing opportunities. Small presses, niche presses, print on demand (POD), e-publishing, app publishing, transmedia, and, of course, self-publishing have exploded onto the scene, and we find ourselves hip deep in a publishing revolution.

Many authors—primarily those who were living high under the old publishing model—have bemoaned these changes. Large traditional publishers are folding or being purchased and combined. Bookstores are closing in droves. Consequently, the remaining traditional publishers are being even more conservative than they were before. Advances are smaller, they're taking fewer chances on new authors, and beloved midlist authors—many of the names you know—are finding themselves without new contracts. Publishers compete for the few surefire home run hitters, and everyone else is left in the dugout.

So it's no wonder that authors are complaining about these changes. But I have maintained for years that there's never been a better time to be a writer. Never, as in ever. As in since the dawn of mankind.

Until today, restrictions on how easily a writer could reach a reader with her message existed. Before Gutenberg, the restriction was that only the clergy and a few others even knew how to write or had access to mass production of printed material. Then you had to have great wealth to use that movable type press and get the books out to people far and wide. Back then, it was the large publishers who put up the money for books to be made and distributed, and so they were the ones who controlled what got published and what did not. And what got published was what would sell enough units to pay off the large cost of producing and distributing the book.

Nowhere in there did the small-time author sitting at his desk have the ability to get his book broadcast to the world. Sure, we've had self-publishing for a while, but it was exceedingly rare for a self-published book to reach a wide readership. Most such books ended up in boxes gathering dust in the (poorer) author's garage. And yes, we've had the Internet for a while, but so long as the old publishing model was going strong and e-readers were rare, most electronically published books never reached a wide readership, despite the technical possibility for it to happen.

But now, today, for free, you could upload your manuscript to Amazon, and people across the globe could be reading it on their Kindles in minutes. You could begin collecting money from your writing before you went to bed tonight.

But wait. There are a billion reasons why you might not want to do that and why you probably wouldn't make much money tonight. Still, the point remains that you *could*. You have at your disposal the potential to reach tens of millions of readers without any up-front cost to you and without any middleman (other than Amazon or whoever).

It's a great day especially for the previously marginalized sort of book and the previously marginalized sort of author. Before, if you weren't writing what was perceived to be "hot," you couldn't get published at all. Those lightly esteemed off-genres like true crime or Western or military or Christian fantasy/SF or whatever were simply out of the question.

Now it's possible to get *your* novel to *exactly* the readership who wants *exactly* what you like to write.

There's never been a time like this in history, and I hope you take advantage of it.

The question for you, then, becomes whether you want to pursue traditional or nontraditional publishing.

My counsel is to try to get paid before deciding you're going to pay. Unless you know without a doubt that your book will simply never, ever find a publisher who wants to take it on (and pay you for it), I recommend giving that option a try.

Here's the hierarchy you might consider:

- Find a large traditional publisher who will pay you an advance, give your book a full edit and a good cover and marketing support, and all the trimmings.
- Find a midsized traditional publisher who will pay you an advance and do as many of the other things as possible.
- Find a small traditional publisher who will pay you an advance and do as many of the other things as possible.
- Find a niche publisher who will either pay you an advance or at least not charge you anything. Hopefully they will give you a decent edit and cover and other stuff, but very little marketing, probably.

- Find a custom publishing company that will allow you to self-publish for free or very little expense (research CreateSpace and Lulu for starters).
- Cobble together your own publishing team (editor, cover designer, copy editor, typesetter, marketer, printer, and any others you need), each of whom you pay as freelancers; you bear the expenditures but you retain complete control and can pull the plug whenever you wish (so long as you pay what you owe, of course).
- E-publish only (hopefully after using a freelance editor and cover designer, at the least) and see if there is enough reader interest to go to a print version of the book through print on demand.
- Pay lots of money to a self-publishing company that offers a package you like and can afford.

Each of these options has advantages and disadvantages, and each one could be the right solution for you at different points in your publishing career.

If you go with self-publishing—either in print or electronic form, or both—understand that there is no guarantee you'll make back your money. In fact, probabilistically speaking, you won't recoup your expenses (unless you go the free route). To have the best chance of recovering your money, you'll need to do lots of marketing, which we'll address later.

The myth being propagated out there today is that all you have to do is e-publish a book and it will be hugely successful. But the "If you build it, they will come" approach is, indeed, a myth. Sure, the guys who already have big sales can put out a new e-book and it will sell a million copies. But that same dynamic doesn't work for 99.99 percent of the rest of the authors putting out e-books.

Many authors turn to self-publishing ("custom publishing," it's called now) for strategic reasons. They're hoping to make such a big splash with their self-published book that it will attract the interest of those few remaining traditional publishers, who will come calling with a six- or seven-figure advance. (I refer you to the 99.99 percent figure again—but it does sometimes happen.)

Or perhaps they are already published but they are feeling stymied by their traditional publishing contracts. The going wisdom used to be that someone known for writing legal thrillers shouldn't start writing zombie books, but the author may frankly want to write zombie books, so he does it on his own via custom publishing. And in some cases, it works fabulously.

The other great thing about custom publishing is that you keep most of the dough yourself. Yes, you have to pay out to get the thing published, but after that, all the profit comes to you. You'll have to give some to Amazon or whatever, but the lion's share of the profits finds its way to your *pocketses*. And if you do recoup your expenses, you have the chance for serious money.

The clout of traditional publishing houses is fading. Even if you do land a contract with one of them, it may not include an edit! You almost certainly won't get much marketing support. You could end up paying for those things out of your own pocket, after all. And as for getting your book into bookstores, there are fewer and fewer of those establishments every day. Suddenly novelists are beginning to look around and say, "Wait, tell me again why I need a publishing house?" The answer is usually a silence punctuated only by chirping crickets.

Now, again, it's more blessed to be paid than to pay. But times have changed in publishing, and traditional publishing houses have gone from being the only legitimate game in town to being merely one of many good alternatives.

exploring the publishing industry

Simultaneous with your efforts to raise your manuscript to the highest level of fiction craftsmanship you can attain, you should begin working to learn the publishing industry.

The best ways to do that are to 1) read industry magazines and blogs and 2) go to writers conferences.

The primary publishing industry magazine is *Publishers Weekly*, which you can usually find in your library, or you can buy a subscription and read it online. *PW* has great book reviews and articles on trends, but it also covers news in the industry. It is the magazine that publishing professionals themselves read. Another good one is *Library Journal.*

With a little snooping around online, you can find blogs written by influential people in the publishing industry. Peruse a copy of *PW*, note the names of editors and agents being quoted, and then search for blogs by those people online. Some terrific material awaits you.

Then consider writers conferences again. If you attend three major writers conferences in the field of publishing that you hope to break into—and if you put yourself out there while you attend, actually introducing yourself to faculty, pitching your novel's idea to agents and editors (even if it's not "ready," you can do so just for practice and feedback), and having appointments with faculty in which you just ask for advice—you will quickly gain a working grasp on the publishing industry.

If you could attend all three conferences in a six-month period, you'd really have your finger on the pulse of it. Or, at least as much as someone on the periphery can have a finger on the pulse of any industry.

Plus, going to writers conferences allows you to become familiar with people who are in a position to help you get your book published through the traditional publishing route (i.e., the one where you receive money for your book). After the conference, you can contact those people via e-mail, remind them about your great meeting at the conference, and ask if they'd like to see your latest manuscript or proposal. Agents and editors are more likely to respond to you well and in a timely manner if they've met you.

marketing

Right away, let me say that no one knows how to market fiction successfully. Oh, sure, if you're in charge of promoting the next J.K. Rowling book and you have an unlimited budget, you can do it. But when it comes to an author whom most people haven't heard of—and when you're doing it on a limited budget—it's not so easy. Indeed, it defies understanding.

If there were a surefire way to successfully market a novel, everyone would be doing it and every book so marketed would be a runaway bestseller. But such is not the case. No one knows.

However, it is possible to do a number of things that can give your novel a statistical chance at becoming a bestseller. Most of the time, those things don't work. But books that do them are more likely to be successful (or less likely to be unsuccessful) than books that don't.

This isn't a book on marketing, and I'm no expert on it. (That's why I don't run the marketing portion of Bestseller Society.com.) But I will say that marketing is all about letting people who would like your product know that your product exists. All of your marketing efforts, no matter how your book has gotten published, should be directed toward getting it in front of potential lovers of your book in a way that makes them want a copy for themselves.

I'll give you my 30:1 Rule of Marketing. For every thirty things you do to market your book, one of them will work. Unfortunately, you probably won't know which one of the thirty it was that worked, and even if you did know and you repeated it, it wouldn't work again. So you have to keep doing your thirties to get the ones.

But this rule works very nicely when applied to a monthly discipline. Every day, do one thing to market your book. Even if it's small, like sending an e-mail to a newspaper asking if they'd be willing to review your book. After roughly thirty days, you will have done roughly thirty things to promote your book ... and one of them will have found traction. You will do this until you finally have enough ones piled atop one another that word of mouth takes over.

If you can get to that point—and most books never do—it will take on a life of its own. I wish you every success!

what about before my book is published?

In the meantime, even before your book is published, you can and should be working to build your so-called publishing platform.

Books have been written on the subject of *platform*. Essentially platform is how many people will automatically buy your book as soon as it's available.

A writer who is also a national media personality—with, say, a syndicated radio talk show—has a massive platform. As soon as a book by this person it available, even for preorder, millions of people will buy it.

Most of us have a less impressive platform. Most of us, if our first novel came out, could count on a whole five or six people buying it. A platform of that size is not going to impress any publishers. They, of course, prefer authors who have large built-in audiences.

What can you do to build your platform? Start doing things that will cause more people to become aware of you. (Legal things, preferably.) Begin a blog that is not just about you and your writing journey but is about something that will appeal to the same reader who will love your novel when it comes out. Try to get speaking gigs that pertain to your book topic and ask if you can sell books at a table in the back. Write magazine articles on topics that appeal to the same readership you'll be after for your novel. For instance, if your novel is about a professional cookie baker, perhaps you'll write an article on delicious Valentine's cookies.

If you're hoping to be traditionally published, you may not be able to build a platform large enough to impress them, not even if you worked on it for a year or more. But if you're in the market for a small press—and especially if you're self-publishing—you'll want as many people as possible to know about you before the book comes out.

Most novelists I know absolutely hate the idea of marketing. Either they shy away from self-promotion on ethical grounds or they're naturally mousy types who would rather write ten novels (or walk across a football field of hot coals) than market even one. If that's you, maybe save your energy from the blogging and speaking and instead save up money to hire a freelance publicity/marketing person (preferably one who rocks the social media sites) to do it for you if and when your book is released.

But even the mice among us can follow the 30:1 rule.

literary agents

It used to be that getting an agent was tantamount to getting published. If you could land an agent, it was thought, then getting published was just a matter of *when*, not *if.* Having an agent was the mark of an author with real promise. It also used to be that you pretty much couldn't get published if you didn't have an agent.

Times have changed. Now there are so many agents out there that simply having one doesn't mean much anymore. Indeed, anyone can hang out a shingle and say he or she is an agent, so it's harder to know if an author with an agent is any good. It follows that just having an agent doesn't necessarily make it a sure bet that the author will be published. Plus there are many more publishing possibilities that don't require an author to have an agent than there are publishing possibilities that do. Some small and/or new publishers these days don't like authors to have agents.

Some aspiring authors might be predisposed to think about agents as a negative force—those eternally elusive potential allies always on the side of *other* authors, or those people always sending rejection letters, or those great preventers-of-access to big publishing houses (and big publishing deals).

But I assure you that such is not the case.

agents are people, too

Most literary agents love books at least as much as you do. They are professional believers in authors whose hope every day is to help the authors they believe in find publishing success and a wide readership.

Some of us may have an image of literary agents as something akin to high-priced lawyers in expensive suits having power lunches in Manhattan cafés. That is sometimes their experience, especially when they meet with their well-dressed counterparts (editors) at publishing houses. But most of the time they're sitting at a desk not terribly different from yours looking at words on a screen and wracking their brains about how to help these authors fulfill their publishing dreams.

Traditional publishing companies turned to agents not to be exclusivist but simply to retain their sanity. In the old days, when writers could come to the publishing house and literally drop their manuscripts over the transom, publishers would accumulate the so-called slush pile. You can imagine the editor unlocking the door every morning and pushing aside that pile of manuscripts just to get into the office for the day.

Now fast-forward fifty years, and the publisher has had to remove its transom altogether. There came to be so many authors seeking publication that there was more slush pile than office space. Picture WALL-E's skyscrapers of trash transformed into skyscrapers of manuscripts. There's no way a publishing house can manage so many manuscripts, even electronic manuscripts, much less evaluate them with any seriousness, and do the other 90 percent of running a publishing house.

Enter literary agents.

If you're that overworked editor, what would you say to someone—a person who used to be an editor you worked with, let's say—who comes along and says, "You know, if you want, I could take all of these away from you, read through them, identify the very best, and bring to you the ones I know your publishing house would like"? You'd probably say yes before he'd even finished the sentence.

The transom has now been shifted from publisher to agent. They're the ones who get the real slush pile now. Agents perform a true service for publishers. Theoretically, the editor knows that, if an agent brings her a manuscript, it's extremely good. It's already been vetted by an industry pro and paired with this house. That's why most traditional publishing houses won't even accept a proposal for a book unless it comes through an agent. They need to have someone else verify its merit first.

the game changed on agents, too

Today, agents are fighting for their professional lives. With the slow sinking of traditional publishing companies comes the diminishing of agents' livelihood.

Legitimate agents don't make money on your book until you do. They take a cut from whatever money you receive from a publishing house. (That's how you can spot a scam artist agent, by the way: If he charges you money up front, *walk away.* You can also check Preditors & Editors.) Agents make their living by selling books to publishers. All well and good.

But what happens when publishers are folding? What happens when fewer and fewer houses are buying books? What happens when the houses that are holding on buy fewer and fewer books—and when the only authors they want are the guaranteed bestsellers? What happens when all the midlist authors on the agent's client list are no longer offered new contracts?

This is what's happening today, and suddenly agents are seeing their livelihoods dry up around them. There's less money coming in from publishers, which means there's simply less money for agents. When your income goes away, when someone moves your cheese, you're in trouble. It's time to adapt or die.

So agents are busily trying to reinvent themselves. They'll keep aiming for the remaining traditional houses, of course, but they're also feverishly researching new publishers, new publishing models, new publishing options, and, of course, new ways to generate revenue. Some are beginning to offer freelance editorial services. Some are becoming publishers themselves. Some are acting as matchmakers, connecting authors with freelance editors, cover designers, and the rest.

Some are getting out of publishing altogether.

We're in the midst of a publishing revolution. When revolutions happen in countries, the fate of the old regime is always in peril. Can they keep doing what they were doing, but in the new political landscape? Will they be swept aside? Will there be any place for them? Will they be able to reposition themselves and continue to prosper when the dust settles? So it is with agents right now.

should you try to get an agent?

In light of all of that, should you try to get an agent? I mean, if agents can't get contracts for their existing client base, including multipublished novelists you've heard of, will they be able to get a contract for you? Are they even *taking* new clients?

Whether or not you try to get an agent depends on your publishing strategy and your goals. If you dream to publish with a large traditional publishing house, you should certainly attempt to land a reputable agent. Without one, as we have seen, your book won't reach the desk of anyone at the publishing house.

(Going to a writers conference where editors from publishing houses will be on faculty is one way of bypassing this restriction. So if you're going to conferences and are willing to pitch to editors while you're there, you might not need an agent—but you might want an agent for other reasons. More on that in a moment.)

If you're not trying to get published by a traditional house, you may not need an agent. I've found that many agents don't even want to represent authors who aren't trying for the big houses. And you can understand why: If an agent gets paid out of your advance and royalties, and you're targeting houses that don't pay advances or royalties (or don't pay much), why would an agent want to represent you? Fifteen percent of not much is … not much. They have to pay their bills, too.

I said above that you should attempt to land a *reputable* agent. It's a lot harder to become a client of a high-powered agent than it is to sign with someone who is just starting out … or someone who doesn't know publishing at all. Those agents are usually pretty easy to get. But would that be a good thing, if they have no ability to get your book before the acquisitions editors at the major houses?

Researching agents is somewhat like researching freelance editors. One way to find names of agents is to check the copyright page of novels that are similar to yours. Many times, the literary agency is listed there, and you can look them up online once you have their names. This tells you that the agent likes books like yours and might be willing to take another in the same genre. You can also find agents' names in the annual *Writer's Market* put out by Writer's Digest Books, or a similar annual publishing guide.

Once you have names, research these agents online. Visit their webpages, Facebook pages, and especially their blogs. Look for information about who their other clients are (some of whom you might contact to ask about the agent), whether or not they're taking new clients, what writers conferences they might be attending soon, what genres they're looking for, what their writer's guidelines are, and how best to contact them.

Part of your research should include looking them up on Preditors & Editors (pred-ed.com). But keep in mind, again, that some names listed there shouldn't be. And some folks who aren't on there should be. Still, it's a good place to start.

three reasons to try to get an agent

If you're trying to get published by a traditional publishing house—and I remind you again that it is more blessed to be paid than to pay—then you'll probably want to try to land a good agent.

There are three great reasons to do so.

First, agents are the only ones who can get your book in front of editors at the large traditional publishing houses. If you have a relative who works at that publishing house or if you pitch to one of these editors at a writers conference, you can possibly by-pass this reason for having an agent.

But even if you have an in with one or two of these houses, you won't have the full range of options in front of you like a good agent will. Such an agent will be on a first-name basis with every acquisitions editor at every sizable publishing house in their chosen category. She will know every house's reputation, every house's current and previous bestsellers, and every acquisitions editor's preferences. She will know exactly which houses might be the best fit for your book and exactly which editors to pitch it to.

One great thing about having an agent is that she can often get you a higher advance than you could without an agent. However, since 15 percent of your advance will go to the agent's cut, you might not actually feel the increase in advance. But it's still nice to get it.

Let's say you don't have an agent but you are nevertheless able to present your book to an acquisitions editor at a large house, and let's say that editor has championed the book in-house and things are in final deliberations—or maybe you've even been offered a contract. At that point, you'll find it much easier to land an agent. Go up to one and say you got your book through the door at a publishing house, and you'll be much more likely to get his attention. You've done a large part of his job for him, you see.

But before you let that give you a bad taste about agents, consider the other two great reasons for having an agent.

The second reason is that a good agent speaks contract-ese. Publishing contracts are written in a language so arcane that only the priesthood can understand it. A good agent is in that elite group. She knows that a publishing contract is completely geared in favor of the publishing company, not the author, and she knows what areas have wiggle room and what areas don't. She knows how to get the author better terms than what is offered in the initial contract. She can play hardball if she has to. She can secure better e-publishing terms and can be sure there is a true clause for a book being put out of print (you want this, trust me).

The typical new author will look at a publishing contract offered by a house and 1) be so thrilled to have one at all that he'll just sign it and send it off before the publisher changes its mind, and 2) read the first *herewith* and become baffled, giving in to the mind-set that it's all Greek so he'll just have to trust that there's nothing in there that he'd regret agreeing to.

A story I recently heard reveals that doing so is not a good idea. It's about a sixty-page publishing contract offered by a large traditional house to an author who had achieved great success self-publishing. The contract was ostensibly for future books by the author. He didn't realize until he'd signed it and sent it back that buried on page 28 was a clause saying that any new edition of the popular self-published book would belong to the publishing company. Yikes!

Publishers aren't usually out to rip you off, but in this day of sinking ships, they're more likely to try to structure their contracts to help them stay afloat. If you are offered a contract by a publishing house, it would behoove you to have a good agent in your corner translating it and dancing the dance with the publishing house for you.

The third great reason to have an agent is to have her handle conflict with the publishing house. It is a lot more common than you might think for publishers and authors to get annoyed with each other. Maybe the publisher doesn't follow through with something verbally promised. Maybe the author misses a deadline. Maybe the publisher produces a truly awful cover. Maybe the author refuses to be edited. It's wonderful for both parties to have an agent in the mix.

The author calls up the agent and rails to him about a lousy thing the publisher has done to her. The agent then contacts the publishing house and has a calm, businesslike discussion, using the lingo of the biz and a common knowledge of the realities of publishing, to see if he can get things straightened out. Or the editor calls the agent and rails about what a stinker the author is becoming. The agent then calls the author and has a kind and supportive, career-building talk with her to see if she and her editor can come to some workable solution.

Because the agent has acted as intermediary, the next time the author and editor talk, they can do so as old friends and as if nothing had ever gone pear-shaped between them. Ah, peace.

I hope it's clear that a good agent is all but necessary if you're aiming for a traditional publishing deal. But if you're shooting for one of the lower bullets on our publishing hierarchy list, do you still need one? *Can* you still get one?

I'd say that it's best to have as many friends in publishing as you can. If you can land an agent with her understanding that you might not be aiming for traditional publishers (most agents will stop the conversation right there)—it's rarely going to be a bad thing. Agents can often give you not only career guidance but an insider's perspective on the publishing industry, both of which are very good things. So if you can do it, do it.

Keep in mind that the agent works for you, not the other way around. I know it's almost impossible to keep that perspective, especially when agents are the ones determining whether or not you can even enter into a contract agreement to work together. I mean, how many McDonald's employees made McDonald's jump through hoops before they'd agree to work there? None, probably.

So it is with an author-agent relationship. You may not feel like she works for you, but she does. If she doesn't do what she promised, or if she just can't seem to get your book in front of any of the right editors or houses, you can fire her. Signing with an agent isn't like getting married, after all. It's more of a business relationship, sort of like signing on to a cable TV service provider. If you find another one you like later, cut ties and go with the new one.

Of course, publishing is not so large an industry that you can burn any bridges you want, so if you do cut ties with an agent, do so amicably. Keep it in mind, however, that you can cut ties if you're not happy or if it's just not a good fit.

conclusion

The last step on the path I recommended for you earlier in this Victory is to shop the book around in an intelligent manner and take charge of your publishing career.

what to do next

You have written a novel. Amazing. Congratulations are well deserved. If you've done it in thirty days, you've earned a champion's laurels. Most of this book is about helping you accomplish that.

But the second part of this book's title is about what to do with your book now that you've written it.

So far in Part Three I've helped you revise the book, understand the publishing climate, and consider your options. It's time to pull it all together.

This Victory, our last together, begins with my thoughts and concludes with quotations from people across the publishing industry—agents, editors, and novelists alike—offering counsel on what you ought to do with this baby now that you've given birth to it.

whither wander you?

From the Bard:

> Puck: How now, spirit! whither wander you?
> Fairy: Over hill, over dale,
> Thorough bush, thorough brier,
> Over park, over pale,
> Thorough flood, thorough fire,
> I do wander every where.

As a novelist with a completed manuscript in your pocket, you are a powerful individual. You're like Senator Thompson in *The Ides of March* who has 356 convention delegates to give to whichever candidate he chooses to support. You have a whole lot of goodness that you want to bestow upon the reading public. But how to best do it? Whither wander you now?

I find myself shaking my head as I reread that paragraph. Just a few years ago, I wouldn't have been able to truthfully write such a thing. The publishing monolith worked very hard, even if not always intentionally, to make the individual author feel insignificant. A mere cog in the wheel. A secondary player. Something rather like a person's appendix. Okay to have, possibly, but just as easily removed and discarded.

In those days, the power resided with the publisher and the bookstore hegemony.

Those days are gone.

Now an author can get her fiction directly to her readership—and collect a much heartier share of the profits. Now authors are finding they may not need a publisher at all. For generations, publishers have looked down their noses at small presses and self-publishers. "When you're ready to be *truly* published," they'd say, "try coming to us. But you'll have to wait your turn like everybody else." Now publishers have changed their tune. They're more likely to say, "Hey, don't forget us! We provide value, too!" The truth that had gotten lost was that publishers need authors, or they die.

I don't mean to pooh-pooh traditional publishing houses. They really do offer great value and prestige, plus distribution, industry acumen, editorial wisdom, and more. Plus, they pay! But no longer are they the only, or even necessarily the best, game in town.

Which is the right publishing solution for you?

In the previous Victory, I listed eight publishing avenues that stretched out before you. Everything from finding a large traditional publishing house to paying for a package deal at a self-publishing house. Before you had a finished manuscript in hand, all of these paths were closed to you. With a finished manuscript in hand, all of them are (at least theoretically) open to you.

Here are four strategies you might consider for you and your book.

strategy #1:
work from the top down

In this strategy, which is probably the most common one employed today, you'd start at the top of the publishing hierarchy I've established and work your way down the list.

You'd first target the largest traditional publishing houses: the big five (or however many are left by the time you read this). You'd have to secure an agent to be considered at these houses, so that would probably be your first step.

I won't lie to you about your chances at these houses. Unless you have some remarkable in or an unlikely stroke of luck, you're probably not getting in with them. Don't misunderstand: I hope you do, and I'd love for you to write me and tell me how you proved me wrong. But I'm not optimistic about anyone new landing a deal at one of those houses.

As a side note: Watch out for these large houses and their self-publishing schemes. Several traditional houses are trying to stay in business (er, expand their portfolio of profit profiles) by offering to publish authors *if the authors pay*. So you might get a book out by one of the most famous publishing houses in the country, but not in the way you'd dreamed. When you foot the bill, you're self-publishing, no matter what it's being called ("premier publishing," "hybrid publishing," etc.) and no matter what publisher's name is on the spine.

I suspect this option is most popular with authors who are out mainly to impress people. They're willing to pay a premium for the prestige of being associated with a famous publisher.

I'm a fan of self-publishing, as you'll see below, but I don't want anyone to think that paying to be published by X publisher is the same as getting traditionally published by that same publisher.

If you and your agent strike out with the major players in your targeted publishing category, you'd simply move down to the next tier: midsized traditional publishers and see if you can get one of them to take your book and give you the best possible deal. If that doesn't work out, you'd move down to a small traditional house, and if that doesn't work, you'd try every advance-paying niche publisher who might be interested.

At that point, your agent might be out of ideas. The most honorable of them will continue to seek publishing opportunities for you, even if it means you getting published but not receiving an advance (which means the agent wouldn't receive an advance, either). Most will quit before this happens, however, since the agent needs to generate income from book contracts. Still, I've seen it happen.

Most times, if you've struck out with the advance-paying houses, the agent will have a conversation with you. She'll want to know if you still want to work with her. Perhaps you have another project she can shop around, and you could start the process all over again with that book. Some agents will just cut you loose. You'd get a "We no longer feel it benefits both parties for us to continue our agent-author relationship" letter.

Don't let that throw you. Don't let all the rejections send you into depression. There are far fewer publishing opportunities available through traditional channels anymore, but that doesn't mean you have fewer publishing opportunities in general. Quite the opposite.

But if you do exhaust the options in which a publisher will pay you to publish your book, you should consider the options in which 1) you pay the publisher or 2) you publish it yourself, either by paying or by pursuing a free option.

The easiest but most expensive self-publishing alternative is to go with a full-on custom publishing solution: a subsidy press or vanity press. Examples include AuthorHouse, Xulon, FriesenPress, and Tate Publishing. These companies typically offer an array of packages ranging from a few hundred dollars to several thousand. Options include a professional edit, professional cover design, some level of marketing support, and a certain number of "free" copies.

If you have the cash and you really don't want to directly mess with any aspect of your book besides the writing, consider one of these. Ask for samples first, though, so you can see what their books look and feel like.

If you prefer to handle things yourself, one of the more hands-on approaches might be best for you. You might not save money doing it this way (or you might), but you'll certainly have more control over the final result.

In these, you provide the editing, cover design, typesetting, and the rest yourself. Either you do them yourself (or skip them—not recommended) or you contract others to do them for you. Then you'd find a printing company, and you'd provide the cover file and the interior file. As far as the printer is concerned, you've done it all yourself. You are the publisher.

two kinds of printing companies

You have two options when choosing a printer. You can go with a traditional printing company (called an "offset" printer), which will print anywhere from two hundred to twenty thousand units for you at a time. Or you can go with a print-on-demand (POD) printer, such as LightningSource or Snowfall Press, which will print as few as one copy for you and up to as many as you want.

The advantage of going with an offset printer is that you can get each copy of the book for a lower price … but only if you order them in bulk. So you might be able to print each copy for $1.75—but you'd have to order ten thousand units to get that economy of scale. This is how authors end up with boxes and boxes of books in their garages. They get enticed by the lower unit price and don't always have a clear idea of how many they'll have to order (and sell), or what it will look like in their garage, to get that unit price.

The advantage of going with a POD printer is that you never have boxes of the book unless you want them. You can order exactly as many to be printed as you have orders for or expect to sell at a speaking engagement or whatever. And if you fix a typo to the text or add an award emblem to the cover, with POD you can upload the corrected files and every new unit that is printed has the changes. With offset, you'd have hundreds or thousands of the "wrong" version sitting and gathering dust. What would you do with them?

The downside of POD is that your unit cost is higher. Instead of that $1.75 you were paying at the offset printer, you might pay $5.50 for a copy of the same book. But you also won't have to rent a warehouse for your inventory. It's up to you.

strategy #2:
start free and go from there

One of the most popular new publishing strategies is to try your book out by publishing it through a free option and seeing if it gains enough popularity (and cash) to upgrade to a print version later.

This is like test marketing. You put your novel out there as an e-book, and see what happens. You promote it as best you can, but then you just hide and watch. You don't offer it for free, of course, but you don't charge much for it. You can do this because you don't have to make back your investment. It was free!

(You may have to pay to purchase an ISBN or to file it with the Copyright office, etc., but we're talking less than two hundred total. If you contract an editor, cover designer, and copy editor, your costs will go up. But these are all optional. Recommended, but not required.)

If the book finds a readership and starts making you some dough, then in this strategy you'd begin thinking about taking the book to the next level. Maybe it was e-book only, but now you have the cash in hand to do a short run at an offset printer or to get it set up at a POD house, and you could see if that version grows legs. If it does, you can upgrade again. Maybe you take your earnings and purchase a deluxe publishing package at a custom publishing company.

Maybe your long-term goal is to sell so many copies that you attract the attention of a large traditional publishing house. In their current trepidations, having someone bring them a proven winner is often quite appealing. The publishing blogosphere is filled with stories of self-published books that were "picked up" by major houses and went on to land seven-figure advances.

Please note, though, that this is so rare as to be almost ludicrous. Yes, it does happen, but supposedly someone wins the Publishers ClearingHouse Sweepstakes every year, too. The buzz around this topic makes it sound like all you have to do is e-publish a book and you'll become a millionaire. Um ... probably not going to happen. Most of the time the book gets listed with Amazon and other online booksellers and then just sits there. After that, it's all about marketing.

Maybe you don't hope to attract a big traditional publisher. Perhaps your goal is to keep the money for yourself. If you're doing all the work to promote these books, and they're somewhat successful, why would you want to hand that income stream to a publishing house? In that case, your eventual hope wouldn't be to land with a major house but to land a major pot of gold. More and more, this is what authors are trying to do.

But the same caveat applies here: The probability is that your books won't go huge. You might generate a nice secondary income from them—and this publishing strategy is designed to turn something small into something large later—but the chances are that you won't make the megabucks a few e-publishing and self-publishing authors are making. Keep your expectations screwed on straight, and you'll be okay.

It almost goes without saying that the stigma that used to be on self-publishing ("vanity publishing" can't be anything but derisive) is gone now. However, now it connotes an equally erroneous conclusion: that if you self-publish you're automatically going to be rich. But that's a nicer connotation than the old one: that self-publishers are narcissists.

Companies like Smashwords can create an e-book, in all the major e-reader platforms, for free.

Companies like CreateSpace can produce print books for you for free. You have to pay for every unit they print, but there's usually no fee for getting the book uploaded and ready to be printed.

If you start your path to publication by going for the big publishers but strike out, you can always try strategy #2 and be a leader in the publishing revolution we're in.

strategy #3:
self-publish and be done with it

This strategy is for the person who just wants to see her book in print and on the bookshelf at home. Maybe she has ten copies printed up to give out as Christmas gifts to family. Or maybe there's some special occasion—someone's retirement party, for instance—and you need a book made up for the event.

In situations like this, custom publishing is the way to go. You can get a professionally produced book for under three hundred dollars and pull it out, beaming with pride of honest effort and workmanship, whenever the urge strikes you.

If you've written this novel simply to prove you could do it, and if you have no further goals for it, this might be the right publishing solution for you. It's quick and easy, and it gives you and everyone else a reminder of your accomplishment.

strategy #4:
form your own publishing company

Think I'm crazy? Well, maybe I am, but that doesn't change the fact that small—even one-person—presses are popping up all over the world.

I hope you've sensed the rising power of the individual author in what I've been describing in Part Three. Take that power and multiply it by ten or more when you do more than self-publish your own book. If you become a publisher yourself, you can certainly continue publishing your own books, but you can also publish other people's books.

Like many novelists, I wrote my own first novel because nobody was writing the kind of book I thought should be out there. Later, I became a publisher because nobody was publishing the kind of book I thought should be out there. This is an age of empowerment in publishing, and going from author to publisher can be like going from a wooden megaphone to a THX sound system.

I could write an entire book on how to start and run your own small publishing house, but we don't have room for that here. So let me just say this: It rocks.

Of course, you have to have a certain temperament to run your own business, no matter what industry it's in. If you have that temperament, and you can assemble a team with all the requisite skills, you could pull it off.

A small publishing house has the same challenges faced by the self-publishing author. You still have to produce the book in a professional way, paying for it yourself and printing copies somewhere, and you still have to figure out 1) how to let people know your books are out there (marketing) and 2) how to enable them to buy your books (distribution, retail channels, online storefront, download, etc.).

But there's an added dignity that comes to you if you're publishing other authors besides just yourself. If your name is Susanne Jenkins and your "publishing house" is Suzy-J's Books, and all you produce are your own novels, people may think it's not a real publishing house. (These days, that really doesn't matter much, but it still happens.)

In my opinion, small indie presses like I'm describing here are the wave of the future. They will fill the void left by all the larger houses shutting down. Most of the disenfranchised or displaced midlist authors will find new homes at places like this.

More than that, though: Small indie presses will go places the traditional houses never went, even in the glory days. Because these houses are so small, they can wedge themselves into any niche imaginable.

Want to create a publishing house that produces only novels about flying dogs? Go for it! If you keep your costs low enough and reach enough paying customers, you're good! See a need for e-books on faucet repair or guitar tuning or horse stall shoveling? Do it! Want to produce novellas? Who cares that "people" say novellas are dead? In this new publishing environment, anything that people want to read about and are willing to pay for is alive. Want to publish epic fantasy poetry in iambic pentameter? So what if only seventeen people will buy it? If you do it right, you can still make your money back.

I'm telling you, in fifty years historians will look back on this time as the dawning of a new golden age of publishing, and they'll try to imagine how wonderful it was to be alive and writing while it was happening.

Whichever strategy or strategies you try, including those you make up yourself or hear about from someone else, I hope you feel how powerful you are as a novelist with a completed novel in your pocket.

wisdom from other publishing professionals

While I was writing this book, I put out a call to hundreds of my publishing friends and colleagues: novelists, agents, and editors. I told them I was writing a book for authors who were going to produce a novel in thirty days, and I asked them what they would say to such people about what to do with that novel once it was complete.

For the rest of this Victory, I'm going to let them have the microphone.

* * *

If they've got the manuscript done, I'd encourage them to have two other pieces: a one- or two-page synopsis, and a one-page bio that focused on platform.

Next, I'd probably say, "The first draft of any novel is usually bad." So I'd encourage them to use the next couple of months to polish it. Take it to a critique group. Have writer friends read and comment. Get it in front of an editor. Pay for a professional critique. Make it as sharp as possible, since that's the best way to get it published.

Then I'd say to them, "Check out *all* of your options." Should they introduce themselves to agents? Sure. Should they try to get it in front of some editors at a writing conference? Of course. Should they consider small presses? By all means. Should they explore self-publishing? Yes. But don't jump on the first opportunity that presents itself. Take your time, get some counsel, and try to move forward professionally.

My take: Too many writers are in a hurry. The writers who get it done and then take steps to get it polished and ready will stand a better chance of succeeding.

* * *

I always tell authors to:

1. GO TO A WRITERS CONFERENCE.

Just because they have a finished manuscript doesn't mean it's publishable. At a writers conference they can submit manuscripts for critique, and they can get feedback. They can meet with editors and learn more about the publishing world. They also can meet fellow writers and connect for prayer and support.

I started attending [a certain] writers conference in 1994, and I discovered friends for life. I've been blessed to work with most of the editors I met there at that time. They saw my progress during the fourteen years I attended! We built great relationships.

But more than that, I connected with friends whom I've prayed with, cried with, rejoiced with, and worked alongside for twenty years. Going to a writers conference isn't just about getting A BOOK published. (That's super easy these days!) Going to a conference is more about yourself—and developing yourself as a career writer. I shudder to think what would have happened if I'd self-published something I came up with those first few years on my writing journey!

2. FIND A CRITIQUE GROUP ...
OR EVEN A FRIEND TO CRITIQUE WITH.

I was on a few online groups back when the Internet was just getting a running start. I was on a secular writing loop for a time, and we'd critique each other's fiction. I learned so much— not only from those who gave me feedback but also by critiquing others. I saw what worked and what didn't work. It made my writing stronger.

3. IF THE MANUSCRIPT IS READY,
I'D START READING AGENT BLOGS AND TRYING TO FIND AN AGENT.

There are some people who go directly to self-publishing or approach editors at publishing companies, but my agent has been my partner on this journey. I have thirty-three books in print, and I wouldn't be where I am without her. She's my cheerleader, my career coach, and my go-to person. I get advice and contacts. She can find a great idea in all the dozens that I send to her, and she knows which idea would be a fit for which publisher.

An agent is another way of going from "just publishing a book" to being a career writer. My agent has an article on her agency's website on choosing an agent. Not every agent is a good agent, and a bad one is worse than no agent at all! I recommend that writers read agency blogs, get to know them in person, and ask for references when deciding.

* * *

Find writing friends, join a writing group, find critique partners—but use critique partners with caution. (I've had critique partners tell me weird things that I knew were wrong.)

Develop a network of reading/writing friends who can read your manuscript not for every little typo but to give you a general feel for it: "Yes, this is good," or, "There are a few plot holes, and some of it needs to be reworked."

Go to writers conferences and join organizations—RWA, Sisters in Crime, International Thriller Writers, or any one of many—and become active online. I would try to budget one conference per year—and then take advantage of everything that conference has to offer. Schedule as many of those "fifteen-minute pitch one-on-ones" as the conference allows—but don't be a bully at meals. Be kind to agents and editors that you meet at meals or in lounges, and other places.

I'm not sure I would immediately approach a traditional publisher. But I think I might "test the waters" by putting maybe a few shorter stories or shorter pieces online. (But those works should be "perfect" as well, as in they should be vetted through friends or an editor.)

Have a professional website, a Facebook page, and a maybe even a blog.

* * *

If you've always imagined you'd have your book published in the traditional way by an established publisher, then start by researching and approaching agents. While you're in the midst of that process, you may want to also research and approach smaller niche publishers.

Meanwhile, get yourself educated about options for self-publishing so that if you eventually decide to go that route, you'll know where to start.

The most important thing to remember is this: Don't get set on just one approach. You don't know which one is eventually going to work for you, so research all of your options.

* * *

(From literary agent Steve Laube) As you would expect, I vote that the writer approach agents first. The agents have a grasp of the scope of the entire industry and can assess whether or not a project has immediate commercial viability.

One can approach publishers (editors) directly, especially if they meet at a conference. But many publishers prefer working with agents and say so (doing so makes it easier for them in the negotiating process since many issues have already been settled in past negotiations). The weakness here is the slush pile. Another reason editors like working with agents is that the slush pile has been moved into the agent's in-box.

The self-publishing route is always open to an author. I contend that it would be better to have someone else pay you to publish your work and bear the burden of all editorial, production, and distribution costs. That said, there are many authors who are also entrepreneurs and know how to build and run a small business ... which is what self-publishing ultimately becomes. Tossing a book into the e-book ether is not a panacea solution with dollars falling from the sky. That can happen, but just listing titles with Smashwords or Amazon isn't enough.

There is plenty of evidence that if someone self-publishes and has enormous success, either in print or in e-book, that the larger traditional publishers take notice and often come in with a deal of their own. The key to that formula is "enormous success." Selling a thousand e-books at ninety-nine cents isn't going to garner attention per se. But selling ten thousand might.

* * *

As far as what to do next, all options are on the table now. I'd say don't be too anxious. First, edit the thing so it's the best it can be. Then take a couple of weeks to write down all the options, do some research. Make it a business decision as well as a heart decision.

Should the author approach agents? Approach editors of traditional houses? Go directly for self-publishing? Small presses? Create his or her own publishing company?

All of the above.

Most important ... without question ... nonnegotiable ... LEARN what to WALK AWAY FROM in a traditional publishing contract, and don't be afraid to do it if the house won't budge.

Here are the contract clauses to watch out for:

1. **A BLANKET NONCOMPETE CLAUSE.** The publisher is entitled to a fair noncompete clause. They are investing in the book and you should not be directly competing, e.g., a self-published legal thriller when they release the legal thriller you contracted for. But the author should not accept a clause that controls all of his writing and unfairly restricts self-publishing.
2. **AN UNRESTRICTED OPTION CLAUSE.** The option clause should apply only to the next book in a series.
3. **AN OOP (OUT OF PRINT) CLAUSE** that is not tied to minimum income within the royalty period. Offering one hundred dollars isn't serious.
4. **AN OVERBROAD WARRANTY.** Language that does not permit an author to publish anything until after the contracted book "is published," or that the author must have the "permission" of the publisher.
5. **THE 25 PERCENT E-BOOK ROYALTY CEILING** should be negotiable. Because digital is taking over and authors are being asked to do more of the digital marketing themselves, they should share in the back end. This is a hard

one for publishers, I know, because it gives them the long-term willies. But we are in a new era, and flexibility and creativity have to be the watchwords. A writer who still seeks the imprimatur of a traditional publishing contract may decide to go ahead with 25 percent … but should only do so after getting satisfaction on those other clauses.

The most important currency in negotiations is information, so know the ins and outs of contract language. The strongest motivation in negotiations is getting to a win-win. The strongest position in negotiations is the ability to walk away from a deal.

* * *

Having a completed novel is such an important step for a new novelist. Neither a publisher nor an agent is likely to be comfortable in moving forward in offering a contract or representation without reading an entire manuscript. So the manuscript becomes the most important selling tool a novelist could have.

* * *

I would recommend they attend a few conferences that specialize in their genre. Their goal should be to meet with agents and maybe an editor or two of choice. They should have a perfected pitch and present it well to get interest from agents and editors.

I'd suggest they pursue this route for a year or two or maybe more (depending on how aggressive they are), while they also get involved with genre-based groups online.

After a bit, if they end up with a bunch of rejections, they should analyze why they're getting rejected. Is their writing bad? Or maybe their idea just isn't what people are looking for?

If the reasons for rejection don't revolve around bad writing, and if the writer feels he's given agents a really good try, then I think he should e-publish the book. E-publishing is cheaper and you don't end up with one thousand books in your basement. Such writers should then view promoting their book as their part-time job. And if it takes off, they could turn it into a POD so that they can offer physical copies.

Then, if their dream is still to get traditionally published, they should start the whole process again with a new manuscript (forget about the old one). But when they meet with agents, lead with the fact that their $2.99 (or thereabouts) e-book sold 30,000 copies in the first year. Such numbers grab attention.

* * *

As a veteran of the Winchester Writers' Conference (in England) I have been presented with many a manuscript from a newbie, and have never found one that was ready for publication. Many had great promise. One or two went on to attain publication in due course. But their first untutored efforts? No.

Nowadays I make sure the newbies are aware of the basics (that's where the teaching at writers conferences are helpful to newbies), and then I suggest they approach some of the writers' organizations that will give a critique. They have to pay for it, of course. But at least one of these will pass a manuscript on to a suitable agent if it has finally come up to scratch.

If the idea is brilliant but the length is wrong, or there's not enough tension, I direct them to a small publisher on my list of publishers. Different lengths suit different publishers, and putting in the tension or working out how to have a three-way conversation is just a matter of learning the craft, in my humble opinion.

* * *

If wanting to go the traditional route, study what a good query letter looks like, then write one. Then query agents and editors. Go to conferences where editors and agents from targeted publishers attend and take appointments. Volunteer at conferences and begin building name recognition with industry professionals (not necessarily with other writers).

If wanting to self-publish, get the manuscript professionally edited, and buy a professionally designed cover. Develop a
presence through social media and/or author platform. Make
sure the book is done properly with a professional appearance.

* * *

It has to be critiqued! Preferably by published authors so the author can do a round of self-edits and polishing before ever trying to find an agent!

* * *

The first and only thing I would do if I wrote a novel in thirty
days is *find a great content editor*—not a grammar cop (though
that's important, too), but somebody who really understands
the elements of good storytelling.

Then I'd go back and rewrite it a few times. Most of the pros I
know rewrite about seven times before we feel it's fit for human
consumption. Then, and only then, would I find someone who
knows punctuation (think your old English teacher). Again, every seasoned pro I know, regardless of their experience, wants
and needs both types of editors.

After that, I would simultaneously attack all possible outlets,
approaching agents, traditional publishing houses, small presses, and self-publishing options all at the same time. The rumors
of agents and publishers not looking at a project if you're making multiple [queries] is nonsense. They look at more than one
project at a time, so you're entitled to submit to more than one
person at a time. If it fits their needs, believe me, they'll look at it.

Tenacity is the key. Don't give up. Every time I got one rejection letter, I'd use my depression and anger to send out two
more submissions. I used my anger to feed my machine, not
to destroy it. Also, use this downtime to research which direction you'd prefer to go, keeping in mind that the business is
in continual flux.

Only after you've researched and received all the facts are you ready to decide what's best for you. This is a good time to talk to somebody, anybody, in the publishing business—keeping in mind that nobody has all the answers. Everybody's running scared, hoping for success, hoping to keep their jobs. A quote from the seasoned screenwriter William Goldman says it best: "Nobody knows nothing." Don't believe anybody who tells you differently.

And finally, finally, finally, don't forget what's really of value. You, your family, your faith. Getting published is not the end of the rainbow. So many people run the race, get to the finish line, and, after all the sacrifice, sadly realize there's nothing there. After the initial rush, life returns to the same problems, the same questions, the same search for meaning and fulfillment.

Remember as a kid that Christmas toy you'd die for? You received it, but then, after a couple of weeks, a couple of months, you totally forgot about it. That's what being published is like. It isn't a bad thing, but that's all it is, just a thing.

final word

You did it. You've gone from poseur to proven writer. There should be stickers that go on the backs of cars to indicate that you've written a novel, just like there are stickers to show you've run a marathon or competed in a triathlon.

I wish I could hear the experience you had as you worked through this book. If you check us out at FictionAcademy.com, you can contact me through the forums and tell me what your experience was. I hope you found the book helpful on the front end, during the writing, and while you were revising the manuscript and pursuing publication.

Keep the Great Commandment of Fiction in mind: You must engage your reader from beginning to end. It will help you evaluate all the other teachings you hear about—especially those that seem to conflict with other teachings you've heard.

Just keep in mind that someone standing between you and that reader may ask, prefer, or demand that you obey one of the lesser "rules" of fiction, such as no prologues or no "–ly" adverbs or no description. Such will always be the case when there is no consensus about what makes great fiction or how to achieve it.

So here's our unifying principle: Great fiction is fiction that keeps the reader engaged from start to finish, and anything that contributes to that principle is good and to be used by the novelist.

I hope the Great Commandment helps you negotiate all the conflicting teaching you hear and emboldens you to keep the end user in mind.

So you've done it, despite the odds. There are many fears involved in writing a novel, but you overcame them all. No matter what else happens to you, whether this book gets published or not, if you were successful in your quest to write this novel, it is an accomplishment that can never be taken away.

I'm proud of you.

selected index

selected index